RKO

THE BIGGEST LITTLE MAJOR
OF THEM ALL

Betty Lasky

is the daughter of Jesse L. Lasky, one of the founders of the movie industry. She grew up in Hollywood and has been closely associated with many of the major people in the industry. She has worked for *The Players Showcase* magazine as movie editor and writer. The historical accuracy of this book speaks of the three years of painstaking research that went into its writing.

BETTY LASKY

RKO: THE BIGGEST LITTLE MAJOR OF THEM ALL

ROUNDTABLE PUBLISHING, INC.
Santa Monica, California

Second Edition

Original Hardcover Edition Published by Prentice-Hall

ROUNDTABLE PUBLISHING, INC.
933 Pico Boulevard
Santa Monica, CA 90405

First Printing, 1989

Library of Congress Catalog Card Number — 88-64132

ISBN 0-915677-41-5

PRINTED IN THE UNITED STATES OF AMERICA

To my father, who pioneered an industry from a barn in an orange grove: The Jesse L. Lasky Feature Play Company, the roots of Hollywood.

Memory is love.

CONTENTS

ACKNOWLEDGMENTS

My greatest thanks to my agent, Julian J. Portman, who made this book possible, then helped me plot its course and did the initial editing with me. Without Julian's interest, enthusiasm, and ideas, I could not have persevered through the three years of awesome research and writing. This book is his as well as mine.

I am deeply indebted to Saul Cohen, my editor at Prentice-Hall, for the opportunity, for his patience, and for his editorial contribution.

Gina Mendello, NYU Film School Graduate, assisted me by researching the Schary and Hughes regimes. Not only did she unravel their complexities, but she gave me a pattern to follow. She was courageous, cheerful, and a quick worker.

Andrew L. Stone, veteran screenwriter-director-producer and a walking encyclopedia of the industry, helped me, at times, almost on a daily basis. William Le Baron was one of his closest friends; he dined with Tom O'Neil the day O'Neil closed RKO's domestic exchanges in 1957. The door to Andrew's film library was always open.

From beginning to end, Marc Wanamaker, film historian, gave generous amounts of time and information. His Bison Archives is a treasure trove. I would not have attempted this book without Marc's resources.

Most of my library research was done in the Margaret Herrick Library of the Academy of Motion Picture Arts and Sciences, Beverly Hills. I am indebted to Linda Harris Mehr, librarian, Sam Gill, archivist, and their fine staff.

I am equally indebted to Ronald Haver, Director Film Programs, Los Angeles County Museum of Art, and his executive assistant, Joan Cohen. Again, I could not have written this book without their assistance.

I am also grateful to Anne G. Schlosser, librarian, and her staff, Charles K. Feldman Library, at the American Film Institute's Center for Advanced Film Studies, Hollywood.

I appreciate the particular contributions of Audree Malkin, head, Theater Arts Library, UCLA, and Hilda Bohem, UCLA Special Collections.

Special thanks to the Library of Congress, Reference Service, Washington, D.C.

Many thanks to Rita Norton, librarian, San Vicente Library of West Hollywood.

For interviews and information pertaining to RKO and related information, I am very grateful to: Pandro S. Berman, Adrian Mosser of Cineservice, Inc., Hollywood, John Paxton, Col. Barney Oldfield, Jack Cummings, Eugene Zukor, Henry Pflaum Rosen, Robert Sklar, Richard Epstein, Sol Baer Fielding, Samuel Marx, Oliver Dernberger, Dewitt Bodeen, Kemp Niver, Angela Fox Dunn, Dr. Rod Ryan of Eastman Kodak Co., Hollywood, Marcia Borie of *The Hollywood Reporter,* Jean Garmishhausen of *Daily Variety,* Carole D. Simpson, Randy Rogers, Helen M. McKee, and James and Julie Chinello.

Special thanks to Jesse L. Lasky Jr. and Pat Silver. In particular, Jesse provided an invaluable screenwriter's view of Dore Schary.

J'Nevelyn Terrell never lost faith in what she called "an important book." I can never thank her enough.

I am also grateful to several personal friends for their encouragement and help at various points: Marya Warwick, Bernice Willard, Margery Crosby, Cecilia Presnell, Barbara Vajda, Nance Mitchell, and Alena Murray.

RKO

THE BIGGEST LITTLE MAJOR
OF THEM ALL

PROLOGUE

COULD HOLLYWOOD HAPPEN ANYWHERE BUT HOLLYWOOD?

The ancient water tower that blots out the sky above the walls of the studio at 780 Gower Street carried a brand-new trademark one August day in 1958. No less a Hollywood personage than Hedda Hopper peered at the lone word *Desilu* stenciled on the tank as she turned onto Gower and into an unexpected traffic jam. The famous RKO symbol with its jagged streaks of lightning was gone. Faced with the finality of the situation, Hedda muttered to herself, "That bastard, television."

It was never the easiest studio to understand. For three decades RKO Radio had poured out entertainment against a backdrop of management so fickle that one had to think like a Rockefeller to know who was in command or what the company policy was.

But what entertainment emerged!

An old-timer like Hedda knew how to fill the waiting moments with a montage of memories: quick shots of famous and friendly faces like those of Fred Astaire and Ginger Rogers. Would anything like the impact those two created in their first dance, *The Carioca,* ever happen again? Or Kong atop the Empire State Building. If you haven't heard of that ape, you haven't heard of the movies. A wry expression crossed her face as she thought of Katharine Hepburn, an actress unlike any the public had seen before, and yet the top brass had called Kate "horse face" when she first appeared on the lot. Or was it "scarecrow"? Hedda's expression softened. She thought of ladylike Irene Dunne in *Love Affair,* with Charles Boyer so suave.

Some of the recollections made Hedda grimace, like the furor that boy genius Orson Welles caused with *Citizen Kane.* Or the chaos wrought by Howard Hughes, who abused the studio like the women in his life. Who ever heard of buying a studio for its chain of theaters so he could push Jane Russell's bazooms at the audience? The madman had more *chutzpah* than Sammy Glick, but he never had to run as fast. He even tried to sell the studio to a syndicate and pocketed the down payment when the deal backfired. A few years later, he wrote a check for more than $23 million and made himself Number One. He was the first man to own a Hollywood studio from shrimp cocktail to arc lights. Hughes even made a profit from a dead studio. He ran it into the ground and then sold it for $25 million to a tire company that owned a television subsidiary. Then, the new owner bled the corpse by leasing almost the entire backlog of RKO films to television and left the studio to wither in the sun until it blistered into a ghost town.

Hedda straightened as the traffic moved inside the main gate. A grassy square reverberated with signs of life: prop men, carpenters, extras, a smiling collie that looked like Lassie. It was part of the sights of what the press would soon call "the most astonishing production empire of the decade." As she hurried toward Lucille Ball's dressing room—the domain of Ginger Rogers in the old days—Hedda glanced at the Administration Building, where Desi Arnaz was probably creasing his elegant slacks in David O. Selznick's old office. Or Dore Schary's.... Or Howard Hughes's....

Desiderio Alberto Arnaz y de Acha III was once easy to discount. He was yesterday's conga drummer with a Cuban beat, yesterday's town clown. Now nobody laughed at Desi Arnaz, proud landlord of a four-block-long studio wedged between two legendary giants, Columbia and Paramount. He had acquired the RKO studio and the lot in Culver City as well. The latter was the old Selznick Studios where once Atlanta burned and Vivien Leigh shone as bright as Oscar's gold. From *Gone With the Wind* to *I Love Lucy.* Could Hollywood happen anywhere else but Hollywood?

The deal he made with General Tire & Rubber Co., the previous owner, Desi bragged, took only twenty-four hours to consummate. He did it while he was filming a *Lucy–Desi Hour* television special. The asking price was a huge bargain: $6,500,000 for both studios and everything inside—office furniture, cameras, props, the works. General Tire had made some schlocky pictures and lost. They wanted to unload the studios fast. Still, Desi wasn't sure he wanted to go ahead. He felt a little mistrust for *gringos* in those days and decided to call the former landlord, Howard Hughes.

"Grab it, Cuban!" Hughes screamed when he heard the price. "Buy it, or I shall! At that price, you can tear them down and make them both into giant parking lots. You've gotta make money!"

Almost convinced, Desi picked up the $2 million down payment with a quick phone call to the Bank of America, which had helped him buy control of Motion Picture Center, the former General Service Studios, a while back so that Desilu could have a solid roof over its head. They were happy to help him again. Even with that, Desi admitted he began to worry—it was proving too easy! He took a not-so-wild gamble at wheeling and dealing. He telephoned General Tire and said he would buy only if the price were adjusted to $6,350,000.

By 9 P.M., during a break in the shooting of the *Lucy–Desi* show, Desi realized he had to close the deal. His twenty-four-hour exclusive, which he had asked for, was running out. When General Tire did not turn down his last offer, Desi walked across the hall from the sound stage to his office and decided to press his gambling instinct harder. Dressed in the costume of a comic English lord, with jaunty plumed hat, short velvet pants, and buckled shoes for the Shakespearean episode they were doing, Desi telephoned his final offer—$6,150,000—and waited, he said, "with my silly costume and plumed hat."

The phone rang as Lucy entered the office to get him for the second act. He took the call. Lucy asked, "What the hell was that all about?"

"We just bought RKO Studios," Desi told her, and they went off to finish the show.

What happened next was sillier. For tax reasons General Tire decided that it couldn't accept so much money in the current fiscal year. So, the down payment dropped to $500,000 instead of $2,000,000. In effect, Desi saved himself borrowing and paying interest on $1,500,000.

"One and a half million for ten years at 6 percent is $900,000," he figured. "We actually bought the place for almost a million dollars less."

In the same spirit, Lucy reminded Hedda that RKO was the lot where she and Desi had been hired eighteen years before.

"You were a former Goldwyn girl," Hedda recalled as she started to scribble some notes.

"I was making fifty dollars a week when I went to RKO," Desilu's vice president volunteered briskly. "I was there for seven years and seven regimes. When Charlie Koerner sold half my contract to MGM, I was almost pushed out." The big blue eyes that were on everyone's TV screen in the country blinked confirmation. "I didn't care whether they were B or D pictures, as long as I was working.

"I even tested for *Gone With the Wind*. On my knees.... I was too nervous to stand up."

"You met Desi—"

"When we starred in *Too Many Girls*. He was in the Broadway show."

Soon, the actress-tycoon bundled Hedda into an electric golf cart and they set out to see the splendors of Desilu Gower. The summer of '58 sparkled with promise. It was a time of new beginnings, just as it had been three decades earlier, when RKO, the last major studio in Hollywood, was born.

PART ONE

THE MERGER, COURTESY OF JOE KENNEDY (1925-1928)

Benjamin Franklin "B. F." Keith, king of vaudeville.
Courtesy Marc Wanamaker, Bison Archives.

David Sarnoff, radio's guiding genius and the mastermind behind the RKO merger.
Courtesy Marc Wanamaker, Bison Archives.

Edward F. Albee, B. F. Keith's Richelieu, who inherited his throne.
Courtesy Marc Wanamaker, Bison Archives.

Gloria Swanson is welcomed back to Hollywood in 1925 with her third husband, the handsome Marquis de la Falaise. The royal couple is flanked by Paramount bosses Jesse Lasky on the far left, and Adolph Zukor on the right.
Courtesy Marc Wanamaker, Bison Archives.

FBO Western star Fred Thomson and his horse, Silver King, in *That Devil Quemado*, 1925.
Courtesy Marc Wanamaker, Bison Archives.

FBO Studio, 780 Gower Street, 1926. A jumble of standing sets can be seen in the rear.
Courtesy Marc Wanamaker, Bison Archives.

Jesse Lasky poses with Joe Kennedy at the symposium on the movies, Harvard, 1927.
Courtesy Marc Wanamaker, Bison Archives.

Joseph P. Kennedy and his wife, Rose, bound for Europe in the mid-1920s.
Courtesy Marc Wanamaker, Bison Archives.

Will Hays sits at the center of this gathering of movie industry figures, with Jesse Lasky and Jack Warner (in dark suit) on his left, and Louis B. Mayer on his right. Seated, far left, next to Lasky, is studio executive Michael C. Levee; Irving Thalberg stands behind Hays; Samuel Goldwyn is seen standing second from left, rear.
Courtesy Marc Wanamaker, Bison Archives.

Joseph P. Kennedy presents
THE GREAT MAIL ROBBERY
Slashing Melodrama of the Roaring Rails and Uncle Sam's Marines.
U.S.M
Directed by George B. Seitz
An FBO Picture

Joseph P. Kennedy presents *The Great Mail Robbery,* starring Theodor Von Eltz, seen on the poster, 1927. From a press kit for exhibitors.
Courtesy Jean Grant.

Nineteen-year-old FBO actress Jean Morgan, signed by Joe Kennedy in the East, is seen here with Ranger, the popular FBO dog star, in one of his movies, circa 1927–28.
Courtesy Jean Grant.

Joe Kennedy is seen seated just to the left of center next to his henchman, E. B. Derr, at the annual FBO sales convention banquet, FBO Studio, 1926.
Courtesy Marc Wanamaker, Bison Archives.

1

The winds of change were sweeping through Hollywood in 1927. Consolidation was in the air, and with the arrival of Joseph P. Kennedy, consolidation became the biggest game in town. RKO was not even a speck in his range of vision, yet Kennedy revealed his remarkable sense of timing in a few remarks he made at his alma mater, Harvard, in March. Asked to forecast the future of the movies, during a question-and-answer session introducing a series of lectures on the motion picture industry, he casually told the assembled students, "We are on the eve now of big consolidations. They have become practically necessary.... Ours is an industry that lends itself very easily to consolidation...."

Having conquered Wall Street from the vantage point of the Boston office of Hayden, Stone and Company, the Kennedy founding father had eagerly taken on Hollywood. And because it was, if anything, a fast-buck paradise, it was made to order for this financial shark who always wore a wide grin on his face to camouflage the dollar sign implanted in his heart. He had dabbled in Hollywood from a distance. Securing the aid of Guy Currier, a Boston millionaire attorney with fabulous connections, he had commandeered a group early in the twenties that bought a chain of thirty-one New England theaters, along with the local franchise for Universal Pictures. A profitable enterprise, it served as an introduction to the new breed of mogul, the founders of the big movie business. "Look at that bunch of pants pressers in Hollywood making themselves millionaires," Kennedy bluntly observed to an associate at Hayden, Stone. "I could take the whole business away from them."

Another associate observed that "from the theater side of the business, Hollywood could wring you dry.... [Kennedy]...wanted to get to where the wringing was done."

By the summer of 1925 Joe Kennedy heard of a motion picture company that appeared to be sinking simply because its British owners were unable to afford reasonable financing. FBO, Film Booking Offices of America, Inc., was a British production and distribution subsidiary that included a seven-building studio on Gower Street, near Melrose. It had been built in 1920 on land purchased from the Hollywood Cemetery Corporation and opened in early December of that year. The owner, Robertson-Cole, a British firm, distributed Rohmer automobiles and imported and exported motion pictures. In 1922, with reorganization, the film company changed its name to Film Booking Offices. Patrick A. Powers, ex-blacksmith, wheelwright, and a founding father of the Universal Film Manufacturing Company, became president after Rufus S. Cole and H. F. Robertson resigned from the corporation. Before the letters *FBO* could be placed on the roof of the administration building, Pat Powers, in a display of native immodesty, put his name up there. When the modest little studio came to Joe Kennedy's attention, it had acquired a new owner, the British banking firm of Graham's of London, and Powers's name was off the roof and his successor, a Major H. C. S. Thomson, Graham's representative in India, had arrived.

Kennedy, arming himself with a syndicate of powerful friends, including the regal Guy Currier, Louis E. Kirstein (head of Filene's department store), and Frederick H. Prince (multi-millionaire railroad manipulator), raised the money to swing the deal. After intense negotiations that took him to London with his lawyer in August 1925, Lord Inverforth of Graham's capitulated. The terms were unbelievable. The British owners had invested more than $7 million in FBO, but Kennedy had snapped it up for a mere million dollars!

The "pants pressers" greeted the Wall Street star with astonishment. "A banker! A banker!" Marcus Loew, the dean of movie moguls, exclaimed. "I thought this business was just for furriers." Doubtless, he had been reading Kennedy's publicity. Back in 1913 at age twenty-five, Joe Kennedy had made himself president of the Columbia Trust Co., a family affair, in East Boston. Intrigued, the press labeled him the youngest bank president in the country.

But the flashing Kennedy grin, ingratiating friendliness, and slangy, profane speech reassured the Hollywood hierarchy. None of them had seen a banker with that kind of personality before. So *what* if he was an Irish Catholic; at least he was not related to that terrible Jeremiah J. Kennedy, leader of the Motion Picture Patents Company, whom the moguls had battled for survival in the early days of filmmaking.

Hollywood's most knowledgeable journalist, Terry Ramsaye, announced Kennedy's arrival with a suggestion of irony in the September 1927 issue of *Photoplay:* "Now comes this banking person Kennedy...a very young person with freckles on his face and nonchalance in his manner. He comes not as an angel hopefully backing a star-to-be, nor by any of the other many side-door entrances, but bolting through the main gate, acting as though he knows just what he is doing. Apparently, he does."

Official endorsement came from quarters no mogul could ignore, Will Hays, President Warren G. Harding's postmaster general, whom Hollywood selected to deal with its "morality panic." (He was a comfortable choice since Harding's administration had proved as scandalous as Hollywood.) "General" Hays's opinion of Kennedy's qualifications for entry into the motion picture business was quoted in *Motion Picture World* on December 11, 1926. Hays, it seemed, had many reasons for wishing his good friend well. "Most of all," the article stated, "General Hays wanted his friend to come into the motion picture business because he regarded him as...a man who, in his business ideals and concepts as in the fine character of his home life, would bring to the industry much that it has lacked in the past."

In the spring of 1926 Kennedy moved his family—Rose, his devoted wife of twelve years, and their seven children—via private railroad car to Riverdale, a countrified community in New York City with a view of the Hudson.

The profile of Kennedy in *Motion Picture World* ended with the statement that "Joseph P. Kennedy's shadow looms larger every minute." Indeed, his shadow took on real substance in Hollywood with the purchase of FBO. In fact, Kennedy had bought himself a solid work-horse of a studio that favored making low-budget "second features" that only now and then broke the habit with an unforgettable picture of the higher caliber, such as Dorothy Davenport's *Broken Laws*.

Kennedy was satisfied with FBO's mediocre status quo. Let mighty Paramount's Zukor and Lasky, and the great Mayer–Thalberg combine in Culver City, get their brains scrambled trying to outdo *Birth of a Nation*. He had no intention of competing with "producers [who] were fighting to get their pictures on Broadway, and State Street in Chicago," he said in 1928. "I concentrated on getting and keeping Film Booking Offices' pictures on Main Street,...[U.S.A.]."

The FBO films listed in 1927's *Film Year Book* bear him out. Titles like *A Poor Girl's Romance, Red Hot Hoofs, Rose of the Tenements,* and *The Flame of the Argentine* hardly belonged on the same marquee with *Seventh Heaven, The Big Parade, Wings,* or *Underworld*. But they were good enough for unsophisticated small-town audiences, and that was good enough for Joe. No wonder he was bewildered when a journalist complimented him with, "You have had some good pictures this year."

Grinning broadly, he shot back, "What the hell *were* they?"

The rescue operation Kennedy mounted was swift and shrewd. The British owners of FBO, stymied by the prospect of short-term borrowing at a killing rate of 18 percent, had no recourse but to call for the undertaker. Kennedy, the former banking prodigy, knew how to refuel. In record time he set up a division, Cinema Credit Corporation, for raising capital by issuing stock. His wealthy friend Freddie Prince, who shared Kennedy's ravenous appetite for the movie industry's profits, purchased a hefty bundle of Cinema Credit preferred stock and then arranged a loan of a half million dollars through one of his companies, the Chicago Union Stockyards. Kennedy, using his important contacts, matched this amount with a half-million-dollar line of credit at four different banks. FBO's funding needs were now satisfied for the coming year at nominal interest rates. The little company could turn out as much mediocre product as Kennedy wished.

Major Thomson, the India import brought over by the former British owners, had departed, and Kennedy appointed a new FBO production chief, Edwin C. King. He represented the third replacement in two years, following B. P. Fineman, whom Thompson had hired, and J. G. Hawks, his temporary successor. Life at the top at FBO was proving to be short and bitter. But the seed of RKO received the impetus it needed to blossom with the arrival of the next production chief, William Le Baron.

Kennedy ran studio affairs with the tools of a banker. To fill key positions, he brought in his loyal crew, men who shared his wizardry with figures and were willing to carry his secrets to the grave if necessary. E. B. (Ed) Derr, treasurer of FBO, Eddie Moore, Charles Sullivan, John Ford, and Pat Scollard were well-tuned, working-class replicas of the boss—in effect, an Irish Mafia of the day. With this working team, and pros like the seasoned production executive Bill Le Baron to translate their orders into action, FBO increased its movie production to practically one picture a week. They were "program pictures," low-budget Westerns, action pictures, and stunt thrillers, 1927 releases like *Deadman's Curve,* in which Douglas Fairbanks Jr. played a young racing driver; *Hook and Ladder No. 9,* a fire thriller with Cornelius Keefe, Dione Ellis, and Edward Hearne; and *The Bandit Son,* a Bob Steele Western.

These bread-and-butter pictures were actually "the backbone of the industry," as Paramount mogul Jesse L. Lasky readily explained in his lecture at the Harvard movie series in March 1927. In small towns, the films had the life expectancy of half a week, sometimes less. But there were two other classifications that interested Lasky more: "Rialto specials," the pictures that ran as long as the public wanted them, and the several yearly "roadshows"—pictures that lent prestige and good will to the industry.

"I know this is a business, and our stockholders expect their dividends," Lasky said. "But my theory is we can pay dividends and still improve and advance with each picture."

Unlike some other filmmakers, this former vaudeville producer took the art of the films seriously and so had eagerly accepted Kennedy's written invitation to speak at Harvard. He would go anywhere there was an audience he could touch with his enormous personal enthusiasm for the "art industry." The mogul for whom motion pictures were a passionate commitment was a far cry from the Wall Street banker bent on exploiting the new frontier for profit. Meantime, Kennedy reeled off statistics to his Harvard audience to prove that he had found gold in the hills of Hollywood. "The moving picture industry is the fourth largest in the country," he pointed out with relish.

A bewildered student asked him to elaborate.

"My statement is based on the report of H. M. Lord, director of the Bureau of Budgets, Department of Commerce," Kennedy fired back. "The investment is approximately one billion five-hundred million dollars. There are twenty-one thousand theaters [in America] with an attendance of more than 60 million people a week."

With these fantastic figures at his fingertips, Kennedy had considered it mandatory to sign FBO Western star Fred Thomson and his white horse, "Silver King," to a new contract for $15,000 a week.

"He has the widest distribution outside of the big cities of any actor on the screen," Kennedy informed the flabbergasted students. "Fred averages ten thousand [exhibitor] contracts a year for every picture he makes."

Richard Talmadge, Evelyn Brent, and a former Yale football star, Maurice "Lefty" Flynn, were reliable FBO regulars who did not require Kennedy's personal services since they were not big box-office draws. The cowboy movie stars, like ex-minister Fred Thomson, who parlayed his message of clean living to fame and fortune on the screen, were.

Thomson's moralistic Western *The Two-Gun Man,* in which he resisted the natural urge to seek revenge with his guns for his father's death and the theft of his homestead and cattle, made it to Broadway, where it played the Warner Theater in July 1926. Kennedy deserved and took credit for the miracle. He had overcome the New York exhibitor's desire for "flesh and the devil, and plenty of both," he told his Harvard audience with an owlish grin, by asking him to make a small sacrifice. " 'Try this Thomson picture,' " he said he had urged the exhibitor. " 'It won't cost you anything.' "

Kennedy broke into a hearty laugh, and the students chuckled uneasily, not fully understanding. "He put it on," Kennedy continued. "Now he plays Westerns every week. He simply did not know his own audience."

Other sagebrush heroes enhanced FBO's reputation as a leading exponent of silent Westerns in the twenties: Tom Tyler, champion weightlifter and strongman with a relaxed acting style; Bob Steele, a bantam youngster who came across as the very embodiment of the movie cowboy; and Bob Custer, a phenomenon in the sense that he was neither photogenic nor an actor but still satisfied the naïve requirements of Saturday movie matinee fans. On top of this roster, the king of the Westerns, Tom Mix, checked into FBO after leaving Fox in 1928. But the lavish Fox production values were missing in his FBO product, and some critics hinted that "the bloom was off the sage." So the champ wisely decided to take a vacation from films for a while. Sound was encroaching on his territory; the recording devices might reveal the whiskey tenor.

Not surprisingly, the moguls cast hungry glances at FBO's Fred Thomson. Ex-furrier Adolph Zukor, a brilliant strategist and plunderer famous for his sweeping raids on ailing companies and choice stars, bided his time. When Thomson's contract expired in 1928, the diminutive mogul outbid Kennedy for his services, bringing Thomson into the Paramount fold, where he ended his career (and, sadly, his life, after he caught pneumonia) in big, spectacular Westerns.

For Kennedy there was little time to mourn. By then he was onto bigger game, for in March 1927, Joe Kennedy had stormed the hallowed halls of Harvard in the crass name of Hollywood. He launched a symposium on the movies for a senior class of the Business School. The weekly lectures given by more than a dozen chiefs of the industry were not a selfless exercise. It was part of Kennedy's scheme to win for himself the whole pot of gold in Hollywood.

FBO Pictures Corporation hardly presented an imposing face to the ruling circle in the movie capital. As FBO's president, Joe Kennedy was no more accepted than he had been in Brahmin Boston. There, in spite of having distinguished himself in the banking profession, where few Irish strayed beyond the working classes, the exclusive clubs were still closed to the Kennedy family. It was the same for him at Protestant Harvard. He could never make the prized undergraduate clubs, yet he had climbed to a degree of business success no Irishman had attained at that citadel of old Boston society. Money, Kennedy realized, was the cornerstone of power and the social position previously denied him. In Hollywood, the big deals were kindled in the inner sanctum of the Jewish movie lords. He wanted to gain admittance.

After exhaustive research, innumerable telephone calls, and seesawing negotiations that made his assistants and secretaries frantic, Kennedy arrived at a guest speaker list of VIPs that he felt would not be offensive to the prestigious university. Naturally, it excluded some whose accents or bearing might prove less than genteel. Prominent among the rejects were Joseph M. Schenck, the affable head of United Artists, who unfortunately spoke with an overpoweringly guttural accent; Louis B. Mayer, the production chief of Metro–Goldwyn–Mayer, who, Kennedy had been told, at times behaved like an emperor and could be cloyingly sentimental; and Irving Thalberg, Mayer's brilliant young associate, who was excluded because Louie B. was excluded.

The final list cleverly mixed elder statesmen, younger pioneer filmmakers, a distributor, an exhibitor, an actor, a banker, and a "czar." Paramount—

Famous–Lasky Corporation president Adolph Zukor and the great showman who ruled the Metro–Goldwyn Pictures Corporation, Marcus Loew, made up the elder statesmen. Kennedy also included, with some trepidation, rival magnate William Fox. The president of Fox Film Corporation had a reputation for being a loner whose drive for power equaled the intrepid Zukor's; but Joe had also learned that Fox was in the throes of buying that "cathedral of Motion Pictures," New York's Roxy Theater, for $12 million, and Kennedy was intrigued.

Next came Warner Brothers Pictures president Harry M. Warner, a tough businessman who, according to reports, had something big up his sleeve called the Vitaphone. Kennedy had heard that the little studio wavered on the edge of bankruptcy while Harry and his brothers poured their own fortune into developing a sound system that synchronized motion pictures with music or voices. Kennedy wondered if they were guessers or gamblers. Unknown to Kennedy, the moguls had already explored the Vitaphone technique and retreated. The majors had met in secret in December 1926 and agreed that if and when they did venture into sound, they would select the same system—but not the Warners' system. The moguls were not aware that the wily Adolph Zukor had tried to make a private deal with the Warners in October by offering the theater-poor brothers the use of the 600 choice Paramount Publix theaters to display their silent and Vitaphone pictures. However, true to form, the brothers priced themselves too high.

The younger pioneers were the genial Jesse Lasky, Paramount's first vice president, and his former partner, Cecil B. DeMille, president of DeMille Studios. DeMille, now a tough independent, had just completed *The King of Kings,* with the backing of the Wall Street aristocrat Jeremiah Milbank, and it was rumored to be the greatest picture the world would ever see. The next two executives Kennedy chose to attend were Robert H. Cochrane, a vice president of Universal Pictures Corporation, who had been the trusted right hand of the company's fabled founder, the pugnacious little Carl Laemmle (one of Kennedy's rejects), and Sidney Kent, Paramount's super-salesman who bore the title "general manager of distribution." At the same time Kennedy added Samuel Katz, the ambitious, driving young president of Publix Theatres Corporation, Paramount's glittering theater chain, who, according to inside sources, was igniting a feud with Sidney Kent. Both men were important figures in the industry, and Kennedy rightly suspected that neither would turn down his invitation.

Kennedy had searched long and hard for a "highbrow" actor to climax the course—someone with dignity and background and not at swords' points with any of the movie moguls. He settled on Milton Sills, the First National Pictures star and a graduate of the University of Chicago. He intended to introduce him with the words "We want you to get the impression that we are a very highbrow crowd in Hollywood."

To represent the banking interests, Kennedy invited Dr. Attilio Giannini, a former surgeon and member of a powerful California banking dynasty, himself president of the Bowery and East River National Bank of New York. And should Harvard eyebrows be raised over the quality of Hollywood entertainment, Kennedy's next selection served as a buffer. Although Earle W. Hammons, a businessman and the president of Educational Pictures, specialized in releasing short-reel comedies that might be considered crude by Harvard standards, he was also dedicated to promoting educational nontheatrical films, a subject certain to appeal to the University.

Naturally, Kennedy included his friend Will Hays, president of the Motion Picture Producers and Distributors of America. The industry's censorship "czar" would act as a magnet to both Hollywood and Harvard. Kennedy planned to introduce him as "a distinguished lawyer, national figure, and elder in the Presbyterian Church." The inclusion of General Hays was certain to hasten the endorsement of the University, for it had taken a steady flow of diplomatic effort to persuade Harvard to consider the unusual undertaking.

Finally, Dean Wallace B. Donham of the Harvard Graduate School of Business Administration agreed that "a study of the industry" would be pertinent for "the course known as Business Policy...required for the degree"; and brusque President A. Lawrence Lowell gave his nod of approval.

The studio chiefs reacted to Kennedy's invitation with a certain resistance. Lawsuits exploded daily in the upper echelons of the business, so the moguls required definite assurance that deadly enemies were not among those invited. Nonetheless, the opportunity to address the senior class at the great principality of learning promised to be an ego massage no unschooled mogul could resist. Even Marcus Loew climbed out of a sickbed to fulfill his commitment and became so emotional when he stepped to the lectern that he ignored his written speech and blurted out, "I cannot begin to tell you how it impresses me, coming to a great college such as this to deliver a lecture, when I have never even seen the inside of one before." As one speaker, Robert Cochrane, a former newspaperman, remarked, a trifle condescendingly, "I came into the motion picture business at a period when someone said, 'The only two-syllable word a film man knows is *fill-um.*'"

Kennedy combined the virtues of an ingratiating host and stimulating tour guide. He introduced his speakers with finesse, dwelling on their accomplishments flatteringly, and deftly fielded questions from the audience. He strolled with his guests along Harvard's tree-shaded walks, pointing out the historic splendors of the old yard. In a matter of weeks, the telephones would start to jingle in his New York and Hollywood offices. Invitations to play golf and dine with his important new friends produced the sought-after results he coveted: entree to the inside track leading directly to the big money game in Hollywood.

2

Hollywood was a hamlet of giants, lulled by prosperity—an empire built on the logic of the silent screen. The movie moguls were aware of sound, but they only smiled condescendingly when the subject came up. More than a decade earlier, vaudeville acts played on the same bill with Thomas Edison's "latest and greatest invention, Kinetophone." The great inventor had marketed his Kinetoscope with synchronized sound to peep-show parlors before the turn of the century. Oddly, the sound that viewers heard through the earphones was clearer than the picture. Inventions and inventors multiplied through the succeeding years with varying success, and if news of them occasionally crossed a studio chief's desk, he took heart by quoting the local oracle, *Photoplay*'s James Quirk, who crisply announced to his readers in March 1924: "Talking pictures are perfected, says Dr. Lee De Forest. *So* is castor oil."

The first sound-on-film feature played the Rivoli in New York on April 15, 1923, a program of short films with an enticing array of vaudeville stars: Weber & Fields, Sissle & Blake, Phil Baker, Eddie Cantor, Eva Puck & Sammy White, and Conchita Piquir. The *Variety* ad on the De Forest Phonofilms declared: "Films that actually talk and reproduce music without the use of phonographs!" Unfortunately, the voices were not as clear as the faces.

The following year De Forest produced a two-reel talkie with movie actress Una Merkel, a comedy called *Love's Old Sweet Song*. Again the voices were fuzzy. Sound appeared to be a novelty, whereas the silent picture, which told a story that the eye could appreciate with the aid of embellishment from subtitles, had captured the public's fancy. In response, the moguls erected theater-palaces by the hundreds across the land—opulent settings for their roadshow attractions offering elaborate hour-long presentations with "a cast of thousands." But the fickle public preferred to remain home and turn on a new gadget called radio that began broadcasting in 1920.

The moguls had grappled with competition before; it was in the very grain of show business. If they could adjust to changing times, they could survive and continue to live like kings. New weapons were required, and first-run movie exhibitors hired the finest musical artists, big-name bands, thunderous organs, important vaudeville acts, the most luscious dancing girls to plump their attractions. Still the public stayed away.

Hollywood had other reasons for wanting to remain silent. Millions were invested in silent equipment in the studios. It would take millions of dollars to convert theaters to sound. Who would patronize the class theaters with all their expensive paraphernalia if any movie house could offer the glorious sounds of Carnegie Hall from the screen? It was no wonder Marcus Loew looked crestfallen at the Harvard lecture series in 1927 when a student asked him, "Is the Vitaphone going to cut into the vaudeville and picture business in the near future?"

"That's hard to say," he answered. "I put that on a par with anything else that is new. Personally, I don't think it is."

Another hand shot up. "What will they do with the Vitaphone in developing those pictures for foreign countries? Will the actors be speaking English?" With his voice betraying his agitation, Loew responded to his questioner: "All I can say to you is that it is a mighty good thing some of the actors do not speak."

Marcus Loew had retreated to his sickbed by the time William Fox and Harry Warner paid homage to the new technique. In deference to the University, William Fox limited his vision of the future of the "so-called talking film" to the realm of education. His address ran the gamut from the early period when he had persevered against the Trust of the "big ten" producers that had almost succeeded in monopolizing production and distribution to a heart-rending account of a $100,000 Fox film called *Over the Hill* that delivered a stern message to children who neglect their parents. About sound he said, "We have an instrument called the Movietone, but Mr. Warner seems to be so set on his Vitaphone that I would rather leave that subject to him." Instead, he dwelled on his vision of a renaissance in education. "Imagine professors of this college coming to our studio and delivering lectures. We photograph the speaker and at the same time on the same celluloid we 'photograph' his voice. That lecture can simultaneously be shown, not only in Harvard, but in all the universities of the world."

Personally, Fox was hedging. From turning his back on De Forest and the Vitaphone a few years earlier, he had become a believer by investing $60,000 for the patents on July 23, 1926, after listening to the filmed demonstration of a chirping canary delivered by Theodore W. Case and Earl I. Sponable. Fox unveiled his own sound-on-film process, known as Fox-Movietone, in a series of talking shorts. Furthermore, in a move to eliminate expensive theater orchestras, he had dealt theater audiences another surprise: scored films. Shortly after his Harvard lecture, West Point cadets were seen parading smartly at his Roxy in the first sound Movietone News. By May, Movietone comedian

Chic Sale starred in *They're Coming to Get Me,* the first Hollywood short *with* dialogue. In June, the Roxy featured President Calvin Coolidge with Charles Lindbergh at an ear-splitting hero's welcome in Washington after his flight across the Atlantic. Movietone topped this in September by delivering film of Mussolini raving in broken English that "this [sound] can bring the world together and end war!"

Ironically, in the early spring of that year, Thomas Edison pronounced talking pictures a failure, a statement that Harry Warner sorrowfully reported at Harvard. "It is not so comfortable to have your life's wealth invested in a thing which such a great authority as Edison says cannot succeed."

With their own studio facing financial ruin, Sam, Harry, Albert, and Jack Warner reached for the Vitaphone to save them. Sam Warner "had been fooling around with radio stations" and wired Harry to "go to the Western Electric Company and see what I consider the greatest thing in the world," he told the students. He did and wired Sam back: "I think you are right."

On August 6, 1926, just two weeks after Fox committed himself to the Case-Sponable system, the Warners tested the Western Electric process under the Vitaphone label with a "first-class show" that cost $3 million. The program featured John Barrymore in *Don Juan* with a bounty of 127 soundless kisses, a synchronized orchestral score, Vitaphone shorts, and Mischa Elman, Efrem Zimbalist, and Harold Bauer and the Metropolitan Opera's Giovanni Martinelli, Marion Talley, and Anna Case. Will Hays, in a filmed introduction, dutifully blessed the Vitaphone. But the greatest praise came from a Professor Michael I. Pupin of Columbia University, who solemnly stated that "No closer approach to resurrection has ever been made by science."

Unfortunately, the exhibitors disagreed, and the Warners were forced to dig deeper into their coffers to get key theaters wired for sound. Unvanquished, Harry Warner gravely stated his philosophy to the Harvard gathering: "If you think right, you cannot do wrong. This coming year we are going to make three pictures in which the Vitaphone will play an important part. Our first picture will be *The Jazz Singer,* with Al Jolson."

3

Watching from the sidelines, and by no means idle while the sound revolution climaxed with the first part-talking feature-length picture on October 6, 1927, was the young general manager of Radio Corporation of America, David Sarnoff. In January 1927, only a few months before Joe Kennedy staged his ambitious public relations show at Harvard, Sarnoff had starred in an historic event of his own: the debut of NBC, the country's first national radio broadcasting organization. Mounted from the Grand Ballroom of the Waldorf-Astoria in New York, the free entertainment reached out to twenty-five local stations. Hollywood escaped the debut; the program went only as far west as Kansas City.

As early as 1915 Sarnoff had dreamed of bringing events of national importance into the homes of America, but his proposal for a "radio music box" went unrealized. Finally, in 1920, his bosses at the Marconi Wireless Telegraph Company, then RCA, relented. The RCA board pledged the sum of $2000 to develop a receiver. By 1922, Sarnoff's vision of the future had materialized, and radio threatened to sweep away everything in its path—magazines, phonographs and records, concert and theater attendance. No longer could it be called a passing novelty. And radio had become "a genuine box-office menace" to the movie industry.

Merlin H. Aylesworth, the first president of NBC, introduced the inaugural program at 8 P.M. E.S.T. An incredible array of expensive talent kept the 1000 guests in the ballroom spellbound until midnight: operatic soprano Mary Garden (broadcast from Chicago), Will Rogers (from Kansas City), the renowned Metropolitan baritone Titta Ruffo, the New York Philharmonic Orchestra with Walter Damrosch conducting, Edwin Franko Goldman's Band, Vincent Lopez and his Orchestra, and the Gilbert & Sullivan Light Opera Company.

The next day the *New York Times* estimated the cost of the broadcast at $50,000. Sarnoff, the radio industry's thirty-seven-year-old guiding genius, had achieved his dream of nationwide broadcasting. He planned, fought, and risked the resources and reputation of RCA to make it a reality, and RCA held 50 percent of the stock of the new network.

Nevertheless, RCA and its colossal affiliates, General Electric and Westinghouse, were as shaken as Hollywood by the success of *The Jazz Singer.* Western Electric, their competitor, with its inferior Vitaphone sound-on-disc system, was in triumph. GE's all-electronic sound-on-film, still in the development stages, trailed far behind. Sarnoff zealously whipped RCA to get into the race. As always, his ambition reached far beyond the limits of the corporation. He felt that any offshoot of the science of radio, such as talking movies, ought not to be tethered by contractual boundaries. Why not herd these talkers into the RCA corral? GE observed the crowds outside the Warners' Broadway theater and conceded. RCA, it reluctantly admitted, would be a strong combatant to challenge the Western Electric lead.

Meanwhile, the movie moguls were jockeying for position. In the gray dawn of the talkie revolution, a few had come begging at RCA's door. Zukor and Lasky sent an emissary, Roy Pomeroy, the technical wizard who had parted the Red Sea for DeMille; and crafty William Fox came in person. RCA engineers deftly performed a "goat gland" operation on *Wings,* Paramount's World War I epic, in which machine guns crackled realistically during the dogfight sequences.

William Fox boldly suggested that RCA join forces with his embryonic Movietone system. Sarnoff turned down the offer. Why should RCA share the spoils with this movie magnate? Besides, the Movietone devices were no better than the RCA–GE system at that time.

It was generally felt that the rat-a-tat-tat of the gunfire and the whirring engines in *Wings* were more lifelike than the jazz singer's scratchy Vitaphone voice. Still in all, Vitaphone was king and moving fast, signing the other movie majors to exclusive contracts through its marketing company, Electrical Research Products, Inc. Even ASCAP, the association of composers, had been snatched by ERPI's vigorous executive, J. E. Otterson. Only the small independent studios—the midgets, such as FBO—remained.

Sarnoff set his company on a breakneck course to further develop and refine the sound system. He proposed a sound subsidiary, RCA Photophone, that he brought into being under his presidency in March 1928. But to create a market for RCA Photophone in Hollywood would require a studio, a film company that could be joined with a theater chain. In the fall of 1927 Sarnoff found the midget capable of putting RCA into the picture business, and the financial wizard to manipulate the complex merger he envisioned—Joe Kennedy.

Kennedy was riding high following his clever arrangements at Harvard. He was no longer the chief of a second-class studio but a viable member of the film colony. Moreover, he had important credentials as a former banker who still enjoyed vital Wall Street connections. In the frenzied days of what *Variety* headlined THE GREAT HOLLYWOOD PANIC when the studios were frantically converting to sound film, Kennedy's Wall Street allure proved irresistible. Among the offers that came his way were two that would crown his Hollywood career. One would make him some $5 million richer; the other would enshrine him as the lover of the most glamorous woman in Hollywood.

4

Sarnoff and Kennedy met through a mutual friend, Kennedy's business associate Louis Kirstein, the Boston department-store tycoon. The two shared similar backgrounds—Sarnoff, a Russian immigrant, and Kennedy, son of Irish immigrants—and they were motivated by the same aspirations. Sarnoff could see, beneath Kennedy's public relations grin and glib speech, the strategist who could engineer RCA's passage into Hollywood. For his part, Kennedy could almost feel the weight of the jackpot and hear the tinkle of coins as Sarnoff outlined his idea. And even though Sarnoff was a Jew, Kennedy did not classify him as a "pants presser" type. He saw in the diminutive, round-faced executive the man whose vision had ignited a new industry: the hero of radio who made history with the same deft touch he had demonstrated in his own stock-market manipulations.

So, on a wintry noon in October 1927, the two men huddled at the Grand Central Oyster Bar in midtown Manhattan. Between succulent mouthfuls of Chesapeake Bay's finest, they closed their extraordinary deal. RCA purchased a stock interest in FBO for $400,000. Then Sarnoff sent Kennedy out to joust with Keith–Albee–Orpheum, the once big-time vaudeville circuit that could still offer a desirable, if deteriorated, parcel of several hundred theaters.

By 1926, the curtain had all but descended on vaudeville. It marked the year of disaster for the two-a-day, once the entertainment of the aristocracy. Hollywood's make-believe had devoured 97 percent of America's theaters by the end of the year. Throughout the country, only six big-time vaudeville theaters remained in the East; six others were strewn across the rest of the states. By the end of the following year, there was one big-time theater left in New York, Keith–Albee's majestic Palace, the White House of vaudeville; it too was faltering. On the other hand, Marcus Loew's theater circuit shrewdly capitalized on "the opiate of the people." "It's the film that draws 'em, and the vaudeville that fills in," he exulted. And he deftly purchased Metro to unite his empire.

Strangled between the great picture palaces and the popular-priced movie houses, Keith–Albee feebly grasped at Pathé–DeMille Pictures in May 1927. An ill-matched merger, it propelled the exhibitor's foxy general manager into the president's chair at Pathé. John J. "J.J." Murdock, a dyed-in-the-wool theater man, appeared mystified by movie making. Being a Scotsman, he considered the habitual budgetary extravagance of C. B. DeMille appalling. He was further distressed by the impact of sound, went looking for a mongrel movie mogul who could "make 'em cheap," and latched onto Joe Kennedy early in 1928. J. J. Murdock and Joe Kennedy fell into each other's arms like long-lost brothers. Murdock ranked thirteen on *Variety*'s current list of the twenty wealthiest showmen—right behind the Hollywood moguls—and that made him Joe's kind of man.

Kennedy's banking associates Elisha Walker, president of the banking firm of Blair and Company, and Lehman Brothers, the bankers for Pathé and K-A-O, respectively, obliged Joe by going on a buying spree of Pathé and K-A-O stock. In February 1928, with J. J. Murdock's blessings, the Blair–Lehman banking team was sufficiently fortified to bestow on Kennedy the position of special advisor to Pathé at a weekly salary of $2000.

DeMille beamed benevolently, remembering his gracious host at Harvard. C. B. knew Kennedy's background and reputation. Joe could scarcely contain his pleasure at DeMille's reaction. His backer and Pathé's major stockholder, Jeremiah Milbank, the dignified copper-mining king, would be at Joe's disposal. That same month, Kennedy turned over a sizable interest in FBO to K-A-O. David Sarnoff had not overestimated the prowess of his chosen man.

Now Joe turned his attention to K-A-O's aging president, Edward F. Albee, and sharpened his ax. No longer the kingpin of vaudeville, Ed Albee had kept up his reputation as the most hated man in show business—the label he had inherited after the death of his boss, B. F. Keith, in 1914. Albee's enemies were legion: the performers whom he abused and his associates whose telephones he had tapped. Broadway show people cheered when Marcus Loew set out to beat the man he called "that s.o.b. Albee."

J. J. Murdock, Albee's second-in-command, had won the trust of his boss through his thriftiness and excellent service. As might be expected, he had, on occasion, conspired against him; now, under Kennedy's tutelage, he settled down to betray him in earnest. By May 1928, Kennedy was ready to strike. Murdock held a stock option in K-A-O that Albee had bestowed upon him as a bonus. With little persuasion, Murdock sold the option to Kennedy, who then approached Albee with a tempting offer: $4,200,000 in exchange for 200,000 shares of K-A-O stock! Albee wavered until his erstwhile friends, including his trusted right-hand man, reminded him that he would be receiving $21 a share, while the stock was selling for $16 on the open market. Albee agreeably sold out to Kennedy.

Three months later, Joe's high-pressure broker, Mike Meehan, a ruthless Bull Marketeer, pushed the stock up to $50 a share. Yet Albee disappointed his enemies by refusing to be vanquished. As Kennedy assumed the chairmanship of the K-A-O board, the powerless president delivered a surprising message to the *New York Times* on May 17, 1928: "Mr. Kennedy has shown in a brief but colorful career in the picture business such constructive and organizational genius that we consider him a tremendous asset to our business. He is energetic, dynamic and a straight-shooter."

Subsequently, with Murdock's connivance, the "straight-shooter" furiously knocked Albee's men out of the company and brought in all his Irish cronies, including John J. Ford, to run the Keith theaters. Albee's enemies on the trade journals beamed. With wicked glee *Variety* reported on June 27 that "the Kennedy–Ford machine gun squadron in Keith's has turned its attention to agents and bookers this week, executing many of each, with more to follow."

One day Albee foolishly cornered Kennedy in his office and started to make a suggestion. Kennedy's eyes blazed. "Didn't you know, Ed? You're washed up," he said icily. "You're through."

Albee resigned, and shortly thereafter he died. His funeral was not a major draw.

Meanwhile, Kennedy was capitalizing on his new Pathé connections. Jeremiah Milbank, the noble millionaire who had made it possible for C. B. DeMille to spend almost $2,500,000 on making *King of Kings,* had seen the religious epic come to fruition. Having accomplished his mission, he was ready to pull out. Milbank ordered his banking representative, Elisha Walker, to spruce up Pathé and look for a suitable marriage partner. Walker recommended his friend and associate Joe Kennedy, and Milbank, familiar with his good reputation, consented. Like its fellow independents, Pathé was struggling to make the painful conversion to sound. It suffered from having to compete with the monopolistic majors for screen time. Kennedy rose to the challenge, increasing sales, cutting weekly overhead costs, and shearing the salaries of the employees whom he considered "vastly overpaid." Milbank thought him "clever and quick" but DeMille paled. Even as Kennedy switched his title from advisor to chairman of the board, he named his trusted Irish henchman E. B. Derr executive vice president. DeMille picked up more bad vibrations. Abruptly, he sold his Pathé stock and severed his connections. He beat a path to MGM, taking with him his distrust of things Irish.

By the middle of 1928, Kennedy's career in Hollywood had soared at incredible speed. Now he was heading FBO, Keith–Albee–Orpheum, and Pathé, and the big cash bucks he lusted after were rolling in. Well fortified with stock options that he demanded as part of his salary, Kennedy was in the driver's seat when the durable Bull Market suddenly faltered in mid-June. As the market rumbled ominously and indiscriminate dumpings sent theater stocks plummeting, Joe cocked an ear. He snapped his fingers at his broker, Mike Meehan: His financial strength was not to be tampered with by what he sensed as only a summer storm. In fact, *Variety* reported on the amazing stick-to-it-iveness of Keith and Pathé while "the [theater] stocks which have been the subject of bullish enthusiasm for months [were] retreating in confusion." The trade publication speculated that Mike Meehan, one of the shrewdest pool managers in the whole financial district, had been put in charge of the Joseph P. Kennedy fortunes, and that Kennedy was well fortified to make a stand that would attract attention to Keith and Pathé.

Joe pushed *Variety*'s concern aside with a beefy arm, and the infamous Michael J. Meehan, an uncontested Radio expert, vigorously plied his trade: RCA tumbled more than twenty-three points in a day. So, while other insiders lost their nerve and sold, Kennedy stood his ground and bought. After a few "frantic" days, the market regained its strength and surged ahead.

Incredibly, another movie company hove into view and pursued Joe Kennedy for pontifical advice. First National Pictures, a unique major owned by a powerful alliance of theater owners who banded together in 1917 to fight the ramifications of Zukor's dictatorship, sought him out. As if directed by divine providence, Kennedy's old brokerage firm, Hayden, Stone, was directing First National's reorganization following a takeover by Stanley Rossheim of the Stanley Company of America, an imposing theater chain. *Variety* flinched at the prospect of another Kennedy-piloted company and put out some discouraging words on June 13, 1928: "Kennedy may have concluded it is best for him not to tackle too much work in the show business. Other than his own company, FBO, which is running smoothly, he has undertaken to readjust Pathé, not so easy, and also to rehabilitate the Keith circuit, the latter a stupendous job for anyone at present."

Variety plainly did not know its man. Kennedy greedily eyed the stellar roster at First National: Colleen Moore, Billie Dove, Richard Barthelmess, Corinne Griffith, Milton Sills, Ken Maynard, and more. The prospect of heightened power and a broader landscape of opportunity loomed large in his thinking.

In June, Kennedy accepted the position of special advisor to First National Pictures. He brought with him his tough lieutenant, E. B. Derr, as chief of operations. The terms of his contract, announced on August 10, awarded him an annual salary of $150,000 for five years, plus an option to purchase 25 percent of First National's stock during the period. It also granted him total authority over production and distribution, a stipulation that insiders noted with awe. A merger appeared to be in the offing that would, it was prophesied, encompass FBO and Pathé, a veritable monolith, going far beyond Sarnoff's design. Kennedy's banking associates were reported full of enthusiasm, as the potential merger represented a consolidation that would require a lucrative recapitalization.

Suddenly, the Kennedy bubble burst. First National's board of directors took a second hard look at Kennedy's contract and refused to sanction it. Several of the directors disapproved of his production program. Others felt it imprudent to hand so much power to someone calculating a merger that might give them corporate indigestion. Although Kennedy and his associates held the reins at FBO, K-A-O, and Pathé, their influence failed to impress First National's stockholders. President Irving Rossheim's explanation to *Variety* on August 29 suggested that the company had not "reached that state where artificial respiration was necessary." Kennedy's practiced smile stiffened, and he grudgingly submitted his resignation.

Humiliated and angry, he swiftly booked passage to Europe on the *Ile de France* and telephoned his wife at Hyannis Port. He told Rose to meet him in New York, that he had decided to take a six-week vacation at swanky Biarritz and Deauville. At the dock, the reporters were surprised to find J. J. Murdock boarding the luxury liner with the Kennedys. Joe explained, his good humor restored, that he and his partner were going to take advantage of the leisurely atmosphere of the voyage to put their heads together about the future of their enterprises.

Variety had already eavesdropped. On August 22, a few days before they sailed, it announced that Kennedy and Murdock had signed contracts with David Sarnoff's new company, RCA Photophone. Both FBO and Pathé were now equipped with the new sound system. Not for publication was another agreement: RCA held an option to purchase control of FBO.

5

A bombshell was about to explode across the business world that was not a secret in Hollywood. Forbidden love had permeated the movie colony since its infancy, governed by a code as strict as the Hays Office's*: Nobody talked and the outside world wondered. Kennedy had launched his own romantic liaison at the beginning of 1928, after several months of avid and thorough business preparation.

The first meeting occurred as a lunch date at the Barclay Hotel in New York, in mid-November of 1927, and had been strictly business for Gloria Swanson, the queen of Hollywood. She was in New York shopping for financing and financial advice for her next picture. Her friend Bob Kane, studio manager of her former employer, Paramount, recommended his friend Joseph P. Kennedy. Kane's referral hit the mark: Kennedy *was* available. Now, he wanted to make important pictures—as important as Paramount's *Wings,* Fox's *Seventh Heaven,* and even MGM's *The Big Parade*. His dreams crystallized when Gloria Swanson walked into the Barclay.

Petite and astonishingly beautiful at twenty-eight, with exotic blue cat's eyes, a retroussé nose, and klieg-light teeth that gave her a rapacious smile, she swept the mystery of Hollywood into the sedate dining room, a breath of magic that only the queen of the movies exuded. The earthy beauty and regal bearing that DeMille had first glimpsed in 1917 in the child-woman leaning against a door in a Mack Sennett comedy had been richly exploited. The daring director had carefully cultivated an undertone of carnal sin in her pictures. He had boldly staged a fleeting glimpse of the Swanson breasts in a bathroom scene in *Male and Female,* as well as her enticing (if costumed) posterior in a suggestive,

*The Motion Picture Producers and Distributors Association, the moguls' trade organization, was known as the Hays Office.

sexual pose as a lion's bride. Titilating titles like *Every Woman's Husband, Why Change Your Wife?*, and *The Affairs of Anatol,* boudoir sets, and sophisticated costumes had done the trick. Movie audiences worshipped her: men were her chattel, while women placed her in their dreams. After C.B. had fashioned her, the racy Elinor Glyn influence landed her in Valentino's omnipotent arms and swept her through romantic settings in a gold-beaded gown that ravished the country.* Gloria herself had successfully sidestepped the censorship czar and played a fallen woman in *Sadie Thompson,* her second independently financed picture. In spite of two divorces, several secret abortions, two children—one adopted—she was a coveted prize. Her third and current marriage to a handsome, young French marquis in 1925 thrust her to the pinnacle of Hollywood society. Gloria could claim the distinction of being the first celebrity to marry a title, impoverished though he might be.

Kennedy was properly awed by her presence, but he quickly regained his self-assurance. He knew too much about her to remain starry-eyed for long. Hadn't he heard the bitter tale of her tempestuous Paramount reign? He knew how she had turned against the studio bosses, even damning her patron saint, DeMille. During a dinner party at the Laskys' baronial apartment on Fifth Avenue, Lasky had described his trials and tribulations in trying to prevent the movie queen and her blackmailing second husband from destroying herself and her studio. A star's life must appear above reproach. The ever-present shadow of Will Hays—that "mail order Moses"—stalked the streets of Hollywood like Sherlock Holmes. Scandal belonged behind locked doors, not in the nation's headlines. The studios would take *any* action necessary to prevent it, and in Gloria's case the studio bosses resorted to some creative deception to keep her second husband, Herbert Somborn, from revealing a purported list of lovers that had actually included their names along with that of her current lover, Marshall "Mickey" Neilan, in Somborn's suit for divorce. The Paramount moguls had fabricated a telegram that instructed *them* to settle the Swanson divorce suit out of court, signed Will Hays's name to it, and thereby gained her undying enmity. The petite spitfire wound the studio around her little finger. The ungrateful Gloria had scorned their offer of $1 million a year and had then gone off to join those elitist-lunatics at United Artists—the producer-artists important enough to run their own show. Zukor and Lasky viewed her departure with a mixture of relief and anguish. Like Mary Pickford, a star of Gloria's proportions was a precious commodity that might very well prove irreplaceable.

During the preliminary exchange of pleasantries at the Barclay luncheon table, Kennedy savored his good fortune. He knew how much Gloria Swanson was worth and thought, unlike her Paramount bosses, that he knew how to

*The flamboyant English romance novelist Elinor Glyn introduced her sexual sophistication to Hollywood and created a steamy love story, *Beyond the Rocks,* for Gloria and Rudolph Valentino.

handle her. More importantly, she presented a stimulating and exciting new personal challenge. Through the main course and dessert, he played a cat-and-mouse game, hastily scanning the two proposals she showed him for financing her third picture, without betraying so much as a flicker of interest. Instead, he used his personal charm, intellect, and business acumen to intrigue her. He would have her on *his* terms, and she would help him fulfill his Hollywood ambitions.

By evening, Kennedy was ready to make his move. In the afternoon, he had informed her that he had a proposal of his own to make. Her hopes high, she readily agreed to dine with him where he outlined his plans. He dangled before her the chance of working with the greatest director in America, the Austrian genius Erich von Stroheim. Idle, following three scathing experiences with MGM and Paramount, but under contract to Pat Powers, whom he had also alienated, von Stroheim was champing at the bit to work again. Kennedy also gave her a gift: a copy of the book he had published on his lecture series at Harvard.

By January Kennedy had assumed command of Gloria's life. In less than a month he had dissolved her company, Gloria Swanson Productions, and set up Gloria Productions. Without a murmur, she put her whole life into his hands—an amazing display of trust from one who had been badly burned by men before. Willingly, she signed over her power of attorney to E. B. Derr, who became the chief officer of the production company, carrying out the boss's instructions in secrecy. It was even forbidden to mention her name directly in business negotiations. Her code name was "the client." The usual brutal housecleaning followed, with Kennedy's Irish stock company replacing her own staff. The company would be a model of efficiency, Kennedy assured her, with all the deadwood pared away. The strain of being her own boss—working sixteen to eighteen hours a day on *The Love of Sunya* and *Sadie Thompson*—had been grueling; it must have been a relief to be free to concentrate on the creative side of picture making.

Gloria missed the touch of greatness in the seven years since she had worked with DeMille. So, when Kennedy brought von Stroheim to meet her in Hollywood in December, she told him how she marveled at the transformation he had wrought in the formerly insipid Mae Murray in *The Merry Widow* at Metro. She said she related to the suffering he said he had experienced at the hands of the Paramount bosses. She pointed out that Paramount had mutilated the American version of her *Madame Sans-Gene*. They would make hash of his latest masterpiece, *The Wedding March*, she predicted.

The film story von Stroheim outlined to her in his usual measured diction and haughty manner sounded vividly cinematic and tinged with the decadence that had become his hallmark. It left Gloria a little uneasy, but since Kennedy was anxious to select a property before he returned East for Christmas, she consented. Her part would be that of an Irish Catholic convent girl, Kitty Kelly. The heroine was off trail for von Stroheim, whose specialty was Viennese *fräuleins,* but to get his hands in Kennedy's pockets the difficult artist was willing to make a concession. The character is kidnapped in her nightgown by a young German prince for his amusement on the eve of his wedding to the mad queen of the kingdom. The two are discovered by the jealous queen while they are heating up the royal residence with their passionate glances over a midnight supper. The furious monarch, brandishing a vicious blacksnake whip, lashes the poor girl, who has now draped the prince's coat over her nightie, out of the palace. The colorful story climaxes in a dance hall in German East Africa that Kitty inherits from her aunt. The prince discovers her there, and after a suspenseful chase through the African swamps, they are happily reunited.

Under the influence of von Stroheim's prestige, Kennedy enthusiastically endorsed the powerful story titled *The Swamp.*

"This is going to be a spectacular motion picture," he proudly told Gloria. "Together we'll make millions."

And they *were* successful in every respect—playing out their love scenes against the gracious Beverly Hills skyline. Kennedy rented a house on North Rodeo Drive, three blocks from Gloria's mansion on Crescent Drive. Joe made love on the same wavelength that he made money: fast and successfully. At forty, Kennedy was powerfully built—a six-footer with big biceps and muscular legs—and his boyish charm increased his appeal. Gloria did not lodge any complaints, and they became involved in a liaison that ebbed and flowed according to their schedules and the proximity of their respective spouses. Immediately, Kennedy packed Gloria's marquis off to Paris as European director of Pathé. And, while he was abroad Kennedy arranged to spend as much time as he could in Hollywood. In February, Rose gave birth to their eighth child, and he was of necessity in New York.

In May, von Stroheim announced to reporters, "It will be a typical von Stroheim film, but the shooting schedule is so concise that probably fifteen weeks will see it through."

Kennedy beamed, refusing to be disturbed by the phone calls he received warning him that the eminent director's chief talent was his genius for spending large sums of money. Lasky reported to him that von Stroheim had shot enough film on *The Wedding March* to necessitate intermissions for dinner and breakfast. "After hacking it down to four hours, we may still have to release it as two pictures," he moaned.

Kennedy laughed. "What the hell! J.L., nothing can go wrong. I've got two good men to police the Kraut," he said, speaking of Bill Le Baron, his production chief at FBO, and Benjamin Glazer, his production advisor at Pathé. Lasky merely chuckled.

Even Irving Thalberg, MGM's youthful *wunderkind,* acknowledged von Stroheim's brilliance but launched into a disconcerting description of the aberrational content of *The Merry Widow* that had escaped his critical eye. During a sizzling scene with John Gilbert and Mae Murray, the star's suspenders had dangled on the floor. "That cost us fifteen thousand to blot out," Thalberg said harshly. Then there was the lecherous old fellow in another scene who had sniffed Mae's shoes. Mae called von Stroheim "a dirty Hun."

In late May, Gloria's husband paid a short visit to Hollywood and Kennedy unenthusiastically absented himself. Henri returned to Paris in June, and although nothing was said, their relationship had changed. The affair had claimed its first victim. Gloria's marriage was foundering.

At the end of July, von Stroheim finally selected the young English actor Walter Byron to play the profligate prince in *The Swamp.* The royal palace and the convent were rising on the FBO lot under von Stroheim's supervision, and the wardrobe department was carrying out his intricate instructions to fashion the elaborate costumes he required for the crowds of palace extras.

The picture's budget settled at $228,000, a large figure for the time, and in keeping with the prestigious film Kennedy visualized. It would be shot silent, although a synchronized music track might be added. Neither von Stroheim nor Gloria evinced any interest in talking movies; nevertheless, Kennedy pointed out that Photophone was at their disposal.

Then, on August 6, FBO released its first talkie, *The Perfect Crime,* directed by Bert Glennon and starring the very British Clive Brook to accompanying hoots from the *New York Times.* The reviewer guessed correctly that it had been a silent film that FBO had liberally stuffed with sound. Kennedy closeted himself with David Sarnoff in New York. Late in October, the announcement came: RCA had exercised its option to purchase control of FBO. Radio–Keith–Orpheum, RKO, burst forth as a holding company wielding authority over both FBO and K-A-O, and with assets of $80 million. Within a year, RKO would replace them and become the latest RCA subsidiary.

RCA and its associated companies, General Electric and Westinghouse Electric—all strangers to Hollywood—now ruled a motion picture company that, thanks to the merger, was endowed with several hundred theaters.

Kennedy resigned from his post of president of FBO, as well as that of chairman of the board of K-A-O, and grabbed his personal gesture of appreciation from parent RCA: $150,000 for executing the merger. He cashed in his stock and crooked his finger for Mike Meehan: An option on 75,000 shares of K-A-O stock was burning a hole in his portfolio. Although he no longer occupied the executive suites at FBO and K-A-O, Joe was far from through. Also, he was not ready to loosen his hold on Pathé. So, Kennedy and his "silent" partner, Guy Currier, who had shaped the syndicate to buy FBO, abandoned their holdings in the company for approximately $5 million and bade each other an unfriendly farewell. Kennedy had dealt with Sarnoff behind his back, and Currier felt betrayed.

Then, early in November, Gloria went to the FBO lot where a lovely new dressing room that Joe ordered awaited her. Von Stroheim appeared in excellent humor. He had even agreed to a change of title, the distributor, United Artists, having insisted that his title, *The Swamp,* would drive audiences away. Everything was perfection in his German kingdom; every detail of *Queen Kelly* met with his approval. Will Hays had blessed the script after converting the African dance hall into a "virtuous" hotel. Even Robert Sherwood, playwright and editor of *Life* magazine, pronounced it a masterpiece-to-be. So, while David Sarnoff and the general counsel of Keith–Albee–Orpheum adjourned to White Sulphur Springs to draw up an operating plan for RKO in a vacation atmosphere, shooting began. There seemed to be no dark clouds on the horizon.

Louella Parsons, surveying the impressive scene, blissfully heralded Kennedy as "the coming Napoleon of the movies."

It was a dangerous comparison.

PART TWO

THE TITANIC STUDIO: THE LE BARON ADMINISTRATION, 1929–1931

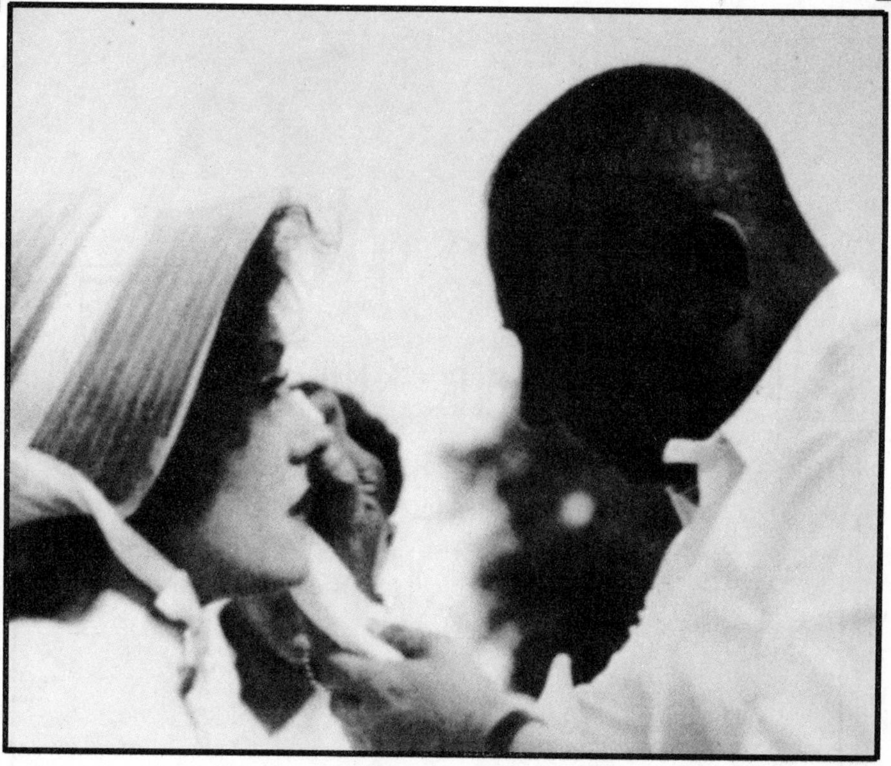

Gloria Swanson and Erich von Stroheim on the set of *Queen Kelly,* 1928.
Courtesy Marc Wanamaker, Bison Archives.

Walkway to the administration building from Gower Street, circa 1929.
Courtesy Marc Wanamaker, Bison Archives.

One of the spectacular production numbers in William Le Baron's *Rio Rita,* 1929. At center stage is Robert Woolsey, half of the comedy team of Wheeler & Woolsey.
Courtesy Marc Wanamaker, Bison Archives.

Members of the little café jazz band in *Street Girl,* 1929, RKO's first official release. From left: Jack Oakie, Guy Buccola, Betty Compson, John Harron, and Ned Sparks.
Courtesy of the Academy of Motion Picture Arts and Sciences.

Vaudeville, musical comedy star, and budding RKO actress Thelma White, poses for a publicity still, shortly after being signed by the studio in 1933.
Courtesy Thelma White.

John Boles and Bebe Daniels in William Le Baron's *Rio Rita.*
Courtesy of the Academy of Motion Picture Arts and Sciences.

A night scene from *Cimarron*, 1929, showing one of the massive sets.
Courtesy Marc Wanamaker, Bison Archives.

Main entrance, 780 North Gower, 1930.
Courtesy Marc Wanamaker, Bison Archives.

Looking down on the Culver City studio of Pathé in 1930, just before the "sacrificial" merger.
Courtesy Marc Wanamaker, Bison Archives.

William Le Baron, RKO's first production head.
Courtesy Marc Wanamaker, Bison Archives.

Joseph I. Schnitzer, Radio Pictures' first president.
Courtesy Marc Wanamaker, Bison Archives.

William Le Baron's massive Western *Cimarron,* 1931, won three Academy Awards. From left: William Le Baron, art director Max Ree, U.S. vice president and awards presenter Charles Curtis, and screenwriter Howard Estabrook.
Courtesy Marc Wanamaker, Bison Archives.

The RKO comedy team of Bert Wheeler, right, and Robert Woolsey.
Courtesy Museum of Modern Art/Film Stills Archive.

Composer Max Steiner during the period he headed the music department at RKO.
Courtesy Marc Wanamaker, Bison Archives.

6

The year of decision had come in Hollywood. By 1929, the silents belonged to the dark ages; the future to sound. The evidence was irrefutable: The moviegoing public had parted with more than $1,500,000 to experience the thrill of the human voice in *The Jazz Singer.* There was no turning back or standing still—and scarcely time to mourn the movie mogul toll of that turbulent period: Sam Warner, who had unwittingly given Hollywood a second act, died on the eve of *The Jazz Singer*'s premiere. Marcus Loew, that Solomon of moguls revered by all, preceded him by weeks. For their fellow moguls it was proof enough that an era had come to an end.

With its silent art now rendered as obsolete as Mary Pickford's curls, Hollywood sold its soul to Wall Street in exchange for $24 million worth of brick and concrete, kiln-dried wood, and other atrocities that shut out the God-given sunlight and sealed in the engineer's tricks in new sound stages. Theaters were gradually consuming another $300 million in renovations, and the consequences were awesome. As 1929 began, more than forty presidents of banks and electrical companies were making their presence felt on the boards of the ten most important film companies. Radio–Keith–Orpheum, because of its mixed blood, had to tolerate nineteen bankers, and a big leather manufacturer—another stranger to Hollywood—as its chief. "Selling entertainment, if you have the goods…is just the same as selling anything else," announced Hiram S. Brown, former president of the U.S. Leather Co. and newly elected president of Radio–Keith–Orpheum.

Radio Pictures, RCA's newly formed production subsidiary, had as its spokesman Joseph I. Schnitzer, whose extensive background in distribution and as a former vice president of FBO made him a likelier candidate than Brown for the presidency. Schnitzer's laconic announcement to *Film Daily,* "*Rio Rita,* talker and singer, to be made by FBO," caused shock waves to hit the executive boardroom of RKO's new offices in the Bond Building in New York. RKO's new chairman of the board, David Sarnoff, shuddered. The world needed to be informed that the second-rate FBO had been transformed into a first-class studio whose initial "super-attraction" would be Flo Ziegfeld's "gorgeous smash hit musical comedy, *Rio Rita.*" Sarnoff ordered a publicity campaign.

Against a scene of flaring lightning bolts and flaming radio beacons, full-page ads in the trades proclaimed:

> The Radio Titan Opens the Curtains of the Clouds and a New and Greater Year Dawns for the Most Spectacular Show Machine of All Time! A New and Mightier Pageant of the Titans is forming...Titanic in Conception...Titanic in Development...Titanic in Reality...Sweeping on to a Mighty Destiny.

So, as the trades continued to reverberate with the little studio's projected bigness, announcing, "Florenz Ziegfeld, greatest showman in the world, gives his genius to Radio Pictures," the flotsam from the defunct FBO lot departed. Old standbys, including the cowboy stars, Ranger the dog, and even the champ, Tom Mix, slunk out the back gate. RKO committed $4 million to overhaul the old-fashioned lot and harvest its initial ambitious crop of thirty sound films for the 1929–30 season. The Titan Gang in New York was hell-bent on getting a sophisticated image for its "titanic" offspring.* The sound musical, a new and prolific film cycle, had just hit Hollywood. RKO intended to jump on the bandwagon with Ziegfeld's 1927 Broadway sensation, *Rio Rita.*

The man of the hour was the studio production chief, Bill Le Baron. To him fell the challenge of competing with and beating MGM's first all-talkie marvel, *Broadway Melody* (February 1, 1929), and a flock of imitative and occasionally original musicals, such as Universal's *Show Boat,* Paramount's *The Cocoanuts,* Fox's *Sunny Side Up,* and Warner's *The Desert Song.* A fortunate holdover from FBO, Le Baron seemed well equipped to lead the little studio to glory. He was forty-six, a scholarly and kindly gentleman—far from the epitome of a movie executive. Le Baron's creativity had first erupted in a 1906 undergraduate show at New York University. Jesse Lasky, then an ambitious young vaudeville producer, caught the show, *The Ides of March.* Lasky overlooked its promising composer, college senior Deems Taylor, and impulsively hired its book writer. Bill Le Baron had a flair for musicals, and by 1918 his association with the great theatrical producer Charles B. Dillingham had brought forth *Apple Blossoms, Her Regiment,* and other nonmusical plays. The following year he embarked on a movie career as a scenarist, eventually directing the Marion Davies vehicles *When Knighthood Was in Flower* and *Little Old New York* for Cosmopolitan Productions in New York, the company William Randolph Hearst maintained for his Maid Marian. In 1924 Le Baron moved to Famous Players–Lasky, where Lasky made him a

*The press, perhaps inspired by the hyperbolic ads, labeled Sarnoff, Brown, Schnitzer, and the others "The Titan Gang."

supervisor, then put him in charge of the company's competitive Long Island studios in Astoria, a post he held until 1927, when he left to join FBO as production chief.

Le Baron's first task for the fledgling studio—that of building a creative force—afforded him the chance to air his good taste. Thus, he hired a stylish art director and costume designer, Max Ree, whose sophisticated and distinctive scenic designs had kindled the New York stage. The Danish-born artist had been brought to the coast by Max Reinhardt in 1925 to design his magical production of *A Midsummer Night's Dream* at the Hollywood Bowl. Max Ree's first big assignment at the studio was to adapt the elaborate *Rio Rita* stage settings for the screen. Harry Tierney, *Rio Rita*'s composer, recommended a gifted Viennese, Max Steiner, to orchestrate the screen version. Steiner was a popular figure in the Broadway pits, conducting and orchestrating for Victor Herbert, George Gershwin, Jerome Kern, Vincent Youmans, and other musical geniuses. Le Baron had invited Steiner to Hollywood as director of music for the studio. By the following year, he headed the music department.

To direct *Rio Rita* as well as write the dialogue, Le Baron chose a stage director and scenarist from his Cosmopolitan Studio days, Luther Reed. Le Baron rightly believed that a silent scenario writer could master the art of scripting a talkie faster than a Broadway playwright, for it seemed that the Broadwayites who had been pulled to the coast were unable to relinquish the stage play form.

For the starring role in their "epoch making" musical, the Titan Gang was eyeing Marilyn Miller, the delectable Ziegfeld darling. The theory that only actors with stage experience could deliver an acceptable accent had swept through the film colony with a vengeance. Broadway talent was hot—Hollywood stars with uncultured and untrained vocal cords were on the hot seat. "Most of the existing screen celebrities have found that all they need is a little gargle water," *Variety* printed in the spring of 1929, in an effort to spread some cheer. Nevertheless, Emil Jannings was ready to pack the Academy Award he had just won for not talking and go home to Germany, Pola Negri refused to try, and Vilma Banky, under duress from her boss, Samuel Goldwyn, talked in a horrid Hungarian accent. The list of candidates playing the waiting game included stars of the magnitude of Greta Garbo, Lillian Gish, and Norma Talmadge. The dashing lover John Gilbert walked a shredded tightrope. Some of the silent era idols, such as Mary Pickford, Douglas Fairbanks, and even Clara Bow were granted a reprieve; for as *Variety* stated on April 3, 1929, "When Clara flashes a gam, all senses are deadened." Not as fortunate were Paramount contract players Thomas Meighan, Richard Dix, and Bebe Daniels, who were cruelly let go when the studio disdained to give them voice tests and Paramount's chief studio executive on the Coast, B. P. Schulberg, allowed their contract options to lapse.

Bebe, spunky and a born survivor who had jumped from Harold Lloyd two-reelers in her teens to big-salaried tomboyish comedy films in her twenties, was not about to be put out to pasture at the ripe old age of twenty-eight. With ten months of her contract left, she dashed around the corner to the Radio lot. In the twinkling of an eye, Bill Le Baron bought her services away from Paramount and signed her for four pictures.

When Bebe heard about *Rio Rita,* she marched into Le Baron's office to ask for the starring role. "I was not aware that you could sing," he said blandly, reserving judgment.

"Oh, but I can," Bebe blurted out. She had been studying with a singing teacher, she told him, and pleaded for a test to prove it. "The talkies don't scare me; I know I can talk and sing."

Le Baron suddenly remembered a party he had attended recently. The actress had done a ukelele number and harmonized in a pleasing soprano with Bessie Love. Bebe's piquant personality fitted her for a peppery Mexican *señorita;* moreover, her brunette beauty would translate effectively in the Technicolor sequences that were planned for the spectacular production numbers in the second half of the musical. Color, almost as old an invention as sound, had been revived as a diversionary tactic in this difficult period. The two-strip color process had already made a deep hole in the picture's $675,000 budget, but Le Baron prayed it would take the audience's mind off any flaws in the new Photophone sound system. Luckily, Bebe agreed to work for a fraction of her usual salary and receive a percentage of the gross.

To ensure her success in her initial talkie, she produced a secret weapon: "the father of sound." Dr. Lee De Forest, her second cousin, frequented the set during the twenty-four-day shooting period, fiddling with the microphone, shifting mikes about, and reassuring the greenhorns that there was life after sound.

Filming a talkie called for heroism. Gone was the comforting whir of the cameras, the stimulation of music from a small orchestra on the sidelines. The diabolic mikes picked up and magnified sounds the actors never dreamed existed. Walter Plunkett, in charge of wardrobe, had to throw out his old palette; the two-color process consisted of cyan and a red-orange, leaving few colors to work with. Then he was forced to eliminate all the "ear-splitting" costume fabrics and accessories such as taffeta, silk, and beads. On the plus side, taffeta could be used for "noise effects": the crackle of fire or the ominous rattle of an earthquake. Petticoats had to be made of felt and wool, and the wardrobe department assembled ingenious coverings of felt and rubber to silence shoes, because the sound of a pair of shoes in action could rival the sound of a herd of stampeding elephants. The hand fans Señorita Rita Ferguson used to flirt with Ranger Captain John Boles in the scenario were particularly irksome. Walter Plunkett had to construct them of clatter-proof material.

Sound stages were still under construction. Bill Le Baron had placed the veteran director Wesley Ruggles's *Street Girl* (Betty Compson's first starring role for Radio) into production along with *Rio Rita*. Both films were forced to share the only available sound channel. Still, morale remained high and the lot hummed with excitement and the sounds of New York accents from the chorus girls and boys who had been recruited to populate the big musical. Best of all, in everyone's opinion, was the presence of Bebe Daniels, an important star from Paramount.

Representing Bill Le Baron on the editing of *Rio Rita* was young Pandro Berman, already on the lot. The cutting room, however, belonged to Billy Hamilton, a veteran cutter who kept his creativity humming with relays of double bourbons at Nick the Greek's Melrose Grotto, behind the studio.

Street Girl, a less ambitious picture than *Rio Rita,* was finished and reached theaters first—its opening ballyhooed by the trades as "an event of historic importance," which took place the evening of July 30, 1929, at the Globe Theatre in New York. On hand to applaud Radio's formal entrance into the heady world of show business were the powerful denizens of RCA and its electrical affiliates who also served on RKO's directorate. RCA's vice president, David Sarnoff, flanked by his boss, Major General James G. Harboard, and a covey of other business leaders, including Westinghouse Electric's Owen D. Young, NBC's Merlin Aylesworth, and RKO's Hiram Brown, lent what the press described as "an atmosphere of dignity and stability seldom observed at a premiere."

There were few movie moguls in attendance—only Sam Katz of Publix Theatres, Harry Warner of Warner Brothers–First National, and Spyros Skouras, Warner's Greek Orthodox man in charge of theaters. In a move that had brought Zukor to his knees the previous year, the triumphant Warners had seized First National along with the Skouras brothers' theater chain, a king's ransom in theaters. Notably absent was William Fox, whose star was on the wane. The go-for-broke mogul had dealt himself the biggest prize of all the preceding spring: Loew's, Inc., the keeper of the most glamorous factory in Hollywood, MGM. Sadly, on this evening he hovered between life and death following a near-fatal car crash a few weeks earlier.

Sharing the limelight and thick as thieves were the Sarnoff "brothers-in-crime," Joe Kennedy and J. J. Murdock. They were still holding down the fort at Pathé. However, the RCA contingent and its Photophone brethren clearly dominated the scene, but Radio's high-spirited Wall Street specialist was not among them. "Financier Mike Meehan," as he was referred to by the trades, had made overtures to purchase Pathé in April. Reports circulated that he was associated with John J. Raskob, the Democratic Party's national chairman, but since RCA, through Radio–Keith–Orpheum, owned a stock interest in Pathé,

Sarnoff was in position to reject the proposed acquisition. Still, Mike Meehan had served the family well. In March, he conducted a great RCA stock pool that netted its eminent participants, including Mrs. David Sarnoff and Raskob, just under $5 million. For his dexterity in driving the stock from 90 to 109 in little more than a week, Meehan and his loyal Irish retainers received a fee of $500,000.

Street Girl, Radio Pictures' first official release, won the unrestrained applause of the packed theater audience. "There are laughs galore....The characters are real," reported *Variety* (August 7, 1929) of the musical drama that was based on W. Carey Wonderley's *The Viennese Charmer,* with dialogue by Jane Murfin. The reviewer cautioned that the story of this street girl—Betty Compson, befriended by a small jazz band quartet that she guides to success—might not represent "a faithful cross-section of theatrical life." The "dour jazz fiddler," Ned Sparks, and the "happy-go-lucky clarinetist," Jack Oakie, were singled out for praise, and John Harron and Guy Buccola completed the quartet. *Variety* acknowledged that Betty Compson's charms were a trifle overripe for the role, but the actress was nonetheless commended for her trouping and vocal efforts.

There was no such hedging of Bebe Daniels's virtuosity in her terrific comeback in *Rio Rita,* which opened the newly wired Earl Carroll Theatre on October 6, 1929. "Despite very strong competition, Bebe is the most glowing personality," wrote *Photoplay* in November. "Her voice, untrained as it is, has a rich quality which an experienced prima donna might well envy." John Boles, plucked off the stage by Gloria Swanson to play her leading man in *The Love of Sunya,* displayed in *Rio Rita* what *Photoplay* called a "dashing tenor voice." Before Photophone he had been a rich baritone. Bert Wheeler, the better half of the stage comedy act of Wheeler & Woolsey, received raves for his "inebriate characterization." Hailed as "the finest of the screen musicals," the film capitalized on the unfailing Ziegfeld stage pageantry and added some open-air touches, the effectiveness of which was not lost on the critics.

Rio Rita grossed $2¼ million and was selected by *Film Daily* as one of the year's ten best films. The Titan Gang was euphoric. Not so Adolph Zukor. The diminutive mogul observed *Rio Rita*'s triumph with displeasure. What was Paramount's *own* Bebe Daniels doing in a Radio picture? Why had B. P. Schulberg let her escape?

A call from his boss in New York brought Schulberg to attention in Hollywood. The shrewd executive listened to the sepulchral voice that had earned Zukor the nickname of "Creeping Jesus." Schulberg was an old hand in the business. As Zukor's press agent for his former company, Famous Players, he had put words into the immortal Sarah Bernhardt's mouth. Chewing his cigar thoughtfully, Schulberg recalled that he had never tested the actress;

therefore he was safe. The boss would have no rebuttal for what he was about to tell him. Removing his cigar with a flourish, he spoke with authority.

"She couldn't talk," said B.P.

7

While relaxing in Palm Beach in January 1929, Joe Kennedy received an alarming telephone call from Hollywood. It caught him unawares. Mike Meehan had performed splendidly in December; Joe's RKO "A" stock, which he had taken in exchange for his big bundle of K-A-O shares, had risen from $21 to about $50 a share, enabling him to clear a comfortable profit of some $2 million. It had not been reinvested. Kennedy, unlike most of the Wall Street fraternity, had read undeniable danger signals in the runaway Bull Market triggered by Herbert Hoover's election victory the previous year. Kennedy's phenomenal sense of timing had served him well during the market slump of June 1928, when he took his stand and defied popular opinion. Now, he disagreed with the boosters who were inflaming the country with their false optimism. The big-time suckers could have the Street all to themselves. He was pulling out. However, his brief sabbatical had been interrupted by Gloria's disturbing phone call. He had talked to her several times over the Christmas holidays: Henri had been in Hollywood, and he with Rose and the children, and Gloria had expressed concern that the von Stroheim picture was running badly behind schedule. After the holidays, he conferred with Bill Le Baron and Ben Glazer. They were not unduly alarmed. Kennedy thought, Could the filthy Kraut have drugged his guards?

Gloria herself had been mesmerized by von Stroheim's method of filmmaking, his uncompromising quest for perfection that resulted in scenes of inexpressible beauty. At first she understood why he would spend an entire day lingering over the most insignificant detail, only to reshoot the scene the following day; the rushes bore a three-dimensional quality, pulsating with life. The scenes in Griffith Park, which doubled for the convent neighborhood in his German kingdom, reminded her of landscapes she had seen in the Louvre.

Then something shocking occurred. It was the scene of Kitty's first encounter with the prince; she curtsies to him and her panties slip down. A bit of innocent byplay follows in which Kitty tosses the undergarment at the amused monarch. Von Stroheim had actually directed the actor, Walter Byron, to caress the panties against his face. Still, Gloria could not bring herself to protest when she saw the rushes—the aesthetic values surrounding the erotic business overshadowed it.

However, in December, she began to feel that the director's passion for artistic perfection might be having an adverse effect on the budget, and she found herself counting the number of takes, noting how many days the meticulous director spent to film a page of script.

In January the company moved to the Pathé lot, where Gloria was thrilled to find a lavish bungalow completely outfitted with a grand piano—an extravagant surprise from her lover. Her pleasure was short lived. As shooting commenced on the African sequences, Gloria again took stock of the situation. Figuring that von Stroheim had already shot more than ten hours of film—yet only one-third of the two-hour picture, after editing—she realized it might take another four months before he completed shooting!

Then, her worries were overpowered by the shock and revulsion she felt when the new rushes unrolled. The seedy hotel in East Africa had taken on the characteristics of a brothel. What Will Hays had deleted had mysteriously reappeared, including a scene of a black priest giving last rites to the dying aunt. Hays had feared that this association, although valid in Africa, might displease Catholics and was sure to antagonize the Ku Klux Klan. Unable to subdue his passion for realism, the erratic director had proceeded to improvise a "typical" von Stroheim story.

For the next few days, Gloria tolerated the new script in which von Stroheim had her marrying a lecherous old cripple in a wedding scene that might have been set in the precincts of Hell. On the morning of the third day, she could stand it no longer. Under the director's ardent tutelage, Tully Marshall, playing the dirty old bridegroom, drooled tobacco juice on her hand as he forced the wedding ring onto her finger. Sick to her stomach and seething with anger, Gloria turned on her heels and fled the set.

As soon as Kennedy arrived in Hollywood, his misgivings were fortified by a call from Will Hays. He closeted himself in the projection room at Pathé, where his worst fears were substantiated. Not only did the African footage disgust him, but the characters and sets were in total contradiction to the European sequences. His shock rapidly gave way to fury. He had been duped and betrayed. The prestige and power that he intended to reap from a truly important picture had been snatched from him. Furthermore, as an eminent Roman Catholic—a fact that Will Hays had stressed —he had been placed in an intolerable position. Worst of all was the overwhelming realization of failure. He had failed, for the first time in his life. Cursing the bastards, von Stroheim and his accomplices, afforded him little comfort. Nor did he find much relief in Gloria's arms. The knowledge that her portrayal of Sadie Thompson in a production he had underrated had earned her an Academy Award nomination served only to rub salt into the wound.

The news of the film Waterloo traveled fast. Von Stroheim's enemies exulted, while Kennedy's friends did their best to salve his wounds. Thalberg, a brilliant tactician, suggested it might be to his advantage to consider ways of salvaging the mess. "The New York critics loved *The Merry Widow* after I restored the Lehár frosting," he told Kennedy.

Lasky seconded the opinion, reminiscing about how he had once been run out of town when he toured with Hermann the Great, the famous magician whose tricks had not always come off. "This is the time to take a firm hand to your rabbit," he advised.

Anxious to redeem his self-esteem, and not unmindful that $600,000 had sunk with *Queen Kelly,* Kennedy clutched at their suggestion that Eddie Goulding, the English writer-director and a great favorite in Hollywood, might be able to turn the fiasco into a triumph. Unfortunately, Goulding failed. He could find no way to reverse the polluted tide, he admitted with a rueful smile. Nonetheless, the obliging Britisher offered to justify the salary he received by coming up with a new picture.

Grim-faced, Kennedy waved him aside and turned to the next candidate, Richard Boleslavski, a recent arrival with impressive Broadway credits.

"This Polack, Boleslavski, tells me that a few songs, some dialogue, and a happy ending will work wonders," he told Gloria after the new director had studied the footage. Kennedy's smile returned. Sound would be the miracle worker.

While the Polish wizard prepared to exorcise *Queen Kelly,* Gloria, with Kennedy's permission, took advantage of Eddie Goulding's generous offer. In a month's time, while Kennedy was in the East, they came up with a little inexpensive talkie—a frothy melodrama—that Goulding titled *The Trespasser* and his friend Laura Hope Crews, the stage actress, helped write. In eighteen days Gloria's quickie was shot on the Pathé lot, then cut and scored in record time and shipped to New York.

The United Artists sales force reacted with such fervor that it was decided, again with Kennedy's approval, to bypass UA's first-run house, the Rialto, which was booked through October, and hold the world premiere in London in September.

At Kennedy's insistence, Gloria, armed with a girlfriend, sailed on the same boat with the Kennedys, and Henri met them in Le Havre. London went wild over Gloria and her little picture, in which she warbled quite prettily for the first time. Eddie Goulding's inspired song "Love, Your Magic Spell Is Everywhere" seemed destined for the hit parade. Kennedy hovered adoringly over Gloria, while Rose looked serene and Henri brooded.

The affair had reached its zenith.

8

Hollywood was aglow with confidence as 1929 faded—ready to believe that it would be untouched by the holocaust that struck Wall Street. Indeed, it appeared that the industry had picked up the checks that financed the expensive sound alterations just in the nick of time. Sound might have been preceded by a worse devil if Hollywood had waited another year. Back in 1926, *Variety* had headlined the phenomena RADIO ARTISTS MAY BE SEEN AND HEARD IN TELEVISION. The banks and electric companies might very well have placed their bets on the more expedient dark horse, home entertainment, with the onset of the Depression.

However, the net profits for 1929 encouraged euphoria; the talkies were proving their worth. Almost every company made big money. Warner led the pack with $17,271,805. Radio-Keith trailed behind, but the returns were not unhealthy: $1,669,564 in 1929. Nineteen-thirty would bring in $3,385,628.

On the occasion of RKO's first sales convention, held in Chicago in June 1929, Radio–Keith–Orpheum's president, Hiram Brown, echoed the braggadocio that had overseasoned the trades for months. The former shoe manufacturer pledged a continuation of "big, first-class productions" and boasted that "Radio is too big to be in pictures without being the dominant factor."

Back in Hollywood, where Bill Le Baron coped with the everyday tussle of running a studio, the effusive statements of the Titan Gang were harder to swallow. In its firm commitment to the song-and-dance cycle through 1929, Le Baron's product reflected the extent to which it basked in the sophisticated New York atmosphere of *Broadway Melody,* the trend setter that had snatched the Academy Award in 1928–29. The entertainment elements and polish of his *Rio Rita* were not duplicated in musicals such as *Syncopation,** directed by Bert Glennon; in *Side Street* and *Night Parade,* both directed by Malcolm St. Clair; nor in *Jazz Heaven,* directed by Melville Brown. The stories, often banal, drew upon a variety of urban ingredients: Tin Pan Alley, racketeers and cops, "Hebe" comedy, "the old prizefight hoke," and in the case of *Syncopation,* the story line merely served as coat hanger for the exploitable music of Fred Waring's Pennsylvanians and radio's Morton Downey.

Le Baron continued the song-and-dance marathon through 1930, paying more attention to comedy (by Wheeler & Woolsey) and some offbeat items, such as *The Case of Sergeant Grischa,* an arty World War I drama, directed by the great Herbert Brenon, and *Check and Double Check,* directed by Melville

*Actually RKO's first picture, preceding *Street Girl* by several months.

Brown, which *Variety* defined as "a freak talking picture with those air [radio] faddists, Amos 'n' Andy."

The musicals were all second-raters and the form was getting frayed. Luther Reed's *Hit the Deck,* still another Broadway-based musical, was dubbed by *Variety* merely "a nice programmer" despite thirty-one minutes of color, Paramount's Jack Oakie, and "a score that tinkles" by Vincent Youmans. *Dixiana,* a big, original, part-technicolor musical with Harry Tierney tunes, also directed by Luther Reed, offered even more production riches—Bebe Daniels as "the most beautiful woman in the South," Wheeler & Woolsey, Everett Marshall, a Metropolitan Opera tenor, and a tap-dancing Negro, Bill Robinson, who took the audience by storm—but it, too, fell flat.

Bebe fared better in *Lawful Larceny,* a "husband stealing" comedy-drama directed by and starring the suave Lowell Sherman. In *Alias French Gertie,* directed by George Archainbaud, she played smooth Gertie to her fiancé Ben Lyon's slick partner-in-crime. A few months later, in June, Bebe married her co-star and her off-screen life was complete, but she was less than happy with her roles at RKO. In *Dixiana* she missed the chemistry she had enjoyed with John Boles, and she wanted another chance to work with him. Le Baron would not oblige, and their rapport disintegrated. In January 1931, he sold her contract to Warner Bros.

Moviegoers had been greeted with an unexpected gift on Christmas Day in 1928. For the first time an audience heard the neighing of a horse—the Cisco Kid's—the clip-clop of its hooves, and all the other provocative sounds that symbolized the Old West, showcased against an authentic Western background. A revitalized Western had delighted audiences jaded from a heavy diet of musicals, and the critical acclaim that followed in the wake of Raoul Walsh's *In Old Arizona,* starring Warner Baxter in an Academy Award–winning performance, signaled a mass movement outdoors with mike and camera. Paramount galloped down the Fox trail the following year with a stunning remake of *The Virginian,* directed by Victor Fleming and starring a taciturn Gary Cooper.

In 1930 Bill Le Baron began production on the biggest project of his career: a massive Western at a cost of nearly $1.5 million that promised to be the answer to President Hiram Brown's sales pitch. Based on Edna Ferber's 1929 best seller *Cimarron,* about the great Oklahoma land rush of 1889 and the forging of the Territory into a state, it covered a period of forty years of American history. It strained the resources of the young studio, but Le Baron's belief in delegating authority to his staff—one trade journal pointed out that he gave them "the right of way to use their God-given mentality and ability"—served him well in bringing forth the super epic. Le Baron handed Wesley

Ruggles the important directorial assignment, and Louis Sarecky, one of several production supervisors he had hired, became his associate on *Cimarron.*

The logistics were staggering. Five months were spent in intensive preproduction preparations, during which time the research department, headed by Elizabeth McGaffey and reinforced by Harold Hendee, worked around the clock while three camera units fanned out across the state of Oklahoma. Max Ree's art department labored through the fall designing, in particular, the three gigantic stages to be occupied by units filming the interiors. Scenes of the Indian Territory were reproduced on the lot as well, with fifty-one members of the Osage Indian tribe, all millionaires from the oil-rich Oklahoma reservation, playing their own ancestors.

Le Baron hired action expert B. Reeves Eason, whom everyone called "Breezy," to engineer the extremely difficult Oklahoma Run sequence. As a second-unit director of big-budget epics, Eason had constructed the hair-raising chariot race in *Ben Hur* five years earlier. For these scenes, requiring 5000 extras and an army of technicians, a vast tent city was built in the foothills near Bakersfield, with corrals for livestock covering forty acres. Fifteen miles of pipe were laid to supply water to the camp; provisions and equipment were transported by 400 railway cars. With all in readiness, nature intervened, and the company fretted while rains fell for four days. On the fifth day, forty-seven cameramen, not including the newsreel contingent, commanded by collegiate-looking Eddie Cronjager, trained their lenses on the crucial scene that the souvenir program advertised as:

> The Greatest Moment the Screen Has Ever Known.... A Thundering Hour That Shook the World.... Fifty Thousand Stampeded Humans Sweep in a Brawling Mass Across the Line....Crazed Men...Frenzied Women...Wild-Eyed Children...Sprawling under Murderous Hoofs...Careening on into a Wilderness That by Sundown Was to Be the Maddest Empire Ever Known!

Richard Dix, whom Le Baron had providentially signed the year before, was handed the leading role of the peripatetic but fascinating Ferber hero, Yancy Cravat. Dix had received mixed reviews for his first two RKO pictures, *Shooting Straight,* in which he played a heroic gangster, a part that suited him, and *Seven Keys to Baldpate,* adapted from George M. Cohan's mystery play, a miscast effort. In Yancy Cravat, he had found the greatest role of his career. Based in part on Temple Houston, the flamboyant attorney who wore rattlesnake-skin ties and could call Sam Houston father, the part had infinitely more depth than the brand of rugged Western hero Dix had played without interruption at Paramount. Long on charm but short on husbandly virtues,

Cravat leaves his faithful, loving wife to run a newspaper he has started and assume his political obligation. He goes off in search of new horizons, only reappearing in time to die in her arms at the end.

Broadway star Fay Bainter, the popular choice for the role of Sabra Cravat, which required her to age from seventeen to sixty, lost out to a lovely and younger RKO newcomer, Irene Dunne. A musical comedy prima donna, Irene had already played another Ferber heroine, Magnolia, in Ziegfeld's lavish road company production of *Show Boat.* Convent bred and a graduate of the Chicago College of Music, she had a dignity, stage presence, and aristocratic beauty that attracted Le Baron when he saw her on the stage in Chicago. Luckily, Irene's marriage to a conservative New York dentist, Dr. Francis Griffin, did not stand in the way of a studio contract. Her first picture, a classic case of miscasting, pitted her against comic Eddy Foy Jr. in an Edmond Loew–Victor McLaglen–style "service" comedy, *Leathernecking.* It prompted the *New York Times* to wonder why "a charming, romantic actress like Irene Dunne" had been cast opposite "a comedian like Eddy Foy Jr." In keeping with studio practice, the new contractee had been thrown into the first available picture. Her next role, announced in June, in Victor Herbert's tuneful operetta *Babes in Toyland,* would have showed her off to advantage. Meanwhile, fate took a hand in Irene's career. The curtailment of Hollywood musicals led to the extravagant production's being shelved. With her instinctive sense of what was right for herself, Irene went after the lead in *Cimarron.*

Richard Dix, who had been impressed with her stage work, launched his own campaign to convince Le Baron and director Wesley Ruggles that Dunne was right for the part. Finally, Irene won the role by proving her versatility in a final screen test as the elderly Sabra, wearing makeup by Ernest Westmore (who was honored by a special cup from the Motion Picture Academy for his work on the picture) and a quaint bonnet she had spied on a little old lady in the wardrobe department.

Premiered at the Globe Theater on January 26, 1931, *Cimarron* reaped unqualified praise. The *New York Daily News* called it "magnificent in scope, powerful in treatment, admirable in action." *New York Times* critic Mordaunt Hall deemed it "graphic and engrossing...a stupendous undertaking, in view of the time that is covered and the host of persons in its scenes." The film had been shot in chronological order, adhering to Edna Ferber's sprawling style, and, in spite of being episodic, the *Times* still felt that it never dragged. *Variety*'s Sime Silverman raved, "An elegant example of super filmmaking and a big money picture.... A spectacular Western, away from all the others." *The Hollywood Filmograph*'s Harry Burns delivered a eulogy, spreading praise evenly over the length of the studio from the leadership of Bill Le Baron and Wesley Ruggles to Clem Portman "for the sound recording" and Billy Hamilton, "film editor on the job." *The Independent Weekly* credited Radio

Pictures for putting "Richard Dix back on the movie map" and said of his performance that garnered an Academy Award nomination, "His Yancy Cravat will live for years!" Burns dubbed Irene Dunne, who also picked up a nomination, "the new Ruth Chatterton of the talkies," and named Edna Mae Oliver, the stage favorite and another *Show Boat* alumna, who played a nosy Colonial dame, "one of the most finished comediennes in filmland."

Max Steiner, whose original music score enriched the picture, was missing from the credits on the souvenir program. However, the preview cards called attention to his vibrant music, asking about the nameless composer. After this breakthrough score, the credits included Steiner's name on all his pictures.

Cimarron collected Academy Awards for best picture, best art direction for Max Ree, and best writing (adaptation) for Howard Estabrook. RKO belonged with the majors now, yet the Titan Gang was hardly elated. Their "cinema gem" had showed a loss of $565,000. Too many of Le Baron's films had met a similar fate.

So Le Baron was dismissed.

9

The affair that Hollywood classified as a Hays Office version of the Hearst–Davies match (since Gloria was safely married and a mother, as well) came to an end with the force of a temblor. Kennedy's mogul friends argued in vain over it, for the convulsion remained shrouded in mystery. Louella dutifully looked the other way, but Hedda, of a more independent turn of mind, eventually reported that Rose's doting father, John F. "Honey Fitz" Fitzgerald, the former powerful mayor of Boston and a leading political boss, had taken certain steps to restore his philandering son-in-law to the family fold.

The triumphant New York opening of *The Trespasser* in late October 1929 left Kennedy feeling strangely troubled. Gloria's little talkie had not been introduced on the screen with the words "Joseph P. Kennedy presents" because, at the start, he considered it a small picture, surely not important enough to bear his name. Its success surprised him, and although it did not displease him, it made him more anxious than ever for *his* picture, *Queen Kelly*, to be the stupendous motion picture he visualized.

Gloria, too, felt uneasy. She still loved Henri and prayed that she would not lose him. At the same time, she felt powerless to end her affair with Kennedy. There were other forces at work as well. Before she left New York in November, Gloria was served notice by His Eminence Cardinal O'Connell, archbishop of Boston, the same prelate who had officiated at the wedding of the Kennedys in 1914. One of Kennedy's henchmen, Ted O'Leary, took her to meet the prelate in his hotel. All O'Leary told her was that someone of importance wanted to see her. The elderly archbishop did not tell her whom he represented, but his sermon on ending the relationship came across with the force of a brickbat. Afterwards, she quizzed O'Leary. He assured her that Kennedy had not set up the meeting but that the arrangements had been made directly by Cardinal O'Connell.

Early in December the curtain rose on the second act of *Queen Kelly,* under the direction of Richard Boleslavski. The principals were called back, additional sets constructed at Pathé, and, as added insurance, Kennedy lured "a young American musical genius," Vincent Youmans, to the coast to compose a few hit songs for Gloria. Again, excitement ran high until the first rushes were viewed. Unfortunately, the patchwork job stood out like the work of an amateur. Boleslavski's directorial style was fighting tooth and nail with von Stroheim's. It was obvious that the two could never be fitted together in any semblance of unity.

Kennedy shrugged his shoulders, halted the production, dismissed the cast, and admitted failure at a cost of $800,000. He seemed to take it calmly enough. With Christmas approaching, he felt that in January the mess could be turned over to the cutting department to solve; it might be releasable in Europe.

Meanwhile, the holiday season was a lackluster time for Gloria. Henri decided it would be better for both of them if he remained in Paris. In January he expressed in a letter to her his unhappy feelings about the hopelessness of their marriage. At last, Gloria had lost her gallant Marquis.

Intent on stealing a page from Gloria's recent success story, Joe returned to Hollywood at the beginning of the new year with good news. He had assigned Josephine Lovett, a successful Hollywood scribe, to write a sparkling comedy for her. Vincent Youmans, he said, would add some songs—Joe had not lost faith in the composer of *Tea for Two.* With this outstanding combination of American talent—Lovett from California, and Youmans a New Yorker—he confidently predicted a belated victory.

In the meantime, he had afterthoughts on *Queen Kelly.* Approaching Eddie Goulding again, Kennedy this time offered the British director a short-term salary (until March) and half the royalties from his hit song "Love, Your Magic Spell Is Everywhere" if he would remake *Queen Kelly* as an operetta. The affable Britisher appeared shocked, declaring that he wouldn't touch the job if asked by their Britannic Majesties themselves! Furthermore, as he disclosed to the press, he was on his way to his lawyer's office. Accustomed to doing business over tea and crumpets, Goulding explained that he had not bothered to read the contracts he had been told to sign after completing *The Trespasser.* Without his realizing it, Kennedy and Gloria had usurped his royalties from his hit song.

Unfortunately, Kennedy's "American talent" had not produced a scintillating comedy script, so the project gained an Irishman: Gloria's old director, Allan Dwan, whom she called in desperation to take command. Lots of improvising ensued in a relaxed atmosphere reminiscent of the manner in which Gloria's little winner, *The Trespasser,* had been created. In a jocular mood one evening, Kennedy offered a Cadillac to playwright Sidney Howard, who contributed the witty title, *What a Widow!,* at the dinner table. So positive was Kennedy of the success of his latest brainchild that he ordered expensive and ornate animated titles to introduce it. This time, no one would miss "Joseph P. Kennedy presents." But despite Gloria's and Allan Dwan's best efforts, *What a Widow!* failed to effervesce according to the recipe. "A comedy of sorts.... [A] farce that sinks to slapstick," pronounced the *New York Times* on October 4, upon its release.

This time, Kennedy's defeat proved insurmountable, as did his ill humor. His fixed smile disappeared. It took only one trifling incident now to bring the affair to its painful close, and Gloria provided it. Informed by her accountant one day that the Cadillac Kennedy had bestowed on Sidney Howard in payment for his *What a Widow!* title had been charged to her personal account, she called the bookkeeping error to Joe's attention. He took it like a slap in the face. Without uttering a word and livid with rage, he left the room. She never heard from him again, but at the end of the year she received a curt letter from E. B. Derr, the chief officer of Gloria Productions, that revoked his power of attorney and steered him clear of any implication of wrongdoing.

It did not take Gloria long to learn that she had paid for much more than the Cadillac. In fact, the financial disaster of *Queen Kelly* was hers alone to bear. Still, there was one detail she was spared in the orgy of auditing that followed. A bugging device in the ceiling of the dressing room of her luxurious bungalow (which she had paid for) at Pathé awaited discovery until the mid-Thirties, when its new occupant, Russell Birdwell, *Gone With the Wind*'s publicity director, raised his eyes and caught a spy.

So, Kennedy took his leave of Gloria, as crudely as he had courted her, but it was not without premeditation. On May 8, the *New York Times* announced his retirement from Gloria Productions, despite his contract with United Artists for two more Swanson pictures, and as "active head" of Pathé as well. At the invitation of his Pathé associate Elisha Walker, he continued to serve as chairman of the board of that company. Those loyal Irish henchmen, E. B. Derr, Pat Scollard, and Charles Sullivan, whose positions in Gloria Productions shielded Kennedy so effectively, served as his minions at Pathé.

However, Ed Derr displayed an inclination to rise above his title of executive vice president in the continual absence of his boss. Kennedy angrily severed their relationship.

Kennedy's glib explanation to the press that Pathé was "sufficiently established to continue without his executive aid" was deceptive. His own lackadaisical management had, in fact, severely weakened the company. Joe's solution was to extricate his money and let the stockholders hang. As Kennedy began maneuvering with David Sarnoff to place Pathé under RKO's wing, Pathé stock shot up like a geyser; Radio–Keith–Orpheum bought heavily, and a "sacrificial" merger appeared to be in the offing.

Just around the corner (in 1933) lay an aborted investigation of the motion picture industry, instigated by a New York congressman, William I. Sirovich. Incensed by the "exorbitant salaries," "extravagant bonuses," and "amazing financial transactions" of the moguls, Sirovich tried his best to launch an attack that, by the nature of his revelations, threatened to tear Hollywood apart. No mogul escaped his censorious tongue as he endeavored to call the House to arms. Even Will Hays trembled when Sirovich invoked the memory of the Teapot Dome investigation. It remained for Hays's good friend Joe Kennedy to make a noble gesture on behalf of his Hollywood friends (and himself, in particular) by exerting his then considerable influence with President Roosevelt to halt the investigation.

Attacking the "purchase of Pathé by Radio–Keith–Orpheum" and its "practical merger," Sirovich stated that "a group was loaded down with a very substantial block" of Pathé stock quoted at about thirty dollars. "As soon as the merger was announced, this inside group pushed Pathé up to about eighty dollars" and "unloaded [it] on the public, making millions of dollars. The purchase [by RKO] at levels not warranted by any values possessed by Pathé" ("the only property RKO obtained that it did not have was a news-reel service," he said) "practically emptied the RKO treasury."

The deal announced by *Motion Picture News* on December 6, 1930, but not yet a *fait accompli,* named a figure approximating $5 million, a paltry fee in the opinion of the Pathé stockholders not in the Kennedy group. The sale would embrace all Pathé assets, except for its 49 percent interest in Pathé–du Pont, a film manufacturing company with a seemingly brilliant future. Radio–Keith–Orpheum's principal acquisition, besides the indispensable Pathé News and the numerous Pathé Exchanges, would be the sixty-acre Culver City studio with its recently completed productions (beginning with *Sin Takes a Holiday*), and "the services of Constance Bennett, Ann Harding and Helen Twelvetrees, as the three biggest Pathé drawing cards." Male stars Bill Boyd and Eddie Quillan and the half dozen Pathé directors would also be included, along with "the old fighting cock," the Pathé rooster trademark. The studio would be "maintained separately," the announcement concluded.

Radio–Keith–Orpheum's president, Hiram Brown, refused to talk about the deal. But there was no question that the Kennedy–Sarnoff inner circle would win. On January 6 of the following year, Pathé stockholders ratified the $5 million sale. Those on the outside (termed by Sirovich "innocent investors") could only share in the $5 million, but the actual cost of Pathé was considerably higher since control of Pathé's stock had been bought at astronomical prices. A few disgruntled stockholders tried, unsuccessfully, to sue the "financial racketeers" (Sirovich's term). Their outcry that Pathé was worth at least $25 million never reached the courts.

By the end of January 1931, E. B. Derr (who had replaced Kennedy as president of Pathé) and Charles Sullivan found themselves looking elsewhere for employment. Mayer, who disliked Kennedy, was happy to oblige them. Lee Marcus, a vice president of Radio Pictures, became the interim president of RKO–Pathé, with Charles R. Rogers, an independent producer, serving as production head.

Kennedy announced that he would return to Wall Street in association with Elisha Walker, now chairman of the board of the billion-dollar Transamerica Corporation. Although Joe had proved to be inept behind the cameras, he had made the most of his final fling in Hollywood. RKO's future well-being had been sacrificed to add some more millions to his personal fortune.

PART THREE

GIANT'S CRADLE: THE SELZNICK ADMINISTRATION, 1931–1933

Young David Selznick (left) and brother Myron with their father, Lewis J. Selznick, circa 1920.
Courtesy Marc Wanamaker, Bison Archives.

Merian C. Cooper, right, and partner Ernest B. Schoedsack with a member of the cast of *Chang*, 1927.
Courtesy Marc Wanamaker, Bison Archives.

Young Pan Berman, far left foreground, on the set of *What Price Hollywood?*, 1932. Director George Cukor is seated, rear center; to his right, assistant director Argyle Nelson.
Courtesy Pandro S. Berman.

Director George Cukor with Billie Burke and John Barrymore on the set of *A Bill of Divorcement*, 1932.
Courtesy Marc Wanamaker, Bison Archives.

Young Pan Berman with Radio Pictures president B. B. Kahane and an unidentified visitor (left to right), circa 1932–33.
Courtesy Pandro S. Berman.

Kenneth Macgowan, one of Selznick's production supervisors, who later produced the Technicolor short subject *La Cucaracha* and *Becky Sharp* for Merian Cooper.
Courtesy Marc Wanamaker, Bison Archives.

On the set of David Selznick's *The Lost Squadron*, 1932. Erich von Stroheim can be seen standing on a platform playing the Prussian film director Arnold von Furst to the hilt.

Courtesy Marc Wanamaker, Bison Archives.

Constance Bennett as the rising screen actress and Lowell Sherman as the alcoholic director in David Selznick's *What Price Hollywood?*, 1932.

Courtesy of the Academy of Motion Picture Arts and Sciences.

10

Sound beguiled the Depression for more than a year after Wall Street laid its infamous egg, but in 1931 the talkies, no longer a novelty, fell prey to the worsening economy. The economic prognosticators who had preached salvation through the stock market had seen their sermon boomerang. Salvation now lay only in the bread line and the apple cart—a tough act even for a singing Jolson to follow. Motion picture studio losses reflected the drop in film attendance. Warner Brothers, the company that had boasted of profits of more than $17 million in 1929, faced an almost $8 million loss in 1931, while RKO, the little major that had chugged uphill to the tune of $3 million in 1930, now slid backwards into a $5.6 million hole.

Meanwhile, Bill Le Baron had relinquished his post of studio chief to young David Selznick and would shortly saunter back to his former lot, Paramount, where the destiny of a new discovery, Mae West, awaited his guiding hand. Despite the success of *Rio Rita* and the enormous prestige of *Cimarron,* he was ineffectual in trying to grind out sixty or more pictures as executive producer, and he had been subjected to increasing pressure from the front office. The flak from the inevitable internecine disagreements between Joe Schnitzer, Radio Pictures president and its primary troubleshooter, and Hiram Brown, the business-oriented president of parent Radio–Keith–Orpheum, dissipated Le Baron's initiative. In February, Schnitzer moved his headquarters from New York to Hollywood—the better to exercise his executive control over production matters. The voice of authority now landed on Bill Le Baron's doorstep. Already the purchase of the Pathé organization had heightened RKO's financial burdens. Le Baron could see the road ahead fraught with deficits and his own buggy stalled by road blocks he was powerless to remove.

About the time Le Baron reached the end of his tenure at RKO, Paramount studio executive B. P. Schulberg's impassioned executive assistant, twenty-nine-year-old David O. Selznick, blew the whistle on "the studio system" he had studied and grown to hate since he had come to work there in 1928. With the impetuousness inherited from his father, fallen movie mogul Lewis J. Selznick, young David defiantly resigned in June—burning his bridges behind him by incurring the wrath of his father's old enemy, Louis B. Mayer. David Selznick's scheme to bend the antiquated studio system to his will and refashion it into small, dynamic production units, each employing an important director, sounded like insurrection to L.B. Fearing that his new son-in-law (Selznick had married his handsome daughter, Irene, the year before) would bring down his own monolith by planting the seeds of dissent among the ranks at MGM, Mayer hastily called a meeting of studio moguls to make sure that this Jewish Pancho Villa would not be given a release for his independent organization. Jesse Lasky, who had already offered Selznick a Paramount release, was now forced to play the old studio-politics game, and he reneged.

In New York to scout around for some capital in the long sweltering summer of 1931, Selznick felt the force of Mayer's omnipotence: He could secure neither financing nor distribution. Reasoning that only an outsider could escape the Mayer edict, Selznick turned on the family *chutzpah* and charged into the Radio Corporation headquarters at Lexington and Fifty-first Street to see David Sarnoff. Radio–Keith–Orpheum's chairman listened in astonishment as the lusty young maverick presented his futuristic concept of movie making with all the fervor of an evangelist and the fluent delivery of a college professor. His eyes popped when Selznick dropped the name of Lewis Milestone, his initial director-partner. After two smashes, *All Quiet on the Western Front* and *The Front Page,* the director was considered major box-office. Sarnoff put down his long cigar and reached for the phone to give Hiram Brown the word. However, a swift counterblow engineered by Mayer removed Milestone to an important position at United Artists, thus thwarting Selznick's deal.

Selznick met again with Sarnoff, and this time he sold himself alone. Radio's top executive had come through the crash unharmed, having had the same uncanny presentiment as his partner, Joe Kennedy. Recently elevated to the presidency of RCA, Sarnoff found his responsibilities increased along with his power. Excavation was beginning for Radio City, a spectacular Rockefeller enterprise that would place the RCA Building, seventy stories in height, at the hub of a select skyscraper community in midtown Manhattan. Cavernous holes indicated the future headquarters of Radio–Keith–Orpheum, the "International Music Hall," which was designed to outstrip, outweigh, and outdo all other amusement palaces in the world, and a moving picture theater that would offer the largest screen ever built and the last word in sound reproduction and amplifying equipment from RCA Photophone. The theater would be an ambitious showcase for RKO Radio product, considering that RCA's errant offspring still occupied the servants' quarters of the formidable Radio family.

The flamboyant master showman Samuel L. Rothafel, known to the entertainment world as "Roxy" after the great New York theater that bore his name, had already signed on as impresario of both theaters, an indication to Sarnoff that this gargantuan undertaking would triumph in spite of the sick economy.

During subsequent meetings Sarnoff further detected Selznick's extraordinary ambition—his obsession with the picture business that evolved from his unusual upbringing. L. J. Selznick had drawn David and his older brother, Myron, into the movie business at an early age. As a gawky teenager David had actually sat in on conferences and been consulted by his father before decisions were made. The movies had outranked Yale, when the foolhardy tycoon was overthrown in the early wars of the movie moguls; but David had acquired a love of the classics from his father, and he enriched his spare moments with a variety of classes at Columbia University. He had plenty of ammunition to take on Hollywood and redeem the Selznick name when he followed Myron to California.

Selznick's enormous capacity for work—for assuming responsibility—soon became apparent to Sarnoff. What Lasky had seen in the young executive that had prompted an offer of Schulberg's job at Paramount now stirred Sarnoff. Aside from *Rio Rita,* he had hardly been satisfied with Bill Le Baron's performance. A change of leadership was easy to buy in these belt-tightening times.

In October 1931 Selznick signed a contract to head both RKO and Pathé, making him the youngest studio chief in Hollywood. According to his contract, his artist's hands would still be shackled by the New York office, but, propelled by his enormous optimism, he fully believed, with Sarnoff's assurance, that he would have sufficient authority to be able to refurbish the RKO lot into the streamlined production facility he envisioned and let his creative juices flow freely.

The crack Santa Fe *Chief* hurtled back to Hollywood at the end of October, carrying its mixed cargo of RKO executives: new production chief David Selznick, his immediate superior, Joe Schnitzer, and associate vice president Charles Rogers. The announcement of the completion of the merger of RKO Radio and RKO–Pathé Studios had just been flashed to the papers. The Culver City lot would soon be scuttled and production operations combined under one roof. Cushioned by his gung-ho spirit and weekly salary of $2,500, Selznick could disregard the hard truth: He was taking command of a rapidly sinking ship.

Radio–Keith–Orpheum's troubles reached a climax by late fall. Indeed, the RKO board faced a mounting financial crisis since "Joe Kennedy threw a monkey wrench into RKO's sweet future," stated *Motion Picture Herald*'s rhetoric about his sellout to the Titan Gang.

In May 1931, exactly a year after his retirement as active head of Pathé, "the generalissimo of the Rooster family," as the trade journal referred to Kennedy, resigned as Pathé chairman. His last Pathé connection severed, Kennedy prudently sailed for Europe, leaving a pack of angry Pathé stockholders behind with litigation on their minds.

At a minority stockholders' meeting in New York, termed by the press "the annual free-for-all," their lost cause was championed by Joseph Conn, a Rhode Island exhibitor who owned 300 shares of Pathé stock. Conn, described by *Motion Picture Herald* as "an eloquent and vigorous figure," denounced the directors who "quit without considering their obligation to the stockholders who elected them." He stated that his suit charging the Kennedy circle with negligence, waste, and improper management of the company and the transfer of its assets to RKO might never come to trial. "They won't dare to have this mess stirred up," Conn declared, revealing that he had already been approached with a substantial settlement "to keep my mouth shut."

Meanwhile, the fallout from the improvident Pathé deal fell squarely on Hiram Brown's shoulders. It was up to him to refill RKO's empty coffers. On June 20 he announced to the press that he had arranged a loan of $6 million from Chemical National Bank, a feat loudly applauded in financial circles in view of the prevailing economic conditions and a tight money market. The terms of the loan, however, were chilling and therefore not widely broadcast. RKO–Pathé was compelled to pay a bonus of $600,000, since the bank considered the loan risky. Hiram Brown brusquely announced that the financial crisis had passed; the subsidiary's cash needs and new production demands could now be met.

However, by mid-November it appeared that RKO had only borrowed time, and not enough at that. Second-quarter earnings had been consistent with the mood of permanent gloom that had descended upon the nation. On November 5, as Selznick took charge of the studio, RKO stock nose-dived to a perilous low of seventy-five cents a share. A week earlier, the studio's creative staff (writers, directors, and associate producers) was given notice: sixty days of grace, after which the new studio chief would assess their worth and decide their fate.

The action was intense the first weeks of Selznick's reign. His adrenalin racing, the bulky, bushy-haired young executive poked his nose into every corner of studio operation, firing off an encyclopedia of memos. Budgets and schedules had gotten out of hand. The departments were weighted with deadwood. To establish a new order would take time, Selznick informed Joe Schnitzer. It would be impossible for him to slash budgets on the remainder of the 1931–32 program of pictures. These films would still cost a lot. After that—his eyes, behind thick-lensed glasses, gleamed—the big spenders would retreat and he could get lean-budgeted films of quality into production.

In the meantime, a storm erupted in the East. On November 10, RKO stockholders were asked to support a refinancing plan favoring RCA, with deadly side effects. Any opposition, they were informed, would result in a receivership for the company and a total loss of their investment. B. B. Kahane, Radio–Keith–Orpheum's vice president and general counsel, placed most of the blame for the company's chronic illness on the Pathé transaction, although he gloomily mentioned "Hollywood," which covered a multitude of ills, and the decline of overseas business as causes for the desperate situation.

With RCA controlling 22 percent of RKO's stock, Sarnoff dealt from a position of supremacy. The powerful chieftain agreed to sanction a refinancing plan to raise $11,600,000 only if RCA gained stock control of RKO. So, under threat of receivership and a total loss of their investment, RKO stockholders wrung their hands while their shares were reduced to one-fourth of a share of new common stock for each share of Class A stock. They were then entitled to reclaim the remainder of their stock, if they could afford it, through purchase of a $5 debenture for each share of common stock they owned.

Like a replay of the events that followed the Pathé merger, the underprivileged stockholders waged a fruitless war on the recapitalization plan. While they tried to rally the support of their fellow losers throughout the country, RKO's B. B. Kahane defended the Titan's position to a group of newspaper financial editors on November 17. Kahane pointed out that no financial institution was willing to underwrite the RKO debenture. "RCA is making no attempt to assume control but is most reluctant to handle the RKO financing," he said, adding that RKO and RCA would welcome "a more feasible arrangement."

On November 19, while Joe Kennedy maintained a low profile in Palm Beach, a Kennedy ally, the intrepid film pioneer Pat Powers, quickly rose to the defense of the well-meaning Titan Gang. "RKO officers are doing their best to keep the organization going under present conditions and should have the hearty cooperation of stockholders," Powers told *Film Daily* on November 19.

B. B. Kahane's next report, a few days later, was decidedly optimistic. He stated that, with several thousand proxies already received, the company expected its financing plan to be approved.

For a time, the opposing factions—the RKO organization and the RKO Stockholders Protective Committee—became increasingly inflamed. An application for receivership was filed in Baltimore Circuit Court early in December. New pleas for proxies were issued. Hiram Brown entered the fray, denying charges of mismanagement.

On December 3, RKO officials issued a negative report to an alternate plan proposed by the minority group. They claimed that it offered insufficient financing. Before the week was past, the Protective Committee hoisted a white flag and agreed to support the company plan, to be voted upon in a few days.

Victory was in sight: a million proxies were in, two-thirds of the number required to assure passage of the plan. Again, an appeal—this time from both factions—went out, urging all owners of RKO stock to forward their proxies at once.

On December 10, a new voice was raised—that of Washington Senator Clarence C. Dill—demanding a Senate investigation of what he felt was "a tricky financing deal." It seemed to him that the plan calling for each stockholder to subscribe to the new stock or give up three-fourths of his present stock in order to hand RCA a bonus was "taking a dirty advantage of the poor fellow who has stock, but no money to put up."

Still another outcry was heard on December 13. A splinter group of stockholders claiming 500,000 shares called for the ousting of the Titan Gang.

Finally, on December 14, after three days of adjournments due to lack of a majority, the refinancing plan was approved in Baltimore. There was speculation that the receivership suit might be dismissed. However, Senator Dill was reported still intent on a Senate probe, despite approval of the plan.

By the end of the year, RCA had taken complete control of Radio–Keith–Orpheum. As a result of stockholders' subscribing to only about $2 million of the $11,600,000 debentures, RCA emerged controlling 60 percent of RKO.

In June of the following year, the Senate Banking and Currency Committee, which for several months had been investigating the debaucheries of Wall Street and its cast of sinners, got around to the RKO "swindle" and a similar cast of heavies. On June 10, Ernest W. Stirn, an economist connected with the University of Chicago, charged the directors of Radio–Keith–Orpheum with inside selling and freeze-out tactics that enabled RCA to acquire control of the company for a fraction of its value.

"The most drastic squeeze-out in history!" remarked William J. Morgan, former attorney general of Wisconsin, who acted as Stirn's voluntary counsel. Stirn and his lawyer disclosed the short-selling tactics under the management of Radio stock floor specialist Michael J. "Mike" Meehan that they credited with driving down the stock's price. Meehan had already figured in the committee's records for his participation in the great bull pool in Radio in 1929.

Stirn zealously traced the RKO stock decline, from a high of 50 on April 24, 1931, down to 1⅝ and 2 on November 30, the last date for which he had records of short sales. On December 29, the stock declined to ¾, he said, and the following day trading was suspended, the stock then being dealt in over the counter and no longer on the Exchange.

In October, the "short position" in RKO on the Stock Exchange amounted to about 10,000 shares, according to figures furnished by Richard Whitney, the embattled Exchange president. It rose steadily and reached a peak of 148,681 shares in November. "Inferential evidence," cried Stirn, "of an inside rigging operation." He pointed out that the short sales were nearly all covered after the directors put out the reorganization plan on November 10.

In Stirn's accompanying brief, it was stated that "by the refinancing plan, and by the short raids against the RKO stock, the minority stockholders were frozen out of the company, resulting in RCA buying Radio–Keith–Orpheum Corporation practically for the price of the debentures."

In a succeeding committee session, a Baltimore attorney, J. Cookman Boyd, came forward with an account of his legal attack against the Titan Gang that resulted in the purchase of his stock by the company directors for "a substantial sum."

In 1933, when Congressman Sirovich took up his cudgel against the "fraudulent" Pathé merger, he echoed Stirn's testimony, emphasizing that the large part of RCA's gain was "taken out of the pockets of the stockholders of RKO by forced involuntary contribution."

Seven years later, in January 1940, prowling again into the affairs of Wall Street, a Wisconsin Congressman, John Schafer, pinned the blame for the RKO "swindle" on Joe Kennedy. "Read the motion picture industry speeches of the late Dr. Sirovich,"* he urged members of the House. "Then get Moody's Industrials and observe the hook-up in connection with the RKO swindle. You will find that Joseph Kennedy, the multimillionaire New Dealer, was the chief racketeer in that manipulation."

*Sirovich was a practicing surgeon.

11

In January 1932, following their insidious pool operations in Radio–Keith–Orpheum stock, the Titan Gang gathered at the RKO Studios for a conference of coast personnel. A power clash between Selznick and Joe Schnitzer had been narrowly averted by the removal of the RKO Radio Pictures president from the firing line in Hollywood and returning him to the home office in New York. Despite persistent rumors that Schnitzer might be on his way out, Radio–Keith–Orpheum's president, Hiram Brown, was reported as saying that Schnitzer's executive power would not be impaired by the move. Statements were still emerging from New York that Selznick would be given a free hand to see what he could accomplish at the studio.

Indeed, under his energetic leadership the little major had already embarked on a program of rejuvenation that would spark its growth and ensure its individuality for some time to come. Feature picture costs for 1932–33 were expected to be maintained at a lower than average (for Hollywood) $200,000. Although he intended to use bigger-name casts, Selznick announced that there would be no raiding of other studios. His idea was to develop stars and to comb the New York stage for fresh acting talent. Other than the Oscar-nominated fledgling Irene Dunne, the studio had failed to produce new stars of its own, relying instead on buying them full grown. Selznick now had at his disposal the cream of the Pathé lot: sophisticated Constance Bennett, whom he favored since she had worked for his father in 1922; patrician Ann Harding, now ensconced in the most sumptuous bungalow on the lot; and dramatic Helen Twelvetrees. Also at his elbow were some alluring contractees: Mary Astor, Myrna Loy, and Shirley Grey.

Even before the new year Selznick launched a drive to strengthen the writing and directing departments that brought George Cukor, his friend and a former dialogue director, from Paramount and utilized such writing talent as Ben Hecht, Dudley Nichols, Gene Fowler, and Zoe Akins. He managed to borrow William Wellman from Warner Brothers to direct *The Conquerors,* a *Cimarron* look-alike with Richard Dix and Ann Harding that did not measure up to its model. He talked his father-in-law into lending King Vidor to direct a South Sea island picture with the lush title of *Bird of Paradise,* starring Dolores Del Rio and Joel McCrea. *Bird of Paradise* was loosely based on Richard Walton Tully's 1912 play. Vidor used enough locations—Hawaii, Catalina Island, a native village on the RKO–Pathé lot in Culver City (reopened as a rental studio and for use by RKO), and a water tank at First National in Burbank—to spend $732,000. Pathé's art director, Carroll Clark, who had replaced the distinguished Max Ree on the Gower lot, contributed Hollywood-style native charm, and Max Steiner added $20,000 worth of marimbas, ukeleles, steel guitars, and vibraphones. Nevertheless, the picture proved too expensive to return its cost, and it received tepid reviews.

Selznick offered the post of executive assistant to his close personal friend, the thirty-eight-year-old Merian C. Cooper, a former director and associate at Paramount on *The Four Feathers.* Cooper's *raison d'être* was adventure; his pursuit of dangerous excitement as a soldier of fortune, World War I flying ace, explorer, writer, and documentary filmmaker had already carried him to the more inaccessible regions of the globe. In the early twenties, Cooper had teamed with a comrade from the Russo–Polish War, Signal Corps photographer Ernest B. "Monty" Schoedsack, on a trek across a 12,000-foot mountain range in Persia in order to document on film the migratory habits of the Bakhtiari tribe. *Grass,* their lecture film, attracted Jesse Lasky, an impassioned amateur explorer himself, who arranged for its distribution by Paramount. The team's next adventure, with Lasky's enthusiastic backing, took them to the Siamese jungle to make a wild-animal picture that featured a rousing climax of stampeding elephants. *Chang* was a big success, and Lasky next gave the team a major feature assignment. For *The Four Feathers,* Cooper and Schoedsack journeyed to Portuguese East Africa and the Sudan and brought back spectacular footage of charging hippos and baboons that was interwoven with scenes shot at the studio with a cast of glamorous Paramount stars.

Merian Cooper leaped at Selznick's offer. Currently employed as an executive for Western Air Express and Pan American Airways in New York, he was exploring the steel cliffs of Manhattan, contemplating the effects of an overly civilized society on mankind. His philosophical grapplings with this and other themes were expressions of an idea for a film. Cooper intended to make another picture with Schoedsack. Fragments of his travels and bits of memories of a travel and adventure book by Paul De Chaillu, one of the first explorers of Equatorial Africa, that he had read as a child of six, had germinated into a story about a giant gorilla he called Kong. Zukor and Lasky had turned the project down, questioning its appeal and doubting that the serious production problems it suggested could be resolved. As Zukor put it: "You know what a fifty-foot gorilla would see in a five-foot girl? His breakfast!" Cooper had received another turn-down from Fox. Selznick, on the other hand, had reacted with ambivalence. His own brain was seething with picture ideas. Faced with urgent decisions and an accumulation of mundane studio problems, an assistant of Cooper's versatility appeared to be what he needed most. He believed in his friend and he was willing to give his dream a chance to unfold.

Coincidentally, the studio had Willis O'Brien, a special-effects expert with a technical crew of artists, sculptors, and model-makers, under contract, and had invested heavily in O'Brien's animation process. Tests for his film project, *Creation,* which featured a motley cast of prehistoric beasts performing by means of "step motion animation," had left Selznick mystified. He didn't know how to proceed with it, but his friend "Coop" would.

Selznick chose young Pandro Berman, who was by this time an old hand on the lot, to act as his production assistant. After representing Bill Le Baron on the editing of *Rio Rita* and *Cimarron,* the twenty-six-year-old Berman had become his general assistant and had persuaded the boss to let him try his hand at producing. *The Gay Diplomat,* his first attempt, added to the unprofitable string of feeble programmers the studio turned out in 1931, but Berman redeemed himself with *Symphony of Six Million,* his first production for Selznick.

Buried among the backlog of projects that Selznick scrutinized when he arrived at the studio was an adaptation of a short story by the popular novelist Fanny Hurst called *Night Bell.* A typical Hurst tear-jerker, like *Humoresque* and *Back Street,* it mined the traumas of a young Jewish surgeon from the lower East Side of New York who abandons the ghetto clinic for the ritzy ladies of Park Avenue. Mindful of the anti-Semitic feeling aimed at the cinema industry that was stimulated by barbs from the press, Selznick seized the opportunity to enrich the script with a realistic and warm portrait of Jewish home life and tradition.

Selznick handed the directorial reins to Pathé's Gregory La Cava, who had several strikes against him: He was a non-Jew and overly fond of the bottle. As it turned out, La Cava's creative method of working enhanced the picture. To him, the script was a road map to glance at, then cast aside. "Forget about the dialogue," he would tell an uneasy Berman. "I can always spit that out at the last minute!"

Selznick ordered a schmaltzy "symphonic underscore" from Max Steiner to accompany the sob story from beginning to end and ensure a handkerchief finale. The script had been rewritten to accommodate this innovation. To play Felix Klauber, the neurotic doctor, Selznick selected Ricardo Cortez, née Jack Krantz, who ironically had buried his heritage in order to become a Valentino clone. The reviewers thought him capable. However, poor Irene Dunne was forced to play his crippled childhood sweetheart, a meaningless role that, in *Variety*'s opinion, placed her in "forced and unreal situations." Only Gregory Ratoff, blessed with a fertile Russian accent, fitted into the ethnic atmosphere, reveling in the role of Papa Klauber. Katherine Brown, RKO's New York representative, discovered Ratoff playing in the Yiddish Theatre and sent him to the coast on a short-term contract. Anna Appel, a New York actress, also contributed to the positive Jewish image in the role of the mother.

Berman brought the picture in for a sensible $230,000. It opened at the Gaiety in New York on April 14, where the sound of weeping rose to a joyous crescendo over Maxie Steiner's lachrymal score. The reviews were sympathetic. Said *Variety,* missing Selznick's good intentions, "It will go over where there are large Jewish communities."

Pandro Berman's next assignment was a project Selznick lovingly nurtured as a comeback vehicle for Clara Bow, whose career he had helped guide at Paramount. *The Truth About Hollywood,* a story by Adela Rogers St. John that she had based on silent-screen star Colleen Moore's tragic marriage to the alcoholic producer John McCormick, had been written to order. Still, the New York office vetoed the project, citing the poor box-office record of Hollywood stories. Selznick clung to the idea, and when Clara Bow decided to retire (her cupid's-bow mouth refusing to come to grips with the King's English), he hired Gene Fowler to adapt the St. John original for the luminous Constance Bennett and make some refinements. The character of the producer (to be portrayed by Gregory Ratoff), in particular, was too close to Samuel Goldwyn's Goldwynisms for comfort.

Given the more trenchant title of *What Price Hollywood?* and hastily produced, the picture left Selznick somewhat dissatisfied, although it made a profit. The story of the calculating Brown Derby waitress who wangles a screen test from an alcoholic customer, the important director, Max Carey, went off in too many directions. Selznick also felt that the tragedy of the Hollywood milieu, as typified by the waitress's rise to stardom and the director's suicidal downfall, might have been better exploited. Because the tragic ending was still considered a box-office gamble, he had compromised by reuniting the star with the polo player she had married and lost along the road; Neil Hamilton played him with a stern jaw. "The Mayfair Theater this week [July 15] is just a bit of Hollywood in tired old New York," the *New York Times* scoffed. But the effect of the picture left the critic somewhat confused. Parts of it were "very amusing, whether intentionally or despite themselves"; other parts were "very sorrowful, in the bewildered manner of a lost scenario writer." Some of it was "quite agreeable."

Female fans found the Constance Bennett screen image irresistible and were not put off by the *Times*'s opinion: "She yells quite a bit in the more hysterical of the scenes, but performs creditably elsewhere." George Cukor, directing his first RKO assignment, handled the dynamic, blue-eyed blonde with élan and contributed his incisive view of Hollywood. Cukor had assisted Selznick in casting actor-director Lowell Sherman, whom he considered a fine actor with the needed degree of odiousness. Sherman used his brother-in-law, John Barrymore, as a role model, and Gene Fowler's searing dialogue resounded with Barrymore's cutting remarks. The result was a realistic but not unsympathetic drunkard, which softened the critics' blows.

Selznick ran headlong into a tragic ending—in fact, he eclipsed it with a double tragedy by not sparing the life of the hero, stalwart Richard Dix, in *The Lost Squadron.* Adapted by Wallace Smith and Herman J. Mankiewicz from a story by the most famous of the Hollywood aerial daredevils, Dick Grace, it glorified the cinematic stunt flyer while going behind the scenes of an aerial film production on location. The picture itself was still on location in the San Fernando Valley when Selznick came onto the lot, and its improbable combination of elements—stunt flying, murder and mayhem, as well as comedy and romance—intrigued him. Selznick felt that it rated more production values, so he borrowed Norman McLeod from Paramount to polish the screenplay and replaced director George Archainbaud with Paul Sloane.

The Lost Squadron opened to excellent reviews at the RKO–Mayfair on March 10. The sight of Erich von Stroheim playing the ruthless director, Arnold von Furst, callous to everything but his celluloid masterpiece, tickled the critics. Said *Variety:* "A smart assignment, as it's bound to provoke comment from the carping critics who may recall some of Von's costly stuff in the past, without much apparent regard for the economic equation."

In November 1932, Selznick aired his contempt for the "formula picture." "There should be more adult fare," he advised *Film Daily.* "More pictures should be made for selective audiences." His personal productions at RKO supported this belief. *The Animal Kingdom,* chosen to inaugurate the new 3,700-seat RKO Roxy Theatre in Radio City on December 29, was one of these. A faithful version of Philip Barry's 1932 sophisticated Broadway comedy, it was clearly addressed to "the upper levels of fan-dom," as *Variety* stressed, with a story "a bit fine and subtle for the generality." Leslie Howard, the charming British actor who had starred in the Broadway production, played the married publisher with a mistress in a distant city who ultimately comes to grips with the weighty question "Which is really wife, and which is mistress?" "The woman-against-woman tension," *Variety*'s interpretation of the campaign between the self-seeking wife, Myrna Loy, and the self-sacrificing mistress, Ann Harding, ensnared the more mature female fans but failed to generate any sparks from the general matinee-goer. Silver-blonde Ann Harding, meticulously directed by Edward H. Griffith, gave a momentary boost to her flagging career in what *Variety* deemed "a brilliant bit of playing." The Queen of the Weepers had allowed herself to freeze into the wearisome mold of a high-brow martyred lady, unlike the more pliable Irene Dunne, who managed to project a human element through her tears.

In the spring, Selznick made an auspicious purchase, starting a train of events that would bring a startling new screen personality into the RKO fold. *A Bill of Divorcement,* an important play by the prominent British female author Clemence Dane, had long been a favorite of Selznick's. Its harrowing theme of insanity was just the sort of adult fare that appealed to him—the antithesis of the pap he had been forced to swallow at Paramount. The demanding role of the daughter who faces the terror of insanity after her long-vanished father escapes from a mental institution had established the reputation of Katharine Cornell in 1921. Because John Barrymore had been cast as the father, after making a good showing in RKO's earlier *State's Attorney,* Selznick felt that his name alone could reap a box-office return, provided the budget was held fast at $300,000. At this juncture, Irene Dunne, the likeliest prospect for the role of the daughter, was eliminated. The first lady of soap opera now earned $50,000 a picture.

Meanwhile, Selznick and George Cukor, whose background as a stage director gave him particular insight into the project, viewed a test of a twenty-three-year-old stage actress named Katharine Hepburn. She had attracted studio attention after cavorting on Broadway through a short run—and in a short tunic—as a hyperactive Amazon queen in *The Warrior's Husband.* Cukor nudged Selznick, and the risky decision was made. The Connecticut girl with the athletic figure and the raw New England accent was cast at a reasonable salary of $1,250 a week.

A Bill of Divorcement opened at the Mayfair on September 30 to glowing reviews that focused on the new acting discovery. "A kind of vigorous, artless charm," *Variety* rhapsodized, in appreciation of Cukor's long takes that accentuated Hepburn's cat-like grace and expressive gestures as effectively as slow motion. While not letting Barrymore's and Billie Burke's fans down—"two screen personalities that dwell in the aura of fame"—it was the "smash impression made by Katharine Hepburn" that stood out. The reviewer even went so far as to say that she would appeal to women because she was "innocent of formal beauty in the sense of prettiness." The *New York Times*'s Mordaunt Hall went further: "Miss Hepburn's characterization is one of the finest seen on the screen." *Variety*'s reviewer had, however, sounded a warning. Could this "happy break" be the result of a part that fit her so thoroughly? Was "the successful outcome inevitable"? It would take another role to "test the future of the girl," *Variety* advised. Selznick had one up his sleeve: Jo, in *Little Women.*

12

In the spring of 1932, a few months before the bear-hunting Senate Banking Committee aired their skullduggery, some of the ringleaders of the Titan Gang made their exit from the plundered company. The changing of the guards was led by RKO Radio Pictures president Joseph Schnitzer, who departed late in February to enter independent production. It had been known for some time that Schnitzer was not entirely happy in his berth and that much of the blame for the company's financial difficulties had been placed on production—his domain. No immediate successor to Schnitzer was indicated, although the trade papers stated that David Sarnoff had invited Sidney Kent to join Radio–Keith–Orpheum. Paramount's brilliant VP in charge of sales had recently been asked to resign from his trouble-ridden company in the heat of a corporate war. However, Sarnoff promptly announced that his discussions with Kent had terminated. Shortly after, a candidate was pulled from the ranks. RKO counsel B. B. Kahane, who had dutifully supported the RKO "swindle," was named president of RKO Radio Pictures.

In spite of a vote of confidence from the board of directors that restored his complete authority, after a period of uncertainty, Hiram Brown submitted his resignation in April, and a Sarnoff lieutenant, Merlin H. "Deac" Aylesworth, president of RCA's high-powered broadcasting subsidiary, NBC, was elected president of Radio–Keith–Orpheum. It was expected that Brown would be offered the post of head of the executive committee, but the discarded executive rapidly squelched this idea. "I came in RKO as president, and I'll go out as president," said the former leather manufacturer, whose lack of show business know-how had finally caught up with him. Nevertheless, it was reported that Brown would continue as a member of the board of directors along with Aylesworth and the parent electrical concerns nobility: A. W. Robertson of Westinghouse Electric, Gerard Swope and Owen D. Young of General Electric, and RCA's David Sarnoff.

Sarnoff capped Aylesworth's appointment with a formal dinner in his honor, lending considerable weight to the thinking in all quarters that RCA was prepared to defend its motion picture subsidiary to the death, if need be.

The trades speculated about the extent of the new chief's participation in "RKO affairs," since Aylesworth's first week's schedule revealed that his mornings were devoted to RKO and the remainder of the day belonged to NBC. It appeared likely that Aylesworth would limit his involvement, that he would act as overseer. That would leave B. B. Kahane in full command of RKO Radio Pictures. Currently conferring with Selznick on the new season's product, Kahane diligently announced that every effort would be made to hold costs to a $225,000 average per picture, with a contemplated lineup of forty pictures.

In April the studio was on its busiest stretch with six major features in the works and two more planned for the end of the month. All ten stages were occupied, and the payroll bulged with the demands of Radio's contract players. *State's Attorney,* a John Barrymore starrer, had reached the final stages of production. Also in the works were King Vidor's *Bird of Paradise,* Constance Bennett in *The Truth About Hollywood,* and *Westward Passage,* in which Ann Harding was co-starring with Laurence Olivier, a newcomer Selznick hoped to build into a box-office draw. *Kong,* described by the press as "a Cooper–Schoedsack adventure-mystery," was being made on carefully guarded stages; Richard Dix was filming *The Roar of the Dragon,* and Helen Twelvetrees and Ricardo Cortez were working in *Is My Face Red?* In preparation were Harding and Bennett vehicles that were expected to keep their female fans weeping through satisfyingly lachrymose matinees.

Selznick, relishing the challenge of running a studio on nickels and dimes, reported to Kahane in June that expenses had been cut by $50,000 weekly. It was gratifying that the measure of authority he exercised over production had paid off in a reduction of costs and a quality product. In the next year he intended to introduce the unit production system that he had advocated at Paramount. "A production schedule of forty or more features is too much for one man to supervise," he told Kahane. "We plan, gradually, to give the producer more authority—to have him assume complete charge of stories and talent." Two or three units, each producing four or five features, would absorb about half of the next season's product, he reasoned.

By late summer, Selznick's little kingdom was under siege. Harsh voices emanating from the New York office questioned his accomplishments and his judgment. Their faith and understanding had changed to distrust and criticism. On the defensive, Selznick mounted a barrage of paperwork to prove that the studio was a model of well-oiled economic efficiency. But he had closed his eyes to the crippling effect of RCA's dominance over Radio–Keith–Orpheum and the weakened financial structure of the parent.

The radio giant had, for the previous three years, battled a devastating antitrust suit involving its familial relations with GE and Westinghouse. This, coupled with the Depression, had caused RCA profits to descend from almost $16 million in 1929 to a position of indebtedness of more than a million in 1931.

In November, Selznick received a copy of a doomsday message from Sarnoff to Aylesworth that made his blood run cold. The confidential memo set the date of Radio–Keith–Orpheum's next financial crisis (January) and listed the amounts that would come due in payments (more than $2 million). Underscoring the previous month's loss of $650,000, and reminding Aylesworth that all the company's material assets were pledged for loans that RCA had, until now, guaranteed, Sarnoff delivered still another blow: Radio–Keith–Orpheum should no longer expect financial sustenance from the electric affiliates. The subsidiary would have to rely on its own source of supply in future. Despite a better grade of product turned out by RKO Radio Pictures, declining theater grosses made it imperative to slash the overhead of the studio. "I am not concerned with the line of attack you take to reduce expenditures," Sarnoff bluntly stated. "Only the results matter."

The ravaged company hit the shore of receivership on a frosty day late in January 1933. Just as his leader had predicted, Aylesworth was compelled to face the consequences. To the press, Radio–Keith–Orpheum's president coolly conveyed the news that "the company is unable to obtain cash necessary to provide for its presently maturing obligations and for other necessary requirements during the year.... There was accordingly no alternative but to consent to the appointment of receivers...." Judge William Bondy of United States district court in New York appointed the Irving Trust Company receiver, which was also named receiver in bankruptcy for the Orpheum Circuit, an RKO subsidiary, with theaters in twenty-seven U.S. cities and two cities in Canada, and operating at losses approximating $30,000 weekly.

The receivership, which listed assets of $104 million, was based on a petition filed on January 23 by one Alfred West, a division manager of the Bancamerica–Blair Corporation, and the unlucky holder of $5,000 of Radio–Keith–Orpheum's 6 percent gold notes. The company defaulted on $731,000 in bonds due January 1, West affirmed. The gold notes, issued by RKO in 1931 to fund indebtedness brought on by that nemesis, the Pathé acquisition, had been purchased by Chase Securities, Jeremiah Milbank, and Bancamerica–Blair, making West's petition, the press indicated, "a friendly action on the part of the various RKO banking interests."

Aylesworth made it clear that the receivership did not embrace the production, distribution, studio, or newsreel units. Nor did it involve the Radio City properties, he emphasized. Sarnoff had already called on his good friends and landlords, the Rockefeller brothers, to make an adjustment of the leases on the two new theaters (operated by RKO), and office space. A payoff in stock plumped the Rockefeller fortune with 100,000 shares of RKO stock and another 100,000 shares from RCA, making the billionaire family one of the biggest individual stockholders in RKO.

Sarnoff clarified RCA's relation to the juggernaut in a peppy statement that plugged the Radio Corporation's position as a trailblazer in the development of talking motion pictures and the manufacture and sale of sound recording and reproducing equipment. "Because of these interests," he said, "RCA has made a substantial investment in the debentures and stock of the Radio–Keith–Orpheum Corporation. We shall work to rebuild the entertainment industry, in order to serve the best interests of the public and of investors."

Even as Sarnoff spoke, a bank officer representing the receiver, Irving Trust Company, settled into headquarters in Radio City, clipped the end of a cigar, and set about instilling the proper spirit of sacrifice in RKO's investors and creditors.

Meanwhile, Selznick and Aylesworth were headed on a veritable collision course, as Radio–Keith–Orpheum's new president exercised his Sarnoff-given authority. Selznick's initial contract was about to expire, and he had been negotiating a new and fatter one throughout the winter. In late January, after finally coming to an agreement on terms and receiving Sarnoff's assurance that the new contract would be approved, Selznick had his contract. It had, however, undergone radical changes. Instead of gaining the latitude over production he had demanded, Selznick's control was wrested from him. Sarnoff handed over his scepter to his chosen man.

The previous November, Selznick had rejected an offer from his father-in-law to come to Metro. L. B. Mayer had undergone a change of heart as he observed young David assert himself as production boss at RKO. In fact, his son-in-law had begun to look like Thalberg material. Irving's poor health was a constant worry to L.B. Even more distressing was the reverence his former protégé inspired on the lot. The introduction of another genius into the divided camp might diminish the Thalberg glow.

After Sarnoff's double-dealing, Selznick rethought his former objections to moving to the family film factory in Culver City—of riding to success on

Irving's coattails; even more distasteful, the stigma of being a relative. Still, Mayer offered him his own production unit, $4,000 a week, his pick of MGM's stars, and assurance that he would not be a Thalberg vassal.

Ultimately, Selznick's misgivings were cast aside after the death of his father on January 25. L. J. Selznick's last advice to his son had been to accept Mayer's offer. Under great emotional stress, Selznick made the painful decision, but not before delivering a Depression-chaser to the beleaguered studio. At the eleventh hour he endorsed a test of Fred Astaire, a young musical-comedy star with enough charm, he felt, to offset an uncertain chin-line and enormous ears. His biggest financial gamble, Merian Cooper's *King Kong,* had just been previewed to a screaming audience in San Bernardino.

On February 16, Selznick took the fateful step.

PART FOUR

HEIRS TO AN EMPTY THRONE, 1933–1935

Pan Berman as second assistant director, peering from behind the bearded actor. FBO star Patsy Ruth Miller, seated; director Al Santell behind camera, circa 1924.
Courtesy Pandro S. Berman.

Pan Berman, behind the wheel, during the filming of *Midnight Folly*, a 1924 FBO production, starring Evelyn Brent, who is standing beside him. Actor Ricardo Cortez is in the back seat. Leaning against the railing of the camera platform is the picture's director, Sylvano Balboni, who was also a cameraman.
Courtesy Pandro S. Berman.

Anne Shirley and director George Nicholls Jr. on the set of *Anne of Green Gables*, 1934.
Courtesy of the Academy of Motion Picture Arts and Sciences.

Merian C. Cooper with his wife, former RKO actress Dorothy Jordan, in 1934.
Courtesy Marc Wanamaker, Bison Archives.

Merian C. Cooper and John Hay Whitney, here seen with David Selznick in 1935 (left to right), merged their company, Pioneer Pictures, with Selznick International.
Courtesy Marc Wanamaker, Bison Archives.

Pan Berman, right, wi
Mark Sandrich, who directed five of th
Astaire–Rogers musical
Courtesy Pandro S. Berma

Director George Stevens and Katharine Hepburn exchange glances on the set of *Alice Adams*, 1935. Left rear is Fred MacMurray. Hedda Hopper, one of the supporting players, is seated next to him.
Courtesy Pandro S. Berman.

Van Nest Polglase and Carroll Clark's Big White Set—an art moderne version of Venice, flowing luxuriantly between two adjoining sound stages. The "Piccolino" production number from *Top Hat,* 1935.

Courtesy Marc Wanamaker, Bison Archives.

Lobby card. Erik Rhodes is to the right of Fred and Ginger.
Courtesy Marc Wanamaker, Bison Archives.

Promotion for *Top Hat*, 1935.
Courtesy Marc Wanamaker, Bison Archives.

13

RKO Bags a Hero

The economic storms that battered the country with increased ferocity in 1932 dispatched their full vengeance on Hollywood the following winter: Several thousand studio workers were on the streets, and four of the major companies that put them there were in financial disarray, submitting to or fighting off receivership and the threat of bankruptcy. Paramount, Universal, Fox, and RKO, along with their studio chieftains— "the scintillant Supermen," as journalist Terry Ramsaye mockingly called them in print—now faced the day of reckoning.

The moguls, their numbers depleted by the disastrous tides of the Depression, were besieged by troubles. Reduced audiences, dark theaters, I.O.U.'s and produce in place of cash at the box office, and less money coming to Hollywood from the East added up to enough bad news for any company. But to compound their distress, the studio bosses were being blamed for many of the conditions that had placed the industry in jeopardy. Some of the more astute of the columnists who formerly chronicled their escapades with a light touch had been spewing out increasingly bitchy rhetoric. Even the erudite Terry Ramsaye appeared to have lost his sense of humor, dismissing them with a terse announcement of "the death of the recent race of dictators.... The Supermen have fallen!" he jeered, "having littered the path of progress with the debris and empty leaseholds of their tinsel glory."

Motion Picture Herald's influential publisher, Martin Quigley, stopped short of laying the blame for the receiverships taking place in the East on Hollywood's doorstep. Nevertheless, he hit hard below the belt with a message that made many a mogul wince. "The motion picture business issued from the status of a racket in its very early days," he stated. "Many people in it, however, have remained so oblivious to the march of time that to this day they feel they are still in some kind of racket. They are the persons who build petty dynasties about themselves, who are content to see a corporation wrecked provided only they can collect heavily before the day of reckoning arrives, persons who believe that principle and character may be all right elsewhere, but that they have no place in the motion picture business."

So it went, until by March, it seemed that the only direction the tormented tycoons could turn to for relief was to the nation's capital. Surprisingly, Congress ended a three-month session without once denouncing them.

Will Hays, whose job it was (in return for a six-figure salary) to offer the moguls as much protection as the climate allowed, valiantly attacked the problem in his speeches. "One thing has been agreed upon by all in the film industry, as well as the bankers, and that is, the show must go on," he stated on one occasion. In another talk he said he believed that "cooperation and self-regulation would prove the only real cure for the disintegrating symptoms that have seized our industrial structure."

Another mollifying voice was raised in the East offering encouragement to those directly involved in receivership. The same week in February that the Irving Trust Company filed preliminary reports on the Paramount and RKO receiverships, motion picture attorney Louis Nizer presented "The How and Why in Everyone's Language of the Magic of Equity Receivership" for readers of *Motion Picture Herald.* Young Nizer managed to make it sound like painless dentistry. "How sympathetic the law can be, by creating machinery to relieve the debtor!" he exclaimed, before divulging its policy of "slow and sane liquidation" with a graceful figure of speech: "The court places its protective wings around the property." When the time comes for the receiver to sell, in order to "liquidate assets and distribute the moneys to the creditors," suffering was adroitly avoided. Instead of a "forced" sale, a new corporation was organized that bought the assets of the corporation in receivership. "The sale is as friendly as the receivership," Nizer concluded, "saving the corporation from the morass of bankruptcy." He added a cheerful postscript for the victims. Stock and cash of the new corporation, if any were involved, were distributed among the creditors and the stock- and bondholders of the old corporation.

David Sarnoff took this opportune moment to pledge "fair play" on the part of RCA to the friendly receivership. "RCA will see to it that all holders of RKO debentures receive the same treatment as RCA in any reorganization of the adjustment of finances," Sarnoff announced on February 10. The recipient of stockholders' suits and much of the blame for the collapse of "his spectacular show machine," Sarnoff nevertheless was bearing up better than might be expected. His RCA had suffered heavy losses again the previous year. Still, he could take comfort in the knowledge that not a trace of red ink sullied Merlin Aylesworth's territory, NBC; for radio remained the country's entertainment bargain. Moreover, it appeared likely that the Selznick management in Hollywood had succeeded in producing a secret Depression weapon, and it was almost ready for launching.

David Selznick's heir apparent stood ten feet tall in the estimation of the RKO directorate. Now that the preview reports were in on *King Kong,* these lofty executives were loathe to remember how strenuously they had resisted authorizing a budget for his crazy "monkey picture." The crisis-ridden company needed a man in Hollywood who could work miracles, and the New York office was in complete agreement that Merian Coldwell Cooper was that man. RKO's losses had risen to $10.6 million the previous year. Selznick's artistry had certainly not rejuvenated the box office any more than had that of his predecessor, William Le Baron—although Ned E. Depinet, RKO's energetic vice president in charge of sales and distribution, emphasized to the press in February, after first plugging *King Kong* as "the biggest picture in the history of show business," that the features in work, or ready for release, were "exceptionally excellent."

In spite of Depinet's optimistic outlook for the Selznick leftovers, Frank Buck's *Bring 'Em Back Alive,* a straight adventure-jungle vehicle, filmed by the world-famous animal hunter and trainer in exotic jungle locales, and originally contracted as a series of thirteen short subjects, had proved to be 1932's biggest money maker. With this in mind, the Selznick "star" features for February and March release—John Barrymore in *Topaze,* Richard Dix in *The Great Jasper,* Katharine Hepburn in *Christopher Strong,* Lionel Barrymore in *Sweepings,* and Constance Bennett in *Our Betters*—could not be counted on to stimulate the deteriorated box office.

Aside from the extraordinary potential of *King Kong,* the short, burly, personable executive with a sparkle in his eye and a well-chewed pipe clamped between his lips had other qualifications that endeared him to the RKO hierarchy in New York. Cooper moved with ease in the world of the rich—*their* world—appearing as much at home in El Morocco or the St. Regis, chumming with young John Hay "Jock" Whitney and his cousin, C. V. "Sonny," as he was in the jungles of Siam with his lanky partner, cameraman "Monty" Schoedsack. Cooper belonged to the Manhattan social register set, having descended from a long line of Southern plantation owners. His father, an attorney, had been chairman of the Federal Reserve Bank in Florida. Cooper had attended Lawrenceville, an exclusive prep school in New Jersey, then received an appointment to Annapolis from Florida Senator Duncan U. Fletcher. However, his love of flying and overly exuberant spirits caused him to resign in his graduating year and to embark upon his storybook career.

In 1927, having risked his life for the things he believed worth dying for and having quenched some of his thirst for adventure and exploration, Cooper invested his earnings from his two successful films, *Grass* and *Chang,* in aviation stocks, thus bringing him to roost in New York as a director of several of the burgeoning commercial airlines. Cooper credited himself with having helped influence Sarnoff—through a mutual friend, David Bruce, a director of the Union Pacific Railroad—to hire Selznick. With Selznick as production chief of RKO, Cooper felt, he would have the leeway he needed to produce his gorilla picture.

On February 14, 1933, RKO Radio Pictures president B. B. Kahane announced Merian Cooper's appointment as studio production head. Details of his contract were still under discussion; in the meantime he would hold office under a temporary working agreement. No shakeup of personnel was contemplated, Kahane assured the press: "Operations will continue as heretofore." Following his appointment, Cooper announced that he had named Pandro Berman his executive assistant. A smooth transition was in order.

Approximately 50,000 people, well-nigh a capacity crowd, viewed *King Kong* on March 2 in its twin opening at the two Radio City theaters, the Radio City Music Hall (so named by Sarnoff to honor his NBC) and its sister theater, the RKO Roxy. "The *only* picture big enough to play the world's greatest theaters at the same time," the trade ads boasted. After a disastrous opening night that saw its celebrated entrepreneur, Maestro "Roxy" Rothafel, carried out on a stretcher, the Music Hall had been compelled to change its policy to include film exhibition. Patrons could not know that rent on the two theaters had not been paid for two months, and that the receiver was prepared to cancel the leases should current business fall off. RKO's exploitation department in New York had taken precautions to see that this wouldn't happen. Newspapers and radio had pelted the city with awesome hints.

On February 27 New Yorkers opened their papers to confront two giant feet poised, according to the text, to smash into their world "with the strength of a battleship and the fury of a thousand demons." Daily, their radios emitted nasty gorilla roars followed by frightful feminine screams. As the opening drew closer, the sound effects grew noisier and the ads grew more explicit, until March 1, when RKO made the monster's dread intentions known. "King Kong, of a former world, comes to destroy our world—all but the soft, white female thing he holds like a fluttering bird!" At last New York was treated to the sight of the snarling ape balanced on top of the Empire State Building, tearing an airplane out of the sky with one giant paw and clutching a flimsily clad Fay Wray in the other.

New Yorkers were psychologically ready to respond to Kong's fury. The Great Depression hovered over their world like a poisonous fog, permeating the economy with fear and distrust as the final days of the condemned Hoover Administration faded away. So it was in the nature of a catharsis to watch an ape who looked fifty feet tall beat the bejesus out of their faltering civilization—and then to thrill to the sight of the beast's ultimate destruction by the tools of science, the ingenuity and inventiveness of modern man. Even as the words of a new president uplifted the nation on Inauguration Day, Saturday, March 4, negating fear, that "nameless, unreasoning, unjustified terror which paralyzes needed efforts to convert retreat into advance," excited thousands lined the streets four abreast to see "the sensation of the talking screen." The same day, New York Governor Herbert Lehman proclaimed a two-day bank holiday that climaxed a wave of bank closures across the nation the previous month. He advised that in a few days, should it prove necessary, New Yorkers would be issued scrip to use instead of currency. In the meantime, more than 150,000 movie-goers took their pocket money out of their sugar bowls and plunked down more than $100,000 at the box office to see *King Kong* in the first week's run.

Audiences agreed with the critics that Merian Cooper's *King Kong* surpassed any horror picture that had gone before, and they were enchanted by its beauty-and-the-beast theme as interpreted in Ruth Rose's fairy-tale dialogue. The experts were bowled over by the RKO studio and camera technology: the genius of Willis O'Brien and his crew, the magic produced by Vernon Walker's camera effects department, Max Steiner's atmospheric musical score, Murray Spivak's innovative sound effects department. After *Variety*'s rave preview notice on February 17, which claimed "the only way to top this would be to make a newsreel of the Armenian atrocities," the trade paper took another, dispassionate look on May 7. "The work has many flaws which are overcome by the general results," the reviewer admitted. He compared *King Kong* to the late Sir Arthur Conan Doyle and his *Lost World,* a 1925 silent that visualized "the existence of prehistoric monsters in some far corner of the modern world." Another reviewer referred to Fay Wray's "ninety-six-minute screaming session, too much for any actress and any audience." The *New York Times*' highbrow, Mordaunt Hall, understood perfectly what *King Kong* represented: "A fantastic film in which a monstrous ape uses automobiles for missiles, and climbs a skyscraper."

On Sunday, March 5, President Roosevelt declared a four-day national bank "holiday," and the movie industry panicked. Calls went out to the corporation presidents, and an extraordinary session was held later in the day to discuss the ramifications. By late evening, the movie company generals, gathered in Will Hays's Waldorf-Astoria–tower apartment on Park Avenue, had reached a decision. In an uncustomary demonstration of togetherness, they recommended a 25 to 50 percent salary reduction throughout the industry for a period of eight weeks, to become effective immediately. Not one of them would officially admit authorship of the idea. "Tightness of cash and the current inability to transport currency to Hollywood are directly responsible for the drastic action," a spokesman informed the press. "A real effort will be made to keep the studios open. This will be possible *only* if the companies are able to reduce operating costs all along the line."

After a mass meeting in Hollywood the following Wednesday, four major studios affiliated with the Hays organization—MGM, Columbia, RKO, and

Warner Brothers—agreed to the wage cut. Fox employees offered a counter proposal that was accepted: to work for four weeks without pay. But there were rumblings that 8000 union workers would refuse to bow to the moguls' demands. Strikes were talked about, and on Monday, March 13, studio workers took a one-day "holiday" to get the point across. That evening, after a week of wrangling between moguls and union representatives, interrupted by a devastating earthquake the previous Friday that practically demolished Long Beach and shook Hollywood, the two opposing factions agreed to compromise. Employees earning less than $50 a week could keep their paychecks intact.

In mid-March, with a brighter outlook gaining momentum in the industry and the box office showing signs of recovery, Merian Cooper, preceded by B. B. Kahane, flew East for a series of home-office meetings. His had been a strong and argumentative voice for the underdog—opposing the reduction of salaries for low-paid workers—during the stormy meetings in Hollywood. RKO employees, innocent victims of the parent company's receivership, had already been asked to adjust to a two-week interval between paychecks and submit to several 10 percent salary cuts. Now, with the help of scrip issued by Cooper in small amounts for their personal use, and backed with his own money, the studio had weathered the banking crisis.

The New York meetings with the RKO executive board focused on economy in production and of course RKO Radio Pictures' 1933–34 program. Just before Cooper's arrival, Merlin Aylesworth scuttled the Selznick unit production system plan the former studio chief had dreamed of launching in the coming season. But Cooper, who carried weight in the executive boardroom, let it be known that he intended to delegate full authority to his staff of associate producers and directors. "I don't intend to tell them how to make pictures," he said heatedly. "They know just as well as I!"

The RKO board approved a schedule of fifty-two features for the new season, at a cost of about $9 to $11 million, and averaging about $200,000 a picture. Before leaving for the Coast with Cooper, B. B. Kahane, whose position had in no way been weakened, informed the trade press that RKO Radio Pictures would deliver most of its projected program of pictures for the current season. "Other than the discontinuance of a series of six Westerns" [the bloom had again left the sage] "there will be no curtailment of the company's production activities. Mr. Cooper will find eight features ready for immediate production upon his return," he said, reeling off titles that included *Morning Glory* with Katharine Hepburn, *Bed of Roses* with Constance Bennett, and *Little Women*. "The final scenes of Wheeler & Woolsey's newest comedy are completed," Kahane added. "In production are *The Silver Cord* with Irene

Dunne, *Maiden Voyage,* a musical, and *The Black Ace,* a Joseph I. Schnitzer independent production."*

Kahane dropped star-names under contract: Constance Bennett, Ann Harding, Irene Dunne, Richard Dix, Wheeler & Woolsey, who with new-comers to stardom Katharine Hepburn, Francis Lederer, and Leslie Howard and a host of "comers" (contractees being groomed for stardom) would all perform in the new season's production schedule. New contracts had not yet been renegotiated with Bennett and Harding, but Kahane intimated to the press that he hoped agreements would be reached. Actually, he was aware that the star potential of the lustrous and younger Hepburn might seriously diminish their positions. "Miss Bennett's contract calls for another picture," Kahane said, pausing to give his final plug importance. "*Ann Vickers,* Sinclair Lewis's best-seller, starring Irene Dunne, and another Cooper–Schoedsack *special* will highlight the new season's releases."

On April 6, the movie industry leaders who made up the New Deal Expedition, as it would come to be known, led by General Hays, took off on the Twentieth Century Limited to outline to Hollywood on its own home turf the need for a new economic order. A sequel to the so-called Waldorf-Astoria Conferences, it would mark the first time New York and Hollywood conversed with each other on industry problems.

The alarm sounded when word reached the studio colony that the generals from New York were on their way west. Fearing further reductions, or even permanent salary cuts, studio workers affiliated with the Academy of Motion Picture Arts and Sciences (which functioned like a company union) hurriedly convened at the Beverly Wilshire Hotel and vigorously voted to resist any further attacks on their paychecks. Said J. Theodore Reed, of the Academy's technical division, "Let us meet them as a militant fighting group."

Practically all the surviving moguls were on hand to pay their respects to the eastern executives when the Chief rolled into Pasadena the following Sunday afternoon. The invincible L. B. Mayer drove up from MGM to extend a guarded greeting to Nicholas M. Schenck, president of Loew's, the mogul who had conspired behind his back to sell his studio to William Fox. Adolph Zukor, battle-scarred and sporting a new title, that of co-receiver of Paramount, was met by the diminutive Emanuel "Manny" Cohen, Jesse Lasky's treacherous former assistant who had commandeered his post in the company wars. Harry Warner was met by brother Jack and young Darryl Zanuck; Robert Cochrane by Universal's reception committee, Senior and Junior Laemmle. Sidney Kent, William Fox's successor, had arrived earlier, and Columbia's Harry Cohn was

*The title of this mild mystery starring Chester Morris and Vivienne Osborne was changed to *Tomorrow at Seven.*

detained in New York. From RKO came Merian Cooper, who boarded the train to ride into Los Angeles with Merlin Aylesworth. Will Hays, laden with bulging portfolios and accompanied by several assistants, briefed the press, explaining that the forces of the Depression had thrown some of the elements of this industry out of adjustment, and called for reorganization and rehabilitation. "The fundamental problem, of course, is to balance the budget between the outgo in all branches of the industry, and the current income from the box office." As he stepped into his chauffeur-driven limousine, Hays denied that the producers were planning a new wage slash.

Throughout the week, the executives exchanged personal views on a program of rehabilitation at the Hays organization office on Hollywood Boulevard. At the same time, Academy members, continuing their meetings and threats, succeeded in forcing the studios to restore salaries to pre-emergency levels. "The emergency is over!" declared John T. Mott, counsel for the Academy's committee.

By April 18, the coast conferences came to an uneasy halt, with a considerable list of tentative plans—hardly more than suggestions on how to "balance cost and gross." The New York generals, having lost some of their swagger, departed, leaving behind a few token committees, and their leader to implement plans to "hasten the processes of readjustment." Said Terry Ramsaye, who observed the cost in Hollywood stand up to the gross from New York: "Hollywood listened a moment to the retreating footsteps of the uninvited guests, and rang for the butler...."

The Cooper method of aligning cost and gross was to turn out pictures at an assembly-line pace, an approach that had not appealed to his former boss. Selznick had been plagued by RKO's arbitrary overheads, which had made it doubly tough for any picture to return its cost, but he couldn't reconcile himself to increasing his output. "Hell, the more pictures you make," Cooper told Selznick, "the more you reduce your overhead and bring down costs." In April, Cooper's zeal placed RKO in the forefront of the majors in the purchase of stories and plays. The little studio acquired eighteen properties, eight more than the giant Metro plant absorbed.

But Merian Cooper had more on his mind than picture-making that spring. On May 27 the dashing executive eloped to Williams, Arizona, with actress Dorothy Jordan, a very attractive RKO contractee from Tennessee, who had recently sidestepped a marriage to an equally sporty movie producer, Howard Hughes. Cooper postponed their honeymoon until the fall, when the removal of his bride from the production schedule would have far-reaching consequences. Dorothy, a dancer, was set to play opposite Fred Astaire in *Flying Down to Rio,* the studio's "aerial musical," as the trades dubbed it. She had understudied Adele Astaire, Fred's enchanting sister and former partner, in their 1927 stage hit, the Gershwins' *Funny Face*. In July, with associate producer Lou Brock and cameraman Roy Hunt and crew in Rio de Janeiro filming atmosphere and background process shots to be used in Hollywood, Cooper selected a replacement: Ginger Rogers, a vivacious twenty-two-year-old fledgling star, whose path had also crossed Astaire's on Broadway. Fred had choreographed one of Ginger's numbers in another Gershwin hit, 1930's *Girl Crazy*.

Ginger had worked at half a dozen studios, appearing in fourteen pictures in her three years in Hollywood without finding an appropriate studio home. Prodded by her hard-driving mother, Lela Rogers, who had guided her career since childhood, Ginger was now angling for a contract with Columbia Pictures, but studio mogul Harry Cohn was indecisive. Despite her flashy chorus-doll roles in Warner Brothers' *42nd Street*—the movie that revived the public's interest in musicals—and *Gold Diggers of 1933,* Ginger had turned in a terrible performance in her Columbia screen test. While Cohn fiddled, Cooper looked at the inferior test. Ginger had just played the lead in RKO's *Professional Sweetheart,* a minor musical, and it was too soon to check her impact at the box office. Nevertheless, something clicked in Cooper's head and he signed her to a seven-year contract.

The same month—July—that Cooper chose Ginger Rogers for *Rio,* Fred Astaire arrived in Hollywood, just married to Phyllis Potter, a beautiful Eastern socialite, and anxious to work. He had been rebuffed by Hollywood before—after a Paramount screen test for a projected film version of *Funny Face* in 1928. He was thirty-four, knife-thin, painfully aware of his physical shortcomings that he felt would make it impossible to play screen heroes. But his career had reached a turning point with the retirement of Adele, with whom he had built his reputation. Fred had gone it alone for the first time in his life in *Gay Divorce* on Broadway the past winter, and in spite of a show-stopping romantic adagio, Cole Porter's *Night and Day,* performed with blonde Claire Luce, the critics pined for his sister, Adele. It seemed to Astaire that on Broadway he would always be tagged as Adele Astaire's brother. And so he made the decision to give Hollywood another try.

Astaire was in luck. The technological limitations of the first surge of movie musicals had ruled out dancing of any complexity. But with *42nd Street,* the imagination and verve of a self-taught dance director from Broadway, Busby Berkeley, broke the barriers that tied song-and-dance numbers to the proscenium arch, setting them up in incredible displays of symmetrical patterns. Although the new, natural-looking, three-color Technicolor process was ruled out by the New York Office because of its expense, improvements in film stock and lighting could enhance the dramatic effects of black-and-white photography. For *Rio,* RKO's new art director, Van Nest Polglase (formerly at Paramount, and whom Selznick had signed), and Carroll Clark were designing an innovative setting—a big, white, glistening casino set, where Astaire would perform briefly with the new RKO contractee, Ginger Rogers, to the music of Vincent Youmans, who had arrived in Hollywood several months earlier to compose the score.

Rio's associate producer, Lou Brock, had stimulated Merian Cooper's interest in making a musical by utilizing an aviation theme, as well as the exotic South American setting. Brock's last feature, *Melody Cruise* (formerly titled *Maiden Voyage*), directed by Mark Sandrich, another musical enthusiast, and starring radio's Phil Harris, had fared poorly in spite of a spectacular iceboat ballet created by Dave Gould, RKO's answer to Busby Berkeley. For *Rio* Brock and Gould hoped to outshine Berkeley with an aerial circus number in which the RKO chorus girls, strapped to the wings of bi-planes, would execute a precision drill.

In mid-August the trades carried a thick color supplement that featured *Morning Glory,* RKO's first picture of the new season, playing at the Radio City Music Hall. Over a photo of Katharine Hepburn throwing her arms in the air, and with a wild look in her eyes, the ad proclaimed: "You can't run away from Hepburn! Her electric personality will haunt you! She's your favorite star ... after today!" The company's new sales pitch promised "Dynamic fulfillment of our pledge: productions, not predictions." The "titanic" theme, a product of the "shake the world" school of film advertising, had passed away with Republican prosperity.

Bill of Divorcement had indeed shot Kate to overnight prominence, but for her second film and first stellar role, Selznick, with misguided zeal, shoved her into an Ann Harding vehicle, *Christopher Strong,* choosing Dorothy Arzner, a top director, for the picture. Pandro Berman inherited the project after Selznick's departure. A bizarre tear-jerker about a pregnant aviatrix who commits suicide, it failed to rouse the box office, although the *New York Times's* Mordaunt Hall likened Hepburn to an American Garbo. Berman himself had selected Hepburn for *Morning Glory,* and given an identifiable role, that of a stage-struck young girl striving to win out on Broadway, she triumphed over the picture's shortcomings: a trite story adapted by Howard J. Green from Zoe Akins' unproduced play, and unsubtle direction by Lowell Sherman, who shot the picture in eighteen days. The following March, Hepburn would triumph over sixty-year-old May Robson (*Lady for a Day*) and a young British actress, Diana Wynyard (*Cavalcade*), to win the Academy Award.

Little Women, Louisa May Alcott's sixty-five-year-old children's classic of wholesome, New England family life during the Civil War, had been one of Selznick's favorite projects. Before leaving RKO he assigned George Cukor to direct the film; then Merian Cooper took over the entire project with one of his associate producers, Kenneth MacGowan. The felicitous casting of Hepburn as the irrepressible tomboy, Jo, the pivotal character in the household of four daughters and their mother, worked like a charm. The film was superbly cast with Frances Dee as Meg, Jean Parker as Beth, and Joan Bennett as Amy, the other less dynamic sisters, and directed with lyrical tenderness by George Cukor. The delicate mood of the novel was retained with uncompromising fidelity by Sarah Y. Mason and Victor Heerman in their adaptation, and in Walter Plunkett's costumes and the period settings designed by Hobe Erwin, a New York artist and decorator who worked with art director Van Nest Polglase.

Little Women opened at the Music Hall on November 16, and its archaic charm cast a spell over movie-goers and the box office, with an opening-day attendance record of 23,000 people. Critic Richard Watts Jr. of the *New York Herald Tribune* noted that "theater audiences smiled wistfully, much more often wept softly as all the well-remembered figures came to life...." As for Hepburn's stunning impact, Mordaunt Hall summed up everyone's view: "As vital, sympathetic, and full of the *joie de vivre* as one could hope for, Jo, the Jo of *Little Women,* is to be seen in the person of Katharine Hepburn."

On the heels of *Little Women's* record-breaking run came Lou Brock's musical extravaganza "destined to make all show business believe in Santa Claus," *Flying Down to Rio,* ballyhooed in the trades as "a picture that gaily spurns the earth and chases Folly among the stars!" Cooper had secured Thornton Freeland, who had directed two successful early musicals starring Eddie Cantor and Fanny Brice, and with the assistance of a second unit headed by George Nicholls Jr., the movie was shot in four weeks. It came across as "a hearty, lively show," and as Mordaunt Hall also noted, there was "an impressive series of scenes devoted to a dance known as The Carioca" that included "the nimble-toed Fred Astaire and the charming Ginger Rogers." Said *Variety:* "The main point about *Flying Down to Rio* is the screen promise of Fred Astaire. That should be about as important to Radio as the fact that this picture is not destined for big grosses, because the studio may eventually do things with this lad...." Astaire was a sure bet, "distinctly likeable on the screen," and as a dancer, "in a class by himself." Not even Ginger Rogers could enter the golden circle.

Astaire, still uncertain as to how movie audiences would receive him, had gone to London in October in order to play *Gay Divorce* there. During the winter the adulation crossed the sea. He would return to Hollywood a movie star.

14

RKO Bags a Hero (cont'd.)

During the previous August of 1933, the moguls, meeting again in New York—this time at the request of the new administration—had been invited to participate in the formation of a code intended to bring Hollywood in line with the government's recovery program. President Roosevelt, bent on giving the Depression-weary nation a New Deal, had cast his eyes on Hollywood, voicing his concerns about such touchy subjects as big salaries, double bills, and "protecting the little fellow." The moguls had just escaped Congressman Sirovich's latest assault. A resolution, introduced by the hot-headed New York Representative in the spring, that threatened to pry into their private business practices had gone down in defeat in May, with practically *all* the expressed opposition coming from Sirovich's own Democratic party. Now, the controlling hand of the director of the National Recovery Act, General Hugh S. Johnson of "the Blue Eagle office," was raised against them. His deputy administrator, Sol A. Rosenblatt, given the herculean task of composing a single code for their entire industry, had dispensed with sleeping and eating in his eagerness to learn all he could about their operations.

As young Rosenblatt shuttled back and forth between New York and Washington in the fall months, conferring with representatives of the various branches of the industry still locked in argument over the structure of trade practices and labor provisions, the trade press speculated on who would rule the code-show, above and beyond a committee of control that it was assumed would be appointed after its completion. Said Martin Quigley, who considered the code scheme an enormous waste of time, energy, and money: "Washington still toys with the notion of finding some miracle man who would be made dictator over motion picture affairs, and from his lofty pinnacle of an exposition of importance, would quickly introduce the millenium into the picture business." Said Terry Ramsaye, pointedly, after duly recording the September voyage to Europe of Joseph Kennedy with his good friend "Jimmy" Roosevelt, son of the president, and Roosevelt's bride and a pride of Kennedys: "Up in New England on the big country club circuit, where there is much bridge and tea, long before the NRA [National Recovery Administration] was announced, it was being said that 'Joe is going to be the administration's big boss of the movies.'" Ramsaye then recalled numerous reports of Kennedy's considerable contributions to the Democratic campaign. "Something like $35,000 was mentioned." He added: "If Mr. Kennedy were, after just a manner of speaking, a problem, and if the motion picture were also, in a manner of speaking, also a problem, this idea of a post for him at the helm of the Administration's administration of the motion picture might not be a bad idea."

But in November, Ramsaye reversed the rumors that Kennedy was to be (or expected to be) importantly reinstated into the motion picture scene. Under the heading DISTILLERS, *Motion Picture Herald* broke the news. "Joseph P. Kennedy of Boston, and formerly of FBO, Pathé Exchange, and sundry other film projects, who arrived back from a visit to Europe with James Roosevelt and other guests, is currently said to be planning a large scale invasion of the liquor market, specializing in Scotch brands, with which he has made connections with the offices of the young Mr. Roosevelt." The item was corroborated with the word that four of his stalwarts were starting a survey of New England for outlets for the National Distillers Corporation.

By the end of November, President Roosevelt finally got around to signing the motion picture code that Rosenblatt had finally written—but not without alleviating some of its sting. After an eleventh-hour visit to the Little White House in Warm Springs, Georgia, by Eddie Cantor, the president temporarily suspended a decision on excessive Hollywood salaries. The diminutive comedian of stage, radio, and occasionally the screen—and coincidentally president of the recently formed Screen Actors Guild—had launched into a tirade in New York the week before against the idea of fixing star salaries under the film code. Cantor declared that major producers were "one big trust" in which stockholders had no voice, while they were "being used as a smoke screen for the millions lost by the companies."

Cantor notwithstanding, the Code Authority of some fifteen members that Roosevelt announced included a portion of the "big trust," among them Radio–Keith–Orpheum and NBC's Merlin Aylesworth. Eddie Cantor and another White House favorite, MGM star Marie Dressler, were named to represent Hollywood's creative talent. For a brief spell it looked like General Johnson, the by now tired and worn NRA director who viewed the movies as just another industry, would hold dictatorial powers. But after a blockbuster of protest from Hollywood, Roosevelt, who had a wide social interest as well as acquaintance in the movie world, decided to retain the status quo: Cooperation and self-regulation, that well-used Will Hays panacea, would prevail under the Code Authority.

That November, the high-flying "plenipotentiary" of RKO Studios, as the press now described Merian Cooper, sailed leisurely eastward via the Panama Canal with his bride. They had already traveled extensively—to the South, the Northwest, and Hawaii—the latter a vacation trip for Cooper to recuperate from a slight heart attack. Cooper had made up his mind to cast off the backbreaking burden of the studio's large production program, having no desires for the duties of head of production any longer. Like other former exponents of mass production—Jesse Lasky, B. P. Schulberg, Charles Rogers, Joe Schnitzer, Samuel Goldwyn, and others now functioning independently as unit producers at Fox, Paramount, United Artists, and elsewhere—and looking years younger—Cooper had become a convert to the idea of decentralized production. The previous May, he had persuaded his friend "Jock" Whitney to buy a 15 percent interest in the new Technicolor Corporation, which he fervently believed in. Cooper and the Whitney family then formed Pioneer Pictures expressly for the purpose of exploiting the breathtaking and expensive three-color process in a series of live-action films to be released through RKO. With Pioneer absorbing the color costs, RKO, which had a couple of years earlier rejected experimenting with "anything so uncertain" as Technicolor, was now willing to share production expense and handle distribution. Walt Disney had tested Technicolor's viability in a *Silly Symphony* cartoon, *Flowers and Trees,* and won an Academy Award for best short subject in 1932.

Arriving in New York in December, where the lines waiting to get in to see *Little Women* at the Music Hall resembled a mob scene, Cooper huddled with the RKO board, intent on dictating *his* scenario for the studio's 1934–35 schedule. If he was ruffled that the *New York Times* had just called *Son of Kong* "a vaudeville buffoon alongside his old man," he didn't reveal it. The "quickie" sequel, made at a third of *King Kong*'s $672,000, looked to the critics like a "wash-up" of the Kong theme.

Spelling out the new season to the press in his Southern drawl and blunt manner, Cooper announced that the company's aim would be to produce only Class "A" pictures. "I believe there will be no room for the 'quickie' type of product," he said. "Dave Selznick started the trend away from 'quickies' at RKO before I joined the company as executive producer. I'm simply trying to carry out what he started." Declaring that "pictures which subordinate the sex-angle [meaning *Little Women*] are the ones which ultimately show the greatest financial returns," he said that "*that* type of product" would be eliminated. The new schedule would call for a minimum of forty pictures with a possible maximum of fifty-two. "I will not personally supervise any of the pictures on the next year's program," Cooper said, in what was something of a revelation, "although I'll provide executive direction over all production activities."

The lavish color supplements that brightened the trades in January 1934 suggested that Merian Cooper had already started to make good on his pledge of delivering the studio from the "quickies." Leslie Howard in *Of Human Bondage* and *The Lost Patrol,* John Ford's production with Victor McLaglen, stood out against an otherwise lackluster listing of standard, commercial subject matter; although the new Hepburn vehicle, *Spitfire,* which transformed urbane Kate into an illiterate Ozark mountain girl, had a dangerously offbeat ring. Constance Bennett, missing from the schedule, had been dropped after the poor performance of her last three pictures, while Ann Harding, whose contract had been renegotiated, had been eclipsed by Hepburn and Irene Dunne—the latter firmly entrenched as the studio's first lady of soap opera.

Meanwhile, with Merian Cooper's contract running out, insiders were laying bets that he would abdicate his RKO throne for Jock Whitney and his millions. On February 2, the *Hollywood Reporter* ran the tantalizing headline SALARY, PERCENTAGE DEMANDS BY PRESENT PRODUCTION HEAD MAY SPLIT THEM. Negotiations between Cooper; RKO Radio Pictures president B. B. Kahane; RKO vice president in charge of distribution, Ned Depinet; and Joseph R. McDonough, the new Sarnoff-crowned general manager of Radio–Keith–Orpheum, had reached a deadlock.

Cooper had reaped a profit of more than $500,000 in the past twelve months, from his $2500-a-week salary and percentage deal—20 percent profit on every picture the lot had turned out—and was holding out for a similar deal, even though the desk of production chief would presumedly be scuttled. McDonough, formerly president of RCA Victor and executive assistant to Sarnoff, who, according to *Motion Picture Herald,* wore his hat "with collegiate nonchalance" but talked as "crisply as a credit manager on a hard Monday," considered the price of Cooper's "executive direction" too steep and wanted to place some limits on his percentage deal.

The deadlock held. In a move they immediately regretted, the RKO board accepted Cooper's resignation.

15

The Pipes of Pandro

Radio–Keith–Orpheum's president, Merlin Aylesworth, rushed to Hollywood the first week of February 1934 to take a hand in the production subsidiary's latest executive crisis. Under his deft touch, RKO's "jigsaw facade," as it appeared to *Motion Picture Herald,* quickly rearranged itself. "The Aylesworth thinks fast and talks fast, but soothingly," the trade journal advised the movie colony's devotees, following the action on the Radio lot. "The McDonough thinks fast and talks tough."

Rumors abounded in the various water holes of Gower Gulch: In view of Cooper's prestige, Aylesworth would get down on his knees and beg him to come back; David Selznick, although thriving at MGM, wouldn't mind being wooed back; even hotter, young Pandro Berman was being wooed by a rival company; the lot would go entirely unit production if B. B. ("Bright Boy") Kahane got his way!

After four days of conferences, and considerable influential maneuvering said to have emanated from inner circles within the neighborhood of Broadway, Wall Street, and the socialite end of Park Avenue, in particular, the prestigious Merian Cooper was reinstated as production head. At the same time, the blunt-spoken McDonough, now occupying the post of general manager of the parent company, was kicked upstairs. In what was looked upon as a stroke of genius, Aylesworth elevated the Sarnoff favorite to the presidency of RKO Radio Pictures, the post then held by B. B. Kahane, and created a new position for the indispensable Kahane, that of president of RKO Studios, another subsidiary. In effect, Kahane would continue in his same role as head man at the studio. Only his hat had changed.

For the time being the arrangement with Cooper remained loosely defined, since he intended to leave in a few days for a Hawaiian vacation with his wife, and they would very likely go to Europe later. Radio's deal with Cooper and his partner Jock Whitney's Pioneer Pictures to release their first three productions had been set just before his resignation. The studio had announced it would "shoot the works" on the British novelist Sir Edward Bulwer-Lytton's classic *The Last Days of Pompeii,* a spectacle picture featuring a volcanic debacle that Cooper assured the RKO board would be as thrilling as Kong's rampage through Manhattan. Understandably, Cooper wanted to visit Pompeii for the picture's atmospheric scenes. Aylesworth could only guess what would happen after Cooper's return. Would he feel like stepping back into the top spot on the lot? Having snatched a comfortable share of the studio's profits in the last year, and aside from health reasons, Cooper might very well prefer to limit himself to the production of his own two or three specials and escape a high tax bracket.

Left with a figurehead when the studio needed a flesh-and-blood production boss to rush out the remainder of the year's program of about fourteen pictures, Aylesworth made a practical decision. In a move highly favored by Kahane and Cooper, he promoted young Pandro Berman, Cooper's executive assistant, to the position of executive producer. Aylesworth knew that Berman's confirmation by the RKO board would be only a formality. At twenty-nine, Berman, then the youngest executive producer in Hollywood, was as thoroughly versed in motion pictures as had been Selznick when he had come to RKO at the same age. Like Selznick he had grown up in the industry. He was the son of Harry M. Berman and cousin of Joe Schnitzer; his roots ran deep in the Gower Street lot. The senior Berman had been one of the founders in charge of sales of the old Robertson–Cole Corp., forerunner of FBO. Schnitzer, who later became Radio Picture's first president, was the vice president of the R-C Company. From a $20-a-week flunky fresh out of DeWitt Clinton High School in New York, bearing the title of third assistant director, Pandro worked his way up and around the FBO lot as assistant director, assistant cutter, and film editor until Bill Le Baron gave him his first big opportunity by making him his general assistant on *Cimarron.*

The short, stocky young producer, whom everyone called Pan, handled the creative business of turning out pictures in a level-headed fashion, with both feet on the ground, unhampered by the egocentricity that characterized Selznick, or the showiness of the Cooper personality. Aylesworth was aware that Berman had already functioned as executive producer some months earlier during Merian Cooper's absence. He had shown he was capable of making production decisions, including choosing excellent properties for the studio. His decision was further supported by the sensational drawing power of the dance act of Fred Astaire and Ginger Rogers in *Flying Down to Rio.* Negotiations had just been completed for the purchase of Astaire's play *Gay Divorce* for a modest $20,000. Berman, accompanied by his wife, Viola, had seen the play in London in December. Aylesworth had been told how Lou Brock, *Rio*'s producer, had passed up the property, ridiculing its antiquated libretto, but that Berman had viewed it with stars in his eyes. Also acting on his starry-eyed judgment, the studio had outbid Paramount and MGM, paying $65,000 for the new Jerome Kern–Otto Harbach Broadway hit, *Roberta,* another made-to-order Astaire–Rogers vehicle.

Aylesworth returned to New York satisfied that a solid chain of command had been established for the unstable subsidiary. Actually, the restructuring would make it possible to shift his administrative duties onto McDonough, who would have his headquarters in Manhattan, and devote his energies to the company's financial problems. As a director of Irving Trust Co., Radio–Keith–Orpheum's receiver, Aylesworth had borne the brunt of the creditors' attacks. In equity receivership for a little over a year now, the company had whittled down its net loss from 1932's horrendous $10.6 million to $4.3 million in 1933, a substantial reduction. Nevertheless, there were plenty of objectors to the "magic" of equity receivership under the shield of Irving Trust. Several prominent creditors had gone so far as to object to its continuance as receiver, and to charge in Judge William Bondy's Federal court that Aylesworth's dual post resulted in "conflicting and disqualifying interests." As evidence they divulged a transaction completed the day before RKO went into receivership, which Irving Trust had sanctioned. This maneuver, they said, had given RCA a favored lien on certain RKO assets worth $2.4 million. But the court's "protective wings" safeguarded the company, just as attorney Louis Nizer had predicted they would, for Judge Bondy upheld Irving Trust. As would Aylesworth's chieftain.

RCA's annual report to its stockholders, made public late in February, included a positive statement from David Sarnoff that substantial progress had been made in improving the operations of RKO and its subsidiaries. Sarnoff offered hope that the year would produce "conditions warranting development of plans for a reorganization of the company and a discontinuance of the receivership."

Sarnoff's optimistic stance held over into May. "RKO has turned the corner with a net profit of four-hundred and three thousand dollars for the first quarter of 1934," he told RCA's stockholders early in the month. "It is encouraging to have RKO in the black again."

However, Irving Trust disclosed some disconcerting data in its third report, filed with the Federal court on May 22. A grand total of $35 million in claims had been filed against RKO to date. Of these, a meager $2 million had been withdrawn. The invalid company could no longer be passed off as a convalescent.

So on June 7, Sarnoff took a momentous step toward severing RCA's relations with its crippled offspring. On that day, the name of Franklin D. Roosevelt had scarcely dried on the latest bankruptcy law—77B of the National Bankruptcy Act—before Radio–Keith–Orpheum, closely followed by Paramount, streaked to the head of the line in New York. "The President wants each and every prostrate U.S. corporation to have the same opportunity to rise and pray for cheap relief," *Time* magazine stressed, commenting on the new bill. Its principal allurement rested in one provision making it possible to secure the court's approval of a reorganization plan agreeable to two-thirds of the creditors—provided they could be corralled. No longer could a mutinous minority stem the tide of reorganization until they were bought off. The press was kept so busy chastising Paramount that it overlooked any corporate sinning that might have landed RKO on the roster of "embarrassed corporations." "Boom-time theatre rentals got RKO," remarked *Time*, matter-of-factly. No member of the fourth estate, it seemed, wanted to bring up the devastating Pathé merger or its perpetrator. Interestingly, within a month, upon his appointment to head the Securities and Exchange Commission in Washington, Joe Kennedy was pictured by the journalist John T. Flynn as "a blundering wrecker of corporations."

In its petition filed in U.S. District Court, New York, for reorganization under the new law, RKO listed liabilities amounting to approximately $16 million in gold notes and debenture issues, and $35 million in claims, as against assets of $25 million, consisting for the most part of stock and notes receivable of subsidiaries. The application, which bore Merlin Aylesworth's signature, trod the well-worn route: RKO "has no means of borrowing"..., and "RKO alleges there is no prospect that improved earnings will be sufficient...to pay the amounts due and payable."

After giving his approval of RKO's petition, Federal Judge Irving C. Coxe swiftly overruled all creditors' objections to the appointment of Irving Trust as permanent trustee. Sarnoff was now strategically positioned to take advantage of RKO's "anticipated" recovery.

16

The Pipes of Pandro (cont'd.)

In Hollywood, Pan Berman turned a deaf ear to the death struggle of the parent company taking place in the east. Having survived three stormy administrations since RCA captured the studio in 1928, and several in its earlier FBO incarnation, he considered crisis a way of life on Gower Street. Besides producing his own pictures—as executive producer standing in for Merian Cooper—Berman had his hands full supervising the production units that packed every inch of studio space and spilled over onto the Pathé lot in the early spring of 1934.

The studio was still riding on the success of *Little Women,* called by exhibitors "one of the sweetest pictures of the season," and *Flying Down to Rio,* which some swore was "the best musical since Eddie Cantor's *Whoopee.*" Unfortunately, a few of the big specials that B. B. Kahane had touted as the box-office sensations of the 1933–34 season had played to empty houses. Poor Irene Dunne, christened by New York critic Richard Watts Jr. "the lady Gandhi of the cinema stars" after her crop of 1932 "weepers," had stoically suffered with Gandhi-like passive resistance through *The Silver Cord* and *Ann Vickers.* Although the latter had been hastily withdrawn from the "special" class and shoved among the "B's," some exhibitors were still disgruntled: "To be regular fellows, they should have ditched it entirely," said one theaterman in Orwigsburg, Pennsylvania, where it flopped on January 17.

Following Katharine Hepburn's triumph in *Little Women,* Merian Cooper had rejected Jesse Lasky's request to borrow her for his film version of *Warrior's Husband* at Fox, as well as his projected film bio of the life of ballerina Anna Pavlova. Instead, Cooper miscast her in *Spitfire,* an adaptation by RKO's popular scripter Jane Murfin of Lula Vollmer's 1927 Broadway play *Trigger.* It proved to be beyond director John Cromwell's resources to impart much authenticity to Kate's "thieving, praying, hellcat of the hills," as the RKO advertising department hyped her role for its Music Hall opening early in March. Still, the majority of critics remained under the spell of the Hepburn of *Morning Glory* and *Little Women* and sided with the *New York Times*'s Mordaunt Hall, who hailed her "vital and persuasive acting."

Pan Berman believed the stage-trained Cromwell to be a fine and conscientious craftsman who would fit the sensitive demands of the film version of W. Somerset Maugham's 1915 masterpiece *Of Human Bondage,* which went into production early in the year. Berman chose an American actress, twenty-six-year-old Bette Davis—she had played the ingenue in his 1932 programmer *Way Back Home*—for the dramatic character role of the tawdry Cockney waitress, Mildred, who is the pathetic object of Leslie Howard's obsession. Describing the slightly happier and decidedly cleaner screenplay (by Lester Cohen), *Motion Picture Herald* said on April 14: "This drama is the emotional story of a fine man's tragic love for a faithless woman" and suggested that theatermen build a ticket-selling campaign on the "bring the handkerchief along" idea. But "the life-like quality of the story," the "marked authenticity of the atmosphere," so praised by Mordaunt Hall, and Leslie Howard's perfect performance played too forcefully on female heartstrings. The female audience could not forgive the crippled Carey (Leslie Howard) for taking back the despicable Mildred so many times, and the picture fell short of box-office expectations. But it proved a triumph for Berman, the studio, and Bette Davis. The role brought her universal acclaim and an "informal" Academy Award nomination by protest after Hollywood discovered that her name was missing from the list of nominees. In spite of a write-in vote, she lost out to Claudette Colbert for *It Happened One Night,* but she picked up the best-actress award the following year for Warner Brothers' *Dangerous.* In Berman's opinion the award was partly due to her brilliant performance in *Of Human Bondage.*

The previous year Cooper had made a two-picture deal with John Ford, the famed director of the silent Western *The Iron Horse,* more recently, *Arrowsmith,* and a kindred soul. Ford wanted to make a film based on *The Informer,* Liam O'Flaherty's 1925 prize-winning novel about the Irish Sinn Fein rebellion of 1922. However, RKO had acquired the rights to *Patrol,* a harrowing war story by Philip MacDonald that depicted the fate of a British patrol lost in the Mesopotamian desert in 1917. This was Cooper territory; Ford, relishing its realism and psychological characterizations, and finding another kindred spirit in screen-writer Dudley Nichols, agreed to do it first. The strong-willed director took an all-male cast headed by Victor McLaglen and Boris Karloff to the Yuma desert, and with a cardboard oasis as his only set, he wrapped up shooting in two weeks. After the preview, *Film Daily* compared *The Lost Patrol* to *Beau Geste,* generously grading it as "one of the best of its kind." S. Barret McCormick, the studio's zealous advertising and publicity chief, followed his customary policy of telling the whole truth about the company's product. "It's the sensation of the hour in New York! Draws four stars from the *Daily News,* and the greatest rave reviews you ever read!" he plugged when *Lost Patrol* opened at Arthur Mayer's Rialto on Broadway early in April.

However, it proved to be a picture that only the critics could love, and their cheers were drowned out by the protests of the paying customers. One day after *Lost Patrol* had run its sorry course, McCormick was overheard explaining "this good picture with a problem" to a Hollywood correspondent. Said he: "It folded like a Legionnaire's tent about Mr. Exhibitor's ears."

In May, Merian Cooper resigned in earnest from his post of production general in order to concentrate on the more fulfilling and less arduous job of an independent producer. In June, Pan Berman followed his lead after RKO Radio Pictures' new president, J. R. McDonough, overexercised his Sarnoffian authority. The annual sales convention of studio personnel from Hollywood, corporate officials from New York, and sales forces from the field that assembled at the Drake Hotel in Chicago on June 18 learned that RKO Radio Studio's president, B. B. Kahane, had established the unit production system. Selznick's dream had finally come to fruition. Under the new setup, Kahane would supervise all production. Berman would be relieved of that responsibility and placed in charge of his own unit.

Relaxed from mingling with Frank Buck, "the greatest living hero name that ever flashed from your marquee," Amos 'n' Andy (a special treat provided by Merlin Aylesworth's NBC), and those "nitwits" Wheeler & Woolsey, "long may they rave!" the distribution delegates nodded through a scholarly discourse on a new three-color Technicolor system to be tested shortly in a John Hay Whitney two-reeler—a "little feature" destined to be the year's "big sensation." Color expansion and a $500,000 building program, they were informed, were on the impressive agenda for the Hollywood studio. Of more immediate concern to the theatermen was a promise from Aylesworth to deliver pictures that would satisfy the homespun virtues of movie-going America and placate the new Legion of Decency organization that had been boycotting movies the Catholic Church considered impure. "RKO has made clean pictures in the past and will continue to make them," Aylesworth pledged.

Of the fifty features scheduled for the 1934–35 season, titles, talent, and staff assignments of thirty-six were divulged by President Ned Depinet of RKO Distributing Corporation with the usual fanfare. McCormick and Robert Sisk, another first-rate promotional head, had kept their elaborate campaign books under lock and key until the crucial moment. Outstanding among the endless procession of "big pictures" guaranteed to "electrify the industry" and "set new box office records" were the Cooper specials *The Last Days of Pompeii,* "a gigantic spectacle drama of barbaric splendor and savage revelry," and *She,* a "weird, fantastic drama" from Rider Haggard's "world-thrilling book"; the setting for the latter—an extinct volcano—was most certainly Cooper's territory. Sir James Barrie's *The Little Minister,* "the most popular play in theatrical history," immortalized by the great Broadway star Maude Adams, was announced as one of three specials to be produced by Berman in which Hepburn would surely gain immortality. Exhibitors clamoring for a new Fred Astaire–Ginger Rogers vehicle were relieved to hear that "the Carioca stars of *Rio"* would co-star with Irene Dunne in *Roberta,* "Jerome Kern's amazing musical stage success," which would be "ten times as tantalizing" on the screen in the talented hands of Pandro S. Berman. Not surprisingly, the implication of another title, *Gay Divorce,* an Astaire–Rogers vehicle announced for fall release, brought a murmur of disapproval. Kahane indicated, however, that despite its frivolous tone, there was nothing in the screenplay to cause exhibitors to worry. The canny executive preferred not to reveal the close call in Hollywood that had threatened to stall the team before it kicked off.

Fred Astaire had returned to Hollywood earlier in the month anxious to start *Gay Divorce* but had balked at the prospect of having Ginger Rogers as his co-star. His experience after Adele's retirement had convinced him that he shouldn't become part of another team. Then, too, he felt that Ginger would be miscast as the cultivated English girl Claire Luce had played on the stage. Pan Berman, who had decided to produce the picture, offered him 10 percent of the profits, a deal he (Berman) was now getting on his personal productions, and Astaire reluctantly agreed to accept Ginger.

For this film, Berman and his assistant, Zion Myers, set up an interlinking unit, which Berman considered essential to the production of musicals. Mark Sandrich, Myers's cousin, who had been turning out the studio's Wheeler & Woolsey musical comedies and was mad about the musical species, became its director. Trained as a physicist, Sandrich had stumbled into pictures through Zion's sister, silent film star Carmel Myers, and had advanced the "playback" technique,* which expanded the potential for creativity in musicals. Hermes Pan, dance director Dave Gould's assistant, who had clicked with Astaire on *Rio*—having come up with the "Carioca" idea—functioned as the connecting link between Gould, who staged the production numbers, and Astaire, who worked separately, adapting his stage choreography. Hermes Pan became a pivotal member of the Astaire–Rogers team during the production, contributing most of the group choreography, while Gould, the Busby Berkeley disciple, moved to MGM the following year, where he earned an Oscar for a leggy Eleanor Powell dance spectacle in *Broadway Melody of 1936* and the Straw Hat number in United Artists' *Folies Bergère.*

In mid-October the trade ads trumpeted the urgent message: "The nation's gone gay!" alerting exhibitors to the "cyclonic" approach of *The Gay Divorcée,* set to play the Music Hall on November 15. The title had been changed to moderate the harmful effect of the word *divorce;* for in July, Will Hays, dogged by the Legion of Decency, had implemented a new censorship tool, the Production Code Administration, placing one of his own men, Joseph I. Breen, in charge.

Lou Brock may have been right in thumbing his nose at *Gay Divorce*'s archaic libretto, but he had overlooked its potential as an Astaire–Rogers dance film. Berman, on the other hand, envisioned the effect Astaire's dance

*A method of filming the action to a prerecorded sound track.

numbers would have on the screen; and the studio's technical departments knew what was needed to make them sparkle and glow. Berman's contract writers, Dorothy Yost and Edward Kaufman, and a third writer, George Marion Jr., shuffled the stale book and worked up comedy routines for the backup team of comics, Edward Everett Horton, Alice Brady, and from the stage version, Erik Rhodes and Eric Blore. The result was unanimous praise from the New York critics. Only Astaire remained uneasy. For the *New York Herald Tribune*'s Richard Watts Jr. delivered a double-edged compliment: "Miss Rogers almost makes one forget the lamented Miss Adele Astaire."

17

The motion picture code's first birthday arrived in December 1934, but it was hardly cause for celebration. With more than half its trade-practice clauses ineffective, Congress paving the way for its abandonment, and the Supreme Court hurling criticism at the NRA, which had fostered it, the movie code pot appeared ready to boil over.

No sooner had Roosevelt signed the code than its author, Sol Rosenblatt, who now bore the title of NRA division administrator, headed for Hollywood to determine the fate of those big salaries and other unfinished code business. But as the moguls closed rank and prepared the counterattack, another adversary advanced against them, throwing confusion into the camp. An insidious Senate survey on the composition of their payrolls from 1928 to 1933 resulted in the publication of details of Hollywood's fancy salaries and bonuses, which in some cases towered above those of the giants of the country's leading industries. The movie colony's "surprise" at the Senate's revelations was carefully assessed by *Motion Picture Herald* on March 10: "Verbal detonations echoed through the hills of Hollywood. Explosions sounded like trench mortars or cap pistols, according to the individual point of view of the exploders."

Meanwhile, both Rosenblatt and his quarry were challenged by still another opponent: the eminent criminal attorney Clarence Darrow, called from retirement by the president to investigate complaints that the NRA codes were furthering monopolistic tendencies in industry and working against the little fellow. A few months after his appointment in March, Darrow's "Little Man" Review Board mounted an attack against Rosenblatt, charging him with displaying sympathy toward the important major studios and failing to protect the interests of the struggling independents. In its third report to the president at the end of June, Darrow's board proposed sweeping changes in the movie code, demanded the removal of Rosenblatt, immediate dismissal of the Code Authority, and creation of a new body that, he pronounced, "can concede something of the rights of the public, and has some other impulse than the extraction of fat profits."

The report constituted the Review Board's final breath. Roosevelt had already declared that the board had "substantially completed the work for which it was established," and he ordered its disbandment. However, it was not to be Clarence Darrow's last hurrah.

The Independent Theatre Owners Association of New York and other minority groups smarting under the one-sided movie code were preparing to launch "the fight of their lives" against the code ("Give it back to those Indians we worked with in Washington!" was the rallying cry), Rosenblatt, and "the big eight" (the major movie companies). It was reported that they would undoubtedly hire that champion of the underprivileged, Clarence Darrow, as counsel.

Besieged from all sides, Rosenblatt nevertheless completed the mass of statistics that made up his official salary report. In July he submitted it to General Johnson of the rapidly crumbling Blue Eagle office in Washington. Its publication, accompanied by some harsh conclusions about the movie industry's irrational and astronomical salaries—the 110-page listing of movie salaries showed that they (individually) soared above Roosevelt's—failed to arouse an attitude of repentence in Hollywood, for Rosenblatt had discreetly omitted the names of offenders. Said the *Herald*'s correspondent James Cunningham on July 28: "Much sleep has been lost by our tired old frame trying to guess the identity of the actor listed as having received compensation of $315,000 last year." The betting was even along Broadway that "this highest paid person is either John Barrymore, an actor for thirty-one years, or Wallace Beery, whose career also spans three decades."

Ultimately, Rosenblatt weakened his stance by recommending further indefinite suspension of the controversial code clauses that had been proposed to regulate the evils of inflated star salaries. So, until further notice, Hollywood would remain uncodified.

In September the keeper of the NRA's Blue Eagle submitted his resignation. In recent weeks General Johnson had been criticized for his "iron-handed" administration by some members of Roosevelt's "official family." In December the press discovered him in a New York department store promoting some of his old war books, and he willingly interrupted autographing to offer reporters an NRA obituary. Declared the General, "The NRA is as dead as the dodo, which is not only dead but extinct."

In May of the following year, the Supreme Court made it official on the grounds of unconstitutionality. Reveling in the dramatic finale on June 1, the *Herald* fired its finest salvo: "The administration appears to at last have run athwart the United States, and the voice of the Blue Eagle which soared screaming and thundering over the industries of the land has been stilled."

Still basking in the glow created by his box-office champion, *The Gay Divorcée,* Pan Berman returned to the studio late in December from a few days in New York, where he had been looking over properties for his own 1935–36 production program. For the current season he had carried a heavy schedule of thirteen pictures, of which ten had been completed. Even without having the responsibility of the entire studio output, Berman still felt overburdened. "No producer should carry a schedule of more than eight or ten pictures," he told the press. His latest personal production, *The Little Minister,* a tender and charming arrangement of Sir James Barrie's pensive Scottish romance, had launched Katharine Hepburn's new six-picture, $300,000 (two-year) contract. Unfortunately, her performance had underscored the difficulty of finding roles that matched her provocative but increasingly irritating mannerisms. As Eileen Creelman of the *New York Sun* pointed out, "Wistful is not a Hepburn characteristic." To compound the problem, the Legion of Decency campaign had seriously reduced the number of stories and themes open to screen treatment. "Things like the Legion always come to an end," the youthful producer advised the trade press on December 29, "particularly when audiences are faced with a steady flow of saccharine material."

With the church campaign turning Hollywood in the direction of lighter pictures, the film cowboy was riding back to market—RKO had announced several Westerns for the new season. By June 1 of the following year, Hollywood correspondent Victor Shapiro of *The Motion Picture Herald* noticed that "the beat of chorus girls' feet, the warbling of opera stars, or the rhythm of the new theme song" sounded from every lot. RKO had two celebrated songwriters in residence, Irving Berlin and Jerome Kern; Berman was planning the movie debut of petite Lily Pons, "grand opera's most glamorous diva," and rushing out a third Astaire–Rogers starrer, *Top Hat,* to open the new season on Labor Day.

Roberta had premiered to an orgy of acclaim in March, beating the highest grosses of *Little Women* and *The Gay Divorcée* across the country. There was no denying the viability of Fred and Ginger. Nor their impact on exhibitors. "I urge you not to try *Roberta* without this marvelous Rogers. She steps right along with you, and you need her to make it real good." Thus spoke an excited theaterman in Winchester, Indiana, in a dispatch to fellow exhibitors on June 15.

On the evening of June 20, the cream of New York society and artistic circles, anticipating an event as earthshaking as the opening of *The Jazz Singer,* turned out en masse for a special midnight showing of *Becky Sharp,* following its premiere at the Music Hall. It was Pioneer Pictures' first feature production, released by RKO, and a "color experiment" costing close to $1 million. The "generous Jock Whitneys," as one newspaper called the young multimillionaire couple, played host. Pioneer's *La Cucaracha,* an $80,000 two-reeler in the new Technicolor, starring peppery Steffi Duna, released by RKO the previous summer, had been an immediate hit, winning an Academy Award for the best Comedy Short Subject. Robert Edmond Jones, the famous Broadway stage designer, brought to Hollywood by Whitney and his partner, Merian Cooper, successfully lifted color out of the novelty category by utilizing it to intensify the dramatic elements of this story of a Mexican fiesta. Collaborating with the distinguished director Rouben Mamoulian, Jones color-designed a more subdued look for *Becky Sharp.* Fiery Miriam Hopkins, playing Thackeray's "woman of the world," provided plenty of vivid color. Her vigorous portrayal put her in the running at Academy Award time, for the "Oscar," as the coveted gold statuette was now called, but it was Bette Davis's year to win for *Dangerous.* While Hollywood awaited the public's verdict—"As *Becky Sharp* goes, so goes color"—the critics rose to emotional heights, viewing it in the context of "cinematic experience" as they tried to decide whether it was "incredibly disappointing, or incredibly thrilling," and dwelt on the "death throes" of the black-and-white picture, which might or might not vanish overnight.

Unhappily, the eagerly awaited Cooper specials, *She* and *The Last Days of Pompeii,* heavily laden with eye-popping spectacles, reminded some critics of nothing so much as *King Kong* editions of "lost kingdom" melodramas that belonged in the children's section of the film library. The studio's technical virtuosity, never more apparent than in *She's* Kingdom of Kor, presided over by the 5000-year-old queen, "She Who Must Be Obeyed"—stage actress Helen Gahagan in an impressive film debut—failed to rescue the movie. And even Cooper and director Ernest Schoedsack's "history-making volcanic upheaval" could not overcome *Pompeii*'s ineffectual story. Casting aside the Sir Edward Bulwer-Lytton novel, Ruth Rose, who collaborated with Dudley Nichols on *She,* worked with a group of writers to develop a new plot. What emerged from the umbrella of the Legion of Decency was a Roman story without a scrap of orgy, without even a peep at the public baths or a suggestion that the town was devoted to "amorous dalliance," as the *Herald* tactfully put it. Only a few chaste kisses sent Cooper's Pompeii to hell.

In August, Pan Berman's superlative production *Alice Adams,* closely followed at the Music Hall by *Top Hat,* so moved young Andre Sennwald, now filling Mordaunt Hall's movie editor's chair at the *New York Times,* that he gushed his appreciation: "Hollywood bestows a garland on the languishing summer cinema!" Sennwald advised that Hepburn, who had faltered through several bad pictures—her most recent had been a sudsy vehicle called *Break of Hearts,* opposite Charles Boyer, the screen's new idol—had resumed her "high place" by giving a performance in *Alice Adams* that would rank with her "finest work on the screen." The studio ballyhooed Booth Tarkington's Pulitzer Prize–winning novel as "an author for Hepburn! an actress for Tarkington!" Had its director been better known, they would have added "A director for Hepburn and Tarkington!" The film was a triumph for young George Stevens, who had sharpened his tools on the studio's shoestring productions. Berman had literally gambled on him, flipping a coin several times with Hepburn to come up with tails for Stevens, as opposed to their other choice, the prominent William Wyler, who Berman knew could be difficult, and probably expensive. Stevens' uncanny grasp of small-town mores and his ability to guide Hepburn (whose real-life persona was light years away from Tarkington's lonely, frustrated, social-climbing heroine) paid off. Kate was nominated a second time for an Academy Award, although she couldn't surmount Bette Davis.

The studio had pulled out all the stops to make *Top Hat* the most grandiose of the Astaire–Rogers song-and-dance shows. Art-department head Van Nest Polglase and unit art director Carroll Clark's big white set—an art moderne version of Venice, flowing luxuriantly between two adjoining sound stages—included enough extravagant images to banish negative Depression-thinking. RKO's fanciful Venetian canals, spanned by danceable bridges, meandered across both stages. Gondolas looking like confectioner's art floated on black-dyed water. A candy-cane Lido Palace, resplendent with glistening dance floors, terrace restaurants, and balconies, provided a dreamy atmosphere for "Fred Astaire, the dancing master, and Miss Rogers, his ideal partner," as Sennwald billed them, to do "agile justice" to Irving Berlin's charming melodies. The previous year the *Times* had suggested that Britain's Jessie Matthews, "The Dancing Divinity," who looked not unlike Fred's incomparable sister, Adele, would make a better partner than Ginger. "Please consider the matter dropped," said Sennwald. "Miss Rogers is entitled to keep the job for life."

That summer of '35, a veritable avalanche of inquiries rolled against the movie industry as all the anti-film legislators in Washington loosed their wrath on Hollywood. Congressman Sirovich, renewing his periodic attacks, demanded a much broader investigation that would encompass every phase of motion pictures, from their effect upon public morals to the latest bankruptcies and reorganizations. Sirovich even wanted to ascertain whether or not the companies had sought to influence or control legislative actions. His investigating ambitions could only be rivaled by those of Illinois Congressman A. J. Sabath, whose committee, with approval of the president, was immersed in hearings in New York on the current Paramount reorganization.

Curiously, the Securities and Exchange Commission—advising that it would assist Congress in forming new reorganization laws—had begun a "formal" investigation of Paramount's financial history in July. However, *Motion Picture Herald* looked askance at the SEC's motive, pointing out that the Commission was without authority to do anything about "what it may find out." The trade journal hastened to add that "observers of the scene had observed, coincidentally, that Joseph P. Kennedy, as chairman of President Roosevelt's SEC, might himself become a highly informative witness if the Commission were to sincerely engage in academic 'studies' of the industry—since the histories of Mr. Kennedy's FBO and his operations along with banking friends in Pathé Exchange and Gloria Productions might provide as much interesting clinical material as even the [investigation into the] great Paramount."

Congressman Sabath seemed to agree. Although the adjournment in August of the first session of the 74th Congress left Representative Sirovich's grandiose plans dangling in mid-air, Sabath's committee surged ahead, broadening its investigation to include financial reorganizations of other motion picture companies. In December, Sabath suddenly summoned the former SEC head—Kennedy had resigned his Commission post in the fall—from Palm Beach to testify in open hearings in New York on the financial history of both RKO and Pathé. Not surprisingly, the lurid subject was never brought up.

18

In the early spring of 1935, Sarnoff had quietly begun negotiating for the sale of RCA's controlling interest in its doomed offspring. The times favored him. The president, whom Hollywood called "the Barrymore in the White House," had boosted the country's morale by his radio fireside chatter, and his New Deal legislation was beginning to provide relief and jobs. The Depression had loosened its stranglehold on the movie business the previous year; Radio–Keith–Orpheum's net loss for 1934 was cut to $310,575, which the trustees attributed to the earnings of the producing subsidiary, which had a net profit of $570,000. The end of Prohibition had brought the movie-going public out of their homes, and Pan Berman had known how to get them back into theaters: The year's releases had put the little major in the black for the first time in four years!

So, by mid-June, as Irving Trust submitted to the U.S. District Court in New York an upbeat report of the company's financial operations, "exclusive" rumors reached the Hearst papers: Conversation had been overheard on the floor in Wall Street concerning the interest being expressed in RKO's reorganization by Floyd B. Odlum's $110 million investment trust, Atlas Corporation, and the Manhattan banking house of Lehman Brothers. Wall Street considered it highly significant that "two independent studies" of RKO, leaning toward a reorganization, were being made by these two heavyweights, the newspaper stated.

Rumors rapidly fleshed out into figures: Odlum had offered $5 million in cash for RCA's entire investment, with Sarnoff insisting on payment dollar for dollar. Broadway circles recalled that both Odlum and Lehman had occupied prominent positions in the hotly contested Paramount Publix reorganization, and that Odlum and John D. ("Drive till it") Hertz, the Chicago taxicab multimillionaire and a partner in Lehman, were members of the new Paramount Pictures board. Besides Odlum's interest in Paramount, his movie investments and those of gargantuan Atlas Corporation embraced Warner Brothers, Fox Film, and Loew's, Inc. But Broadway recognized the slender, slight, forty-three-year-old financier as a soft-voiced, gentle man whose sole acknowledgment to the Diamond Jim Brady tradition was to buy an extra seat in the theater for his hat. Since Odlum shunned publicity, few were aware that he was the son of a Methodist minister, and that his first job had been a $50-a-month position with a Salt Lake City utility company. Wall Street, however, had pinned a different tag on Odlum. He was "Depression Phenomenon Class A," the seer who, in the summer of 1929, had converted Atlas's holdings of $14 million into cold cash and ready assets. Then, in the darkest years of the Depression, Odlum had scooped up twenty-two investment companies at dime-store prices. In those days, the Wall Street oracle sang: "Little investment company, don't you cry, Atlas will get you by and by."

On October 11, the Atlas–Lehman combination purchased one-half of RCA's holdings in RKO for $5 million cash, with an option to buy the balance at $6 million before the end of 1937. RCA's entire investment of more than one million shares of common stock and roughly $10 million of 6 percent debentures was valued on the market at almost $16 million, after the sale.

Merlin Aylesworth interrupted conferences in New York with Radio Pictures president, J. R. McDonough; RKO's distributing chief, Ned Depinet; and the home office executive corps to publicly express gratitude over the closing of the deal. Congressman Sabath looked up from his seat of interrogation, where he was wading through hearings on the wicked Paramount reorganization, and commented that "Atlas Corporation is now getting control of RKO just as they did of Paramount." But Odlum, whose company had begun buying up Paramount debentures at Depression-bargain prices in 1933, had been recently quoted as saying he did not intend to go into the movie business but merely considered it a good field for investment. In fact, Atlas disposed of some of its Paramount holdings and practically all of its Warner holdings while concentrating on the hefty RKO purchase. Lehmans, of course, had been interested in RKO for many years.

The *New York Times* commented that the sale was in line with the Radio Corporation's policy, adopted several years ago, "to break up the various activities of the concern and allow them to go it alone." Nevertheless, RCA still maintained its successful sound subsidiary, RCA Photophone, since Sarnoff, having finally succeeded in crushing the Vitaphone company, ERPI's monopoly of the movie market, was now broadening his attack against his rival. While Sarnoff's enemies had a field day weighing the failure of RCA's "titanic" show machine against the disaster of the luxury liner of the same name, the radio industry leader went right on preaching the unity of interest of radio and the screen. In fact, NBC was building a new broadcasting studio right in the movie capital's heartland, Sunset and Vine, where the Lasky studio—the future Paramount—had stood.

Motion Picture Herald, carried away by the audacity of the act, emblazoned on its editorial page on December 7 the headline RADIO'S NEW WELL. Viewing the retirement of RCA from the motion picture field as "another demonstration of the ancient axiom that 'possession of the tools does not mean possession of the art,'" the wise old trade journal hit even harder below the belt: "As the RCA goes out of the movies, simultaneously, its NBC makes ready to open a great air studio plant in Hollywood to tap the reservoirs of talent created by the screen in its production center. It is a method well understood in the oil fields too."

PART FIVE

RKO BELONGS TO BERMAN: THE ODLUM-BRISKIN ADMINISTRATION, 1936–1937

Samuel J. Briskin, RKO production chief, at his desk, 1936.
Courtesy of the Academy of Motion Picture Arts and Sciences.

The team of Astaire and Rogers a
its peak. The "Never Gonna Dance" numbe
from *Swing Time,* 193
Courtesy Marc Wanamaker, Bison Archive

Pan Berman with Fred Astaire, 1936.
Courtesy Pandro S. Berman.

Pan Berman seated next to Katharine Hepburn on the set of *Mary of Scotland,* 1936. Foreground, director John Ford.
Courtesy Pandro S. Berman.

Victor McLaglen with Bette Davis, receiving his Academy Award for *The Informer*, 1936.
Courtesy Marc Wanamaker, Bison Archives.®

Former RKO production head William Le Baron (right), with Wesley Ruggles (director of *Cimarron*) and Ruggles's wife, actress Arline Judge, attends the 1936 Academy Awards ceremonies.
Courtesy Marc Wanamaker, Bison Archives.

Pan Berman with George Schaefer, left, then–sales chief for United Artists. In the background, RKO production head Sam Briskin and Jesse Lasky, 1937.
Courtesy Pandro S. Berman.

Pan Berman with Ned Depinet, RKO sales chief, at a regional convention, 1937.
Courtesy Pandro S. Berman.

Pan Berman with director George Stevens and Katharine Hepburn on the set of *Quality Street*, 1937, one of her costume pictures (following *Mary of Scotland*), which failed to restore her ebbing popularity.
Courtesy Pandro S. Berman.

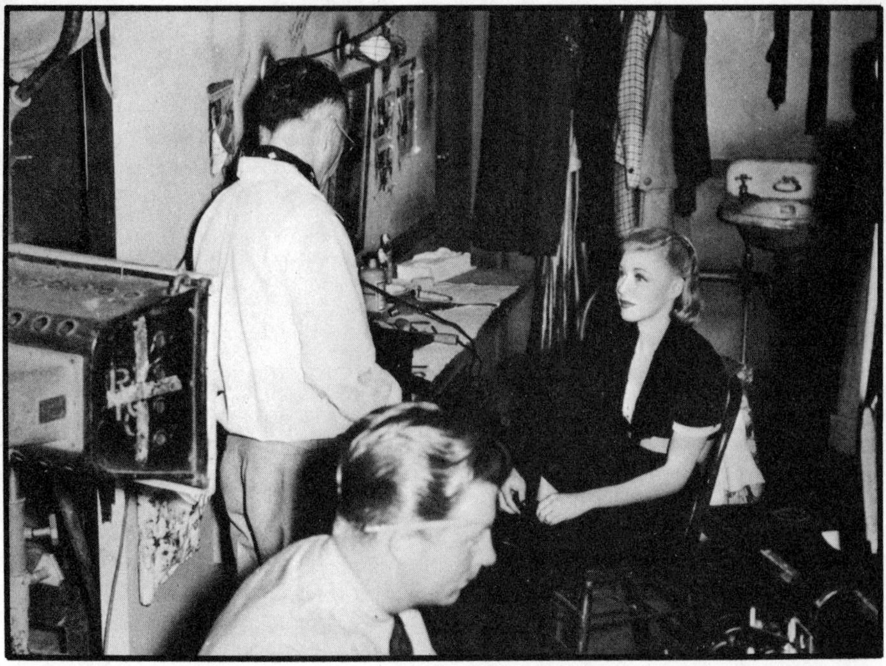

Ginger Rogers on the set of *Stage Door,* 1937.
Courtesy Marc Wanamaker, Bison Archives.

Ginger Rogers rehearsing.
Stage Door, 1937.
Courtesy Marc Wanamaker, Bison Archives.

Irene Castle on the RKO lot in February 1937, signing a contract to be an advisor on an Astaire–Rogers production based on her memoirs. From left: Pan Berman, director George Stevens, and Ned Depinet.
Courtesy Pandro S. Berman.

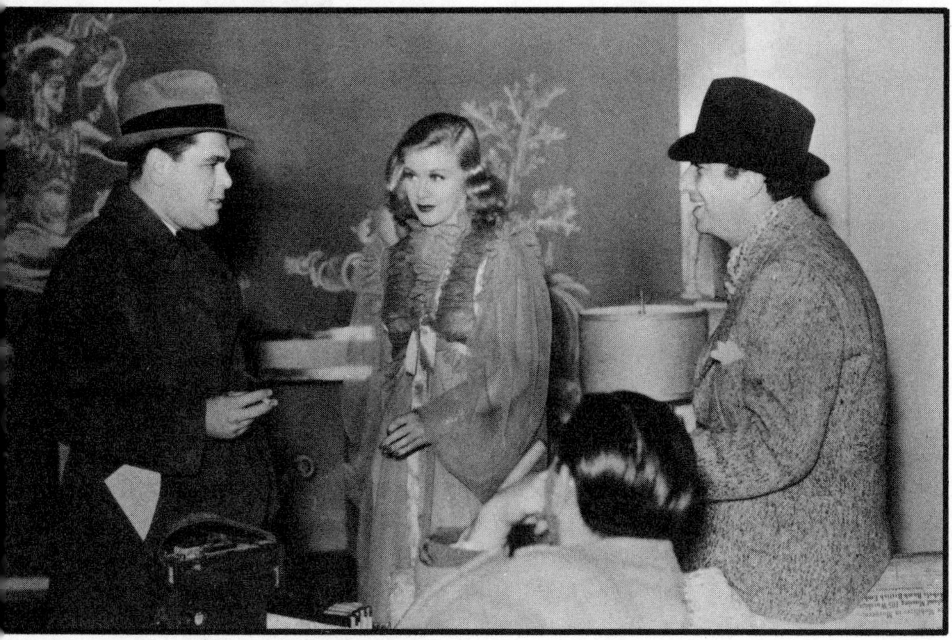

an Berman, left, on the set of *Shall We Dance* with Ginger Rogers and irector Mark Sandrich, right, 1937.
ourtesy Pandro S. Berman.

Practically every light and grand opera star in Hollywood at a movie premiere, circa 1937. From the left: Allan Jones; his wife, actress Irene Hervey; popular radio conductor André Kostelanetz; his wife, petite Lily Pons; Nelson Eddy peering from behind Kostelanetz and Pons; Jesse Lasky; glamorous Jeanette MacDonald; Grace Moore, star of *One Night of Love;* behind the unidentified whistler, Moore's husband, Spanish actor Valentine Parera; Gladys Swarthout, who made five pictures in Hollywood; her husband and manager, Frank Chapman.

Courtesy of the Academy of Motion Picture Arts and Sciences, Jesse L. Lasky Collection

19

Early in February 1936, RKO's newest production chief and a former certified public accountant, Samuel J. Briskin, faced the press, delivering what in Hollywood could only be termed an heretical message. Avoiding hype and rash predictions for overnight success, the steely-eyed vice president bluntly said, "I could do the customary Hollywood thing and scream 'Everything that was done before my arrival is terrible. Throw it out!' But Radio got along before they hired me, and they'll survive after I leave. All I can do is try and improve on the past."

Times had changed since David Sarnoff had called the shots and RCA told the world it was getting "titanic." With the shift in RKO's parentage had come another breed of businessman. In rapid succession, following his acquisition of RCA's ailing movie company in October 1935, Floyd Odlum reshuffled the executive deck to bring the best Atlas-Lehman brains to the fore in the home office. To undertake the formidable task of reorganizing Radio–Keith–Orpheum out of bankruptcy, Odlum named an Atlas associate, N. Peter Rathvon, a corporate attorney of long standing in U.S. industry. It was intimated by the press that the Atlas vice president would be first in line for the presidency of the revamped corporation—when he completed the job of reorganization—nosing out Aylesworth, who according to earlier reports, had been slated for the future throne.

The next appointment—that of prominent motion picture counsel Leo Spitz of Chicago to the post of president of Radio–Keith–Orpheum—more directly favored the Lehman interests and was attributed to Spitz's long friendship with John Hertz, the moneyed Lehman partner and Paramount director. Spitz had followed his friend in and out of Paramount at the time of its financial crisis in 1932 and 1933 and had gained a position of authority while Hertz was tearing into the behemoth's financial organs and purging the company of its top talent: Lasky, Sid Kent, and even Sam Katz, his old Chicago friend who had sponsored him.

The appointment of Spitz to Aylesworth's post immediately led to the Radio chief's resignation. But Odlum was able to offer Deak a consolation prize: the chairmanship of the board of Radio–Keith–Orpheum, a position David Sarnoff no longer wanted, although he continued as a board member. It was stated that Aylesworth's NBC reign would not be disturbed by the demands of his new position, but a few weeks later he abdicated the top spot, remaining as a board member. There was no break in the whirlwind pace of the new Odlum regime. By the time the Radio–Keith–Orpheum directors—who had not been consulted about the Spitz and Aylesworth appointments, but had learned about the changes from the newspapers—formally elected Leo Spitz president (and accepted a couple of resignations from board members), the Odlum–Lehman appointee had already moved from Chicago to New York, settled into the executive suite in the RKO Building in Radio City, and made known Atlas's intentions for an early reorganization. The provision requiring that creditors be given sixty days notice with intention of presenting a plan to the court would give the new president time to study proposals for the settlement of the $9 million Rockefeller Center claim, the largest individual claim against RKO. The management of the Radio City theaters—"those two white elephants," as some of the creditors had taken to calling them—was now dominated completely by the Rockefeller interests, and RKO's place in the future conduct of the Music Hall appeared shaky.

A few weeks following his appointment, Spitz hastily departed for the Coast with the reliable Ned Depinet to inspect the studios, consider the schedule of pictures, and meet the competition: the heads of the other seven majors. During his visit, Sam Briskin was installed as head of production: The Odlum–Lehman talons had quickly reached into Hollywood's small group of proven business talent to pluck the tough, former general manager of Columbia Studios to take over RKO Radio Pictures.

The Russian-born, thirty-nine-year-old movie veteran was made to order for the new regime. Trained on the Columbia lot where the street mogul Harry Cohn ruled by means of desk-pounding and shouting, and nonviolent language was considered morally offensive, Briskin had shouldered his way to the top with the aid of his ledgers. He was credited with Columbia's climb out of the "quickie" ranks to an important place among the majors, and industry insiders felt that it was no accident that such exceptional films as the memorable *One Night of Love,* starring Grace Moore, and the Academy Award–winning *It Happened One Night* had emerged from the studio during his tenure. Briskin had joined the old Cohn, Brandt and Cohn company, Columbia's poverty-row ancestor, in 1920, the days when the Cohn brothers' only ambition had been to see how little they could lose, and it was considered great sport to be thrown out of Doc Giannini's office. This was Briskin's second "vacation" from his home lot. The previous one had occurred in 1924, the first year the company made a profit, and was induced by the partners' reluctance to share it. Briskin's move to RKO was based on their refusal of a new deal that would have taken him out of his managerial spot into a producer's berth at an increase in salary. Even though flooded with tempting studio offers of production units, Briskin succumbed to Odlum's persuasive powers and postponed his producing ambitions.

With this virtuoso installed at RKO, those two Sarnoffian production executives, J. R. McDonough and B. B. Kahane, began to take on the appearance of sacrificial lambs. Brushed aside by new RKO head Leo Spitz, who took over his post of president of RKO Radio Pictures, the unpopular McDonough spent a few powerless months as executive vice president, retiring from the company in June. The popular Ben Kahane followed him out in August.

By February, production plans were beginning to take form, and "the brisk Mr. Briskin," as some astute members of the press called him, was eager to discuss them. Declaring that RKO would invade the A product market with increased vigor, he explained that although a program could easily be top-heavy with B product, "you can never have too many A shows." More A pictures was what the public wanted!

Indeed, the most important change on Hollywood's horizon was, as Briskin theorized, "quality." The moguls were convinced that the public was ready to accept a higher type of product. The best of their second generation—Thalberg, Selznick, and young Darryl Zanuck, who had taken over Fox—specialized in elevated subject matter: big-budget biographical and historical films involving the romantic *Barretts of Wimpole Street,* the illustrious *House of Rothschild,* and the ill-fated *Anna Karenina*. Universal's elderly founding father, Carl Laemmle, predicted that this "high-class, expensive" trend was the wave of the future. On the other hand, the "music cycle is dying," he advised.

Even while "Uncle Carl" was soothsaying, a newly organized and authoritative group, the New York Film Critics, bypassed Hollywood's grandiloquent notion of quality and voted the low-budget *The Informer* the best picture of 1935. Pan Berman had bought the Liam O'Flaherty novel for John Ford for a mere $15,000, and the heralded director filmed it like a B, on a single set erected on two stages that reproduced the Dublin streets and buildings. According to Barret McCormick, RKO's garrulous ad chief, who kept his eyes glued to the set, it had been an easy shoot. It had required no miracle, he said, for John Ford, student of Irish literature and history, to make a polished production from a basically unpolished story. McCormick also discounted the apparent miracle of Victor McLaglen's portrayal of O'Flaherty's "gutter Judas," Gypo Nolan, since the boisterous actor's early life had roughly paralleled the colorful personal adventures of the author. Besides, McCormick had observed Irishman Bob Sisk, newly turned producer, looking in on the set and donating suggestions drawn from his repertoire of Celtic lore. However, as McCormick revealed upon the occasion of *The Informer*'s revival at New York's Little Carnegie Theater in February, the actual miracle had occurred after Ford's work had been done. Reminded of *The Lost Patrol,* "that other good picture with a problem," McCormick this time organized the critics without their knowledge, by an "ad stroke." The first post-production ad of the picture, printed the week of April 27, saluted readers with the prediction that every critic in America would place *The Informer* on his list of the ten best pictures of 1935. "The picture was not a box office champ," McCormick added under his breath. At an overall cost of $340,000—which included studio overhead—it barely cleared the investment, he said when the ten-best lists came out and there was *The Informer,* exactly where he told the critics to place it—thus stimulating new business and pushing it on the profit side.

The Briskin design rapidly took shape at RKO. In charge for a month, he signed the distinguished Herbert Marshall for five years, inaugurating a policy of strong box-office names essential for the studio's increased schedule of A pictures: Where fifteen had formerly been the rule, the A's and the B's would meet each other halfway for the new season—twenty-four in each category. He welcomed Edward Small's production unit and dismissed a fallen star, Ann Harding, admonishing that on the Radio lot there would be no more stories selected by stars. "I've never seen a player who knew anything about stories," said Briskin with finality. Ann's outmoded loveliness and mawkish spiritual sweetness were currently on display in *The Lady Consents,* a box-office casualty that she had pressured the studio to buy for her. Thankfully, hers was the last contract allowing player approval, and it was due to expire with her present film, *The Witness Chair,* a lugubrious courtroom melodrama, just going into production but already projected as a failure by the hardnosed executive.

Regrettably, Irene Dunne had left RKO for a better deal at Universal after completing *Roberta* the previous year. In spite of this, Briskin was swiftly adding "star power" to the studio's sagging list of players, signing Barbara Stanwyck for two pictures; Ann Sothern and Broadway's venerable Fred Stone to seven-year contracts; John Boles, an "outstanding name"; Gene Raymond, and other stellar personalities of stage, screen, and, naturally, radio. Wheeler & Woolsey were announced for "two giggle epics," and more laughs were anticipated from the "flannel-mouthed" Joe E. Brown and Joe Penner, the screen's "perfect idiot." Eight-year-old Bobby Breen, radio's "wonder boy," whose dwarf tenor was inflaming feminine audiences in his film debut, *Let's Sing Again,* an RKO release, would be presented in three more Sol Lesser productions. RKO would also release some action dramas featuring George O'Brien, star of the rugged outdoors.

Briskin's policy banned raiding. "I don't believe in it—it's only a temporary solution at best. We're going to develop people," he emphasized, citing seventeen-year-old Anne Shirley, picked from unknowns for the starring role in a successful 1934 rural programmer, *Anne of Green Gables*. Despite critical enthusiasm for her homespun innocence, Briskin was of the opinion that the studio had used Anne indifferently, "putting her in mild films," rather than giving her a fast buildup by placing her in a movie alongside a strong box-office personality. "Metro took Myrna Loy and made a sensation out of her in one picture with William Powell," he stated, perhaps unaware that Ginger Rogers had bantered with the debonair Powell in RKO's *Star of Midnight* the previous year and had not changed her image as Fred Astaire's girlfriend. "If we could find a yarn for Powell and Anne, we'd have a recognized star after one film." Meanwhile, Briskin boosted Anne's $75-a-week salary to $400.

By spring of the Briskin era, Pan Berman was being heralded as the leading producer of the studio's class-A stories. His old contract, calling for $2500 a week and the 10 percent cut, had been personally torn up by President Spitz in favor of a lavish new deal that awarded him first pick on stories, directors, and cast, placing him in a position comparable, in authority, to Irving Thalberg's berth at MGM. Because of Berman's efforts, RKO Radio Pictures was riding a crest of four straight box-office hits: *Gay Divorcée, Roberta, Top Hat,* and *Follow the Fleet,* the fourth Astaire-Rogers starrer, which had opened to a tidal wave of business in February. The team appeared invincible. They had even landed in the number-four position—right behind Clark Gable—on the exhibitors' list of the biggest money-making stars of 1933–35. Some exhibitors were so carried away by their box-office performance that they had swallowed RKO's entire 1935–36 season's product just to get this "swell show," *Follow the Fleet.*

Unfortunately, it included Berman's two holiday shows, the disappointing movie debut of "pocket soprano" Lily Pons in *I Dream Too Much* and the unconventional *Sylvia Scarlett,* ironically characterized by the *New York Times*'s Andre Sennwald as Katharine Hepburn's latest "personal triumph." The Pons film, in which the soul-stirring Jerome Kern melodies had failed to erase the bad taste of Verdi's "Rigoletto," brought an outcry from exhibitors, whose small-town patrons thought that grand opera sounded like "voice exercises": "We are being high 'C'ed!" Berman resolved to soft-pedal the opera star's coloratura trills in her next vehicle, *That Girl from Paris,* a remake of *Street Girl,* and, as added security, envelop her with comedians.

The youthful producer was still kicking himself for giving Hepburn and director George Cukor, whom he had borrowed from MGM, free rein on the production of *Sylvia Scarlett,* in which Kate masqueraded as a boy ready for any adventure, including falling in love with a cockney Cary Grant. "Watch them, Katharine, or they'll ruin you. One more like this and you're done for!" warned a Nevada theaterman. Despite the picture's disastrous reception, it gave Grant, whose previous work, Andre Sennwald pointed out, had too often been that of a "charm merchant," the opportunity to shine in a comedy role, and Berman signed him to a nonexclusive contract.

Berman next cast the indomitable Kate in the heroic screen image of the ill-fated queen in *Mary of Scotland,* RKO's contribution to Hollywood's outpouring of dignified, historical A pictures. Based on Maxwell Anderson's 1933 poetic drama that had starred Helen Hayes in the Theatre Guild's production on Broadway, it was Berman's most ambitious undertaking and certainly the studio's most widely publicized film of the year. Advertising on it ran the gamut from conventional to hype—"a man of steel [Fredric March as the Earl of Bothwell] meets a woman of fire"—to the apex of majestic self-admiration—a glossy testimonial in the trades featuring formal photos of the production's "creative geniuses" accompanying the proclamation RKO HONORS ITSELF AND THE INDUSTRY. While *Mary of Scotland* was in production in March, the Academy showered *The Informer* with four Oscars. Berman's "epic romance" could boast the presence of two newborn winners: director John Ford and writer Dudley Nichols.

Inevitably, this lofty project lent itself to kidding. *Motion Picture Herald* discovered Ned Depinet that month in New Orleans, of all places, vigorously promoting Hollywood's newly elevated moral standards. "Sex has definitely lost its place in the movies," he informed a convention of exhibitors. "The public doesn't give a hang about sex anymore, if we feed it good, wholesome pictures. My corporation is now making *Mary of Scotland*...." Faking alarm, the *Herald*'s correspondent shot back: "If Mary Stuart didn't have sex, and lots of it, we have been grossly deceived. And doesn't Mr. Depinet know about Elizabeth, the virgin queen? Virgins just have to have sex. They cannot do or be without it. No sex, no virgin. If in truth the public 'doesn't give a hang about sex anymore,' the country is a lot worse off than we suspected."

Mary of Scotland emerged, in the critics' estimation, as "one of the year's notable photoplays"—even if dominantly Hepburn, rather than Scotland's Mary. Frank Nugent, the *New York Times*'s motion picture editor, who replaced Sennwald after his sudden death in January, curbed the impulse to use the word *magnificent,* limiting himself to the less-glowing epithet *impressive.* The exhibitor point of view was put forward in a March 1937 *Herald* squib: "A good show for the upper-class customer, but of no value to the regular cash guest." As a theaterman in Penacook, New Hampshire, had already stated the previous November: "We still can't get our people interested in royalty for entertainment."

Anxious to break new ground and create a wider interest in the motion picture medium, Berman turned his attention to a film version of another

Maxwell Anderson verse play, *Winterset,* presented on Broadway the previous year with Burgess Meredith, Margo, and Eduardo Ciannelli. Going against the norm, Berman imported the three stage leads, overlooking Anne Shirley, whom the studio had announced earlier for the co-starring role. The somber mood of the story—a poetic protest against injustice and mob hysteria based on the Sacco–Vanzetti case—its modern conception, and the handicap of unfamiliar names, gave the trade press cause to wonder how it would be accepted by mass audiences. RKO ballyhooed *Winterset* diligently as "the masterpiece of them all!" and the critics agreed it was RKO's finest achievement since *The Informer.* But for small-town theatermen who had been pleading for fewer "arty" and more "hearty" pictures, *Winterset* personified a program that even Bank Night—that chance game form of enticing theater patronage—couldn't sustain.

For the first time since the magic melding had come about, there were murmurs of discontent with the peerless Astaire–Rogers series. Designating *Follow the Fleet* "the season's best musical comedy," the *New York Times*'s Frank Nugent, for one, missed a few comedians to carry the plot along when Astaire and Rogers were not in there dancing. Rather than comedy, *Fleet,* based on Hubert Osborne's 1922 play *Shore Leave,* substituted a minor romance between Randolph Scott and Harriet Hilliard, a top radio vocalist, whom RKO had recently signed.

Berman had been rushing the musicals into release at the rate of two a year, and at a cost of $520,000 to $640,000, since the momentum established by *Gay Divorcée* in October 1934. Thus, while Fred worked ferociously with his strong right hand, Hermes Pan, and the gifted young studio pianist Hal Borne, to develop the dance numbers and get most of them on film before the principal shooting commenced, the writers solved the seemingly insurmountable problem of inventing fresh story material by a practical formula of rotating the earlier scripts. *Fleet* echoed *Roberta* with a change of locale that swapped Parisian haute couture for San Francisco's waterfront dance halls and cheap little walkups, while *Top Hat* had mirrored *Gay Divorcée* with some alteration.

Then there was the moodiness of the team itself. Astaire had surmounted his physical imperfections, actually creating a romantic image on the screen with the assistance of Ginger. "Adele's kid brother" had vanished; in its place had come another unwanted label, "Ginger Rogers' partner." And as much as Ginger cherished the partnership, the lengthy and strenuous rehearsal schedules prevented her from competing for prime vehicles in which she might prove her dramatic capabilities.

Early in April an anxious exhibitor sent out the message that "Astaire will be very very foolish to insist on his reported intention to seek another partner.

The team of Astaire and Rogers is the drawing card.... If this team should start separately, Ginger Rogers will be starring a long time after Fred has been forgotten," the heartless theaterman wrote. "We're not tired of this combination. We don't know anyone who is, except perhaps Mr. Astaire."

Happily, Astaire, whose 1935 earnings were reported by the Treasury Department to be $127,875, was placed among the highest paid stars in Hollywood. He permitted himself to be lured by Berman into adjusting his differences, and his contract was renegotiated; Ginger received a new five-year agreement at an increase in salary and a promise of meatier roles apart from Astaire. To the relief of exhibitors, the team continued in *Swing Time,* with George Stevens relieving director Mark Sandrich, a lilting Jerome Kern score with lyrics by Dorothy Fields, and a new musical director, Nathaniel Shilkret. The popular conductor of RCA's Victor Salon Orchestra had been hired after Max Steiner had gone to work for Selznick—RKO's former boss having finally won his independence from MGM and established new quarters at Pathé early in the year.

Despite the usual riot outside the Music Hall in late August that signified an Astaire–Rogers opening, intimations of the team's mortality persisted. In December, Astaire's first solo vehicle, *A Damsel in Distress,* was announced. On the other hand, Irene Castle, who had set society-dancing styles with late husband Vernon when Fred and Adele were in their teens, was photographed on the RKO lot in February 1937, signing a contract to advise on an Astaire–Rogers production based on her memoirs.

On May 8 of that year, the *Herald*'s Red Kann reported on the official preview of the sixth Astaire–Rogers musical, *Shall We Dance,* again directed by Mark Sandrich. Held at the Hollywood Pantages Theatre, the studio's professional preview house, it was of course heavily attended by producers, directors, actors, writers, and musicians from the home lot, practically all others, and about a thousand ordinary folk. Red wrote that "no one was heard whistling or humming any of the tunes as the crowd milled out into the street." They were by the prestigious George Gershwin, with lyrics by brother Ira. "There's nothng the matter with the dancing, however, and the comedy content is distinctly superior. After the show, boyish Mr. Berman was here, there, and everyplace in the lobby accepting compliments."

The following month, Berman's production of *Stage Door* went before the cameras with Ginger receiving equal billing with Hepburn. For the first time since the series began, there was no Astaire–Rogers musical in the works for fall; the momentum had been broken.

20

On March 3, 1936, *Variety* ran a newsworthy front-page headline, RADIO CAPTURES DISNEY, that worried Hollywood. Because it had been reported that a dispute on the subject of television was among the reasons why Walt Disney had quit United Artists, the movie industry, which had grown increasingly preoccupied with its relation to the new medium, seized on this as the answer to the alliance with the little major rather than either of those two giants who had bid for his product, Twentieth Century–Fox and MGM. Also, wasn't it Deak Aylesworth, the radio-film executive, who had brought the acclaimed cartoon producer into the RKO fold? The three-year distribution contract Aylesworth had negotiated had called for delivery of from eighteen to twenty-eight animated cartoons and one feature-length cartoon annually, all in the three-component Technicolor process. Adding to Hollywood's apprehensiveness, Aylesworth, whose salesmanship had become the stuff of myths, shrugged off his accomplishment. RKO had not approached Disney. Overtures had been made to RKO by Roy Disney, the company's general manager, he told the press in New York. About Walt's first animated feature, *Snow White and the Seven Dwarfs,* just getting started after more than a year of preparation at his modest Hyperion Avenue studio, Aylesworth, true to form, drawled, "It will be a sensation and revolutionary as an art form."

Disney's own statement, issued in Hollywood following the signing of the contract, clearly revealed his train of thought. "In looking to the future, and that includes television," he said, "we believe our association with RKO offers greater opportunities for the broader and more expansive fields of development." Mr. Disney was due soon in New York to view a television demonstration at the RCA studios, the trade press advised.

Since NBC opened its "air center" the previous December, Hollywood had learned to coexist with radio. As Lasky philosophized after the dedicatory program, "You can't combat progress, and we in the picture business may as well hitch onto it." The movie colony again faced what the *Herald* termed "a second big pumping of its screen talent," this time by CBS, second only to NBC in network size and also settling in the heart of Hollywood.

Still another ominous event now confronted the industry. And since it would star radio's indefatigable genius, David Sarnoff, there was some cause for alarm. RCA had scheduled for June 29 a $1 million television experiment to be conducted from atop the Empire State Building, with experimental receivers placed at various surrounding points. Obviously, Sarnoff believed that television was on its way, even though it would linger in the hands of experimental engineers. Nevertheless, Aylesworth dutifully assured Hollywood it had "nothing to fear from television as a competitive factor," pointing out that "Disney, being primarily an artist, was considering the possibilities of a new medium for his art. He is not alone among film producers who have shown interest," Aylesworth added. "Irving Thalberg likes to talk about television for hours."

Hollywood responded by feigning nonchalance while ordering surveys. The *New York Times* scrutinized "the new development" late in April and reported that although motion picture producers remained unworried, radio was "digging in" in Hollywood as protection against the time when television encroached on their territory. In June of the following year, the special scientific committee under the auspices of the Motion Picture Academy, which had been engaged in the official study of television's status to date, came to a happy conclusion: The television picture was still too small, cost too high, the show poor, and patronage meager. A few weeks later, Will Hays, who had secretly hired A. Mortimer Prall, son of the FCC chairman, to make another survey, released his prognosis. Said the *Herald* in a glaring headline on July 3: PRALL'S "CONFIDENTIAL" REPORT URGES FILMS TO BUY TELEVISION.

In May 1936, Congressman A. J. Sabath was hot on the trail again, his committee having received hundreds of appeals for a thorough investigation of the suspect Paramount and RKO reorganization proceedings. Particularly concerned with the "widespread disregard of bond and stockholders' rights" and further alarmed by charges that the new Paramount management was at that moment engaged in an insidious program of wrecking the company "for the purpose of consummating a merger with RKO," Sabath resumed open hearings in Washington. Again his plans were thwarted, for Joe Kennedy, riding to Paramount's rescue, soon caught up with him.

Early in the year, Kennedy had undertaken his first major job since resigning as chairman of the SEC, a special study of the corporate structure of RCA. This "glorious adventure on the inside of one of the most iridescent spheres of the bubble-blowing era of before '29"—the *Herald*'s lush description of the assignment—took only a month. Joe worked out a masterly recapitalization plan and pocketed a fee of $150,000.

On May 2, as Sabath's committee was renewing its probe, Kennedy accepted an invitation from his old associates, Paramount investors—and major antagonists—Elisha Walker and John Hertz of Lehman Brothers, to make a thorough diagnosis of the movie company's latest ailments, a seemingly difficult situation since both were fighting for control. On June 2, Kennedy took time out from preparing his preliminary report that focused on the chaotic conditions he had uncovered on the Hollywood lot, and the warring factions in the board room, to send Sabath a lengthy plea by telegram for postponement of the scheduled hearing. Acknowledging appreciation of the constructive work of his committee, and his anxiety to cooperate, Kennedy assured Sabath he was "endeavoring to do a constructive job for the ultimate good of the security holders. That purpose would best be served by adjourning this matter with an opportunity to work out their problem. I assure you that I shall be the first to expose any acts which are not for their best interest," said Joe.

On June 2, the Paramount directors received a bruising blow. Kennedy's preliminary report recommended an end to the corruptive influence on Wall Street, exorbitant executive salaries, and trashy pictures—the very same evils that had characterized his own Hollywood career. Kennedy indicated that if the directors didn't act on his recommendations it might be difficult to explain "such inaction to litigious stockholders or to inquiring Congressional committees." To the acute embarrassment of the board, he insisted that his exposé be made public.

During the subsequent wave of executions, RKO's new leader, Floyd Odlum, resigned from the Paramount board, while John Hertz, the tough Lehman partner, hung on. On June 17, during RKO's convention at the Waldorf, Aylesworth told the sales force that there was no truth to the stories circulating that RKO would merge with another film company. In mid-June, Kennedy, who had been mentioned as a candidate for the presidency of the new Paramount, declared that he would not be available. A story that trailed Paramount's venerable board chairman, Adolph Zukor, on his way East to resume active control of production was to the effect that Lasky would leave his independent Pickford–Lasky company to rejoin Paramount. The newspapers reported that New York bankers interested in the company were insistent on Lasky's return, thus reuniting him with the mogul with whom he had founded the company. It was rumored that Paramount's directors had made another bid to Kennedy to become identified with the company as one of its top officers. However, reports were that he was planning to take part in the coming presidential campaign.

In July, Wall Street got its first look at Kennedy's much-discussed and considerably suppressed fifty-four-page study, with such diabolical notions as "Thalbergs and Zanucks cannot be bought or manufactured..." and that one of the finest properties in the industry had "gone into eclipse" while being steered by "the best downtown business brains." Since the report favored Elisha Walker and the old management and damned the new Paramount, which included old friend John Hertz, negative feelings were strong; Kennedy, who had failed to set his fee in advance, had to make do with a paltry $50,000.

By mid-August, it became apparent that Joe Kennedy's job as special advisor to Paramount had been his swan song in the movie business, and politics was now his primary goal. His campaign book, *I'm for Roosevelt,* declaring enthusiastic support of the New Deal, was in the bookstores. The trade press considered it a political document, ably enough done to be called an ambitious document. One statement— "I have no political ambitions for myself or my children"—captured the *Herald*'s interest. "He is answering an unraised question," the journal deduced, "doubtless with all sincerity, but also, one must suspect, without consulting his subconscious mind."

The following November, Wall Street and Broadway took their first look at Radio–Keith–Orpheum's long-awaited reorganization plan, which had been submitted to the U.S. District Court in New York. The figures were impressive. Under the sponsorship of the Odlum–Lehman group, piloted by Leo Spitz, the film company appeared ready to shed its bankrupt image and emerge from its four-year ordeal as a $67 million corporation, with $7 million in cash. The good will of the secured creditors and stockholders, dominated by Atlas, Lehman, and RCA interests, was, of course, assured. The plan for a bright new corporate structure provided capitalization totaling $33 million. One feature simplified the structure: A network of seven RKO and RKO–Pathé subsidiaries would merge very shortly into one new company, RKO Radio Pictures.

An agreement reached only a week earlier with Rockefeller Center, the largest unsecured creditor, eliminated the most serious potential opposition to the plan and was largely instrumental in obtaining the unsecured creditors' approval. In return for 500,000 shares of new common stock, Rockefeller Center would ungrudgingly cancel its $9 million claim, and RKO might again participate in the operation and profits of the two Radio City theaters.

A balance sheet accompanying the plan proclaimed that company earnings had improved sharply: 1935 saw the turnaround with a net profit of $684,733. Considering the strength of RKO's recent performance, net earnings this year might even soar above the $2 million mark. With the Rockefeller claim out of the way, the situation left only sundry independent creditors' groups representing minority interests, as potential thorns. Atlas attorney Hamilton C. Rickaby optimistically indicated that the proposed plan might have the court's approval by March of the following year, but "an insignificant minority"—Rickaby's contemptuous phrase for the remaining opposition, which he voiced in his summation at the end of June—had, by then, become a festering group of dissidents.

Ernest Stirn, a disgruntled holder of RKO's old Class A stock, which had been eliminated by the 1931 RCA refinancing plan he had condemned before the Senate Banking Committee in 1932, came forward to do battle again. Alfred West, the creditor who had brought on the receivership in 1933 with his "friendly" petition, now filed an affidavit to keep the "friendly" suit alive. Joseph Cohen, counsel for common stockholders, attacked the provisions for settlement of the Rockefeller claim as "unfair." The Atlas proposal would hand the Center "one-fourth or one-fifth of the entire stock equity." He claimed that

Atlas was not a "bona fide purchaser" of RKO securities, and that RCA had agreed to reimburse Atlas should the proposed plan fall through. Rickaby heatedly denied this allegation and also denied Cohen's statement that RCA had financed a stockholders' committee that had accepted the plan. Cohen later charged that Atlas became involved solely for reorganization purposes, a point Congressman Sabath, abetted by the SEC, was strenuously dwelling upon in his latest efforts to bring about reorganization reforms.

In August, Special Master George Alger* halted the testimony concerning Atlas's purchase on the grounds that it was irrelevant, but a group of irate Boston stockholders opposed his ruling, stating that the sale involved approximately $30 million worth of securities and debentures for about one-third of their value; they felt that the circumstances warranted investigation.

Floyd Odlum, as was his custom, took an energetic hands-on approach to the work connected with lifting Atlas's latest acquisition from the shackles of bankruptcy. While the attorneys wrangled their way through the reorganization hearings in the East, Odlum participated in conferences at the studio with his key executive, Leo Spitz, who flew west with him in July. Despite the turmoil caused by three studio union strikes in the spring, production had proceeded as usual. In production were four films: *A Damsel in Distress,* starring Fred Astaire and Joan Fontaine, the latter a new and nondancing contract player being exploited as "RKO Radio's sensational new sweetheart"; *A Love Like That,*† a little comedy starring Barbara Stanwyck and Herbert Marshall; *Fight for Your Lady,* a little farce starring John Boles and Jack Oakie; and *Don't Forget to Remember,*‡ an amiable comedy starring Burgess Meredith and Ann Sothern.

Irene Dunne's return to the fold had been announced in June. Having electrified critics with her gift for slapstick comedy—the latest epidemic to hit Hollywood—in Columbia's *Theodora Goes Wild,* she was secured by RKO for two pictures. The first would be *Joy of Living,* a Jerome Kern musical with a comedy plot.

Berman's screen version of *Stage Door,* the Ferber–Kaufman hit play, awaited release in the fall, and the word had spread that it would become "the talk of the movie universe." Visits to the set by Hollywood correspondents had led to the conviction that director Gregory La Cava was making a new Hepburn, and her inspired work would erase the memory of all the "flat, mechanical performances since her first brilliant appearances." Ginger Rogers, it was predicted, was also being born anew. One rhapsodic journalist dismissed Astaire from Rogers' screen career, calling her "a dramatiste with a wastrel

*A court-appointed expert.

†Final title: *Breakfast for Two.*

‡Final title: *There Goes the Groom.*

comedy flare." In addition, La Cava had "created a new star in Andrea Leeds," borrowed from Goldwyn, and had "given the screen a new young comedienne in Lucille Ball," just graduated from the category of "new faces" in training at the studio to small featured roles.

Before his departure, Odlum announced that Sam Briskin had been signed to a new three-year contract, dispelling a rumor that a change in the top studio post might be on the program. Except for the autonomy granted the Berman unit, it was said that Briskin would wield total authority over production.

The preeminence of the A picture was not so much on Briskin's mind these days. Like other Hollywood "geniuses," he talked about the idea of elevating the lowborn B to the point where it could occupy a position of dignity in first-run and single-feature houses. In February, Briskin had announced an increase of 25 to 35 percent in the company's B-picture budgets. The B's provided "a testing ground for new names, and experiments in story and treatment." *Winterset* and John Ford's *The Plough and the Stars*—the latter justified because of its low cost and the success of Ford's *The Informer*—were examples of quality B's. *The Plough and the Stars* was a softened version of a Sean O'Casey play, and its highlight had been a rollicking characterization from the Abbey Theatre's Barry Fitzgerald. *Winterset,* at a cost of about $400,000, Briskin said, gave the studio a personality in Burgess Meredith. At RKO's most recent convention, held in June at the Ambassador Hotel in Los Angeles, Briskin had expounded on the futility of grading pictures in terms of the alphabet. "We have had it definitely proven to us that public opinion is the conclusive marker." Therefore, he announced that he was eliminating individual picture budgets so that "product would not be graded on the basis of expenditures." He handed producer Lee Marcus a heaping assignment of seventeen pictures, almost half of RKO Radio's production output for the next year and based upon an annual budget for the entire portion.

Meanwhile, the rumors of Briskin's desire to resign refused to die. On October 30, the *Herald* took a cautious look at the matter and concluded that "Mr. Briskin and Pandro S. Berman have had repeated differences over policy." The announcement in July that Briskin had signed a new three-year contract now proved false; it was revealed that the papers remained unsigned. Leo Spitz, who had been detained in New York waiting for a report from the court, hurried to Hollywood in the hopes of adjusting the Briskin situation.

But on November 1, *The Hollywood Reporter* advised that the sign staring one in the face at RKO read, "Wanted: A production head!"

PART SIX

STUDIO UNDER SIEGE: THE ODLUM-SCHAEFER ADMINISTRATION, 1938–1942

Costume party at San Simeon, circa 1934. Among the Confederate soldiers grouped behin Marion Davies's Southern belle stand William Randolph Hearst, fourth from the left; Hears editor Arthur Brisbane directly behind her; Joseph Mankiewicz, Herman's screenwrite brother, out of costume, left; director Raoul Walsh, sixth from right; Irving Thalberg third from right; director George Fitzmaurice, fourth from right William Randolph Hearst Jr., second from right. The actor assuming a pose at th extreme right is Buster Collie

Courtesy of the Academy of Motion Picture Arts and Sciences.

Lucille Ball with co-star Jack Oakie (left) and director Ben Stoloff i Lee Marcus's B comedy *The Affairs of Annabel,* in which she played a temperamental movi star. This was one of her seven 1938 RKO release

Courtesy of the Academy of Motion Picture Arts and Sciences

A White House visit by movie industry top brass in 1938. Front row, left to right: Paramount's Barney Balaban; Columbia's Harry Cohn; Nicholas Schenck of Loew's; Will Hays; RKO's Leo Spitz. Back row, left to right: George Schaefer, Paramount sales chief, soon to replace Spitz; Sidney Kent of Fox; Universal's Nate Blumberg; Warner's Albert Warner.
Courtesy Marc Wanamaker, Bison Archives.

Pan Berman, second from left, visiting the *Gunga Din* company on location at Lone Pine, California, in 1938. Seated at far left is Fred Gill, one of the two gag and stunt writers hired by director George Stevens to make the picture more entertaining. Bending over is a *Life* magazine photographer; next to him stands Douglas Fairbanks Jr., one of the picture's stars.
Courtesy Pandro S. Berman.

Pan Berman with director William A. Seiter (center) and the Marx Brothers on the set of *Room Service,* 1938. From left: Chico, Harpo, and Groucho.
Courtesy Pandro S. Berman.

The historic initial session of the board of directors of the new RKO Corporation, held New York in July 1939. Standing, left to right: Frederick L. Ehrman of Lehman Brother Conde Nast, an Atlas representative; L. Lawrence Green, attorney for the uninsur creditors; Lunsford P. Yandell, assistant treasurer of RCA; William Mallard, secreta and treasurer of the new company; Raymond Bill, and John E. Parsons, attorn Seated, left to right: W. G. Van Schmus, managing director of the Radio City Music Ha George J. Schaefer, president of the new corporation; Major General James G. Harbord RCA; Richard C. Patterson Jr., chairman of the RCA board of directors; N. Peter Rathvo president of Peter Rathvon and Company; Thomas P. Durrell of White, Weld, and Compar representing Time, Inc.; and Ned E. Depinet, vice president and director of the new compar
Courtesy Marc Wanamaker, Bison Archiv

portion of the gigantic outdoor replica of the Notre Dame cathedral square, with owds of extras, for *The Hunchback of Notre Dame*, 1939.

ourtesy of the Academy of Motion Picture Arts and Sciences.

Ginger Rogers, flanked by George Schaefer, far left, and her director, Sam Wood, clutches the Oscar she won for her performance in *Kitty Foyle,* 1940.

Courtesy of the Academy of Motion Picture Arts and Sciences.

Orson Welles directs a scene in *Citizen Kane* from a wheelchair after he broke his ankle. The scene features Dorothy Comingore as Susan Alexander Kane.

Courtesy Museum of Modern Art/Film Stills Archive.

Big George Schaefer, Dolores del Rio, and Orson Welles at the New York opening of *Citizen Kane*. Welles was involved in a love affair with the glamorous Mexican actress during this period.

Courtesy Marc Wanamaker, Bison Archives.

"The most eagerly awaited event in motion picture history!" The premiere of *Citizen Kane* at the Palace, New York, May 1, 1941.

Courtesy Marc Wanamaker, Bison Archives.

Joan Fontaine and George Schaefer holding the Oscar she has just won for her performance in Alfred Hitchcock's *Suspicion*, 1941, an RKO release and one of the few happy events of the Schaefer regime.
Courtesy Marc Wanamaker, Bison Archives.®

Orson Welles directs young Bobby Cooper in velveteen and ringlets for his ro as young George Minafer in *The Magnificent Ambersons*, 194
Courtesy Marc Wanamaker, Bison Archiv

21

On a gray Monday late in October 1938, Radio–Keith–Orpheum's work force gathered in the president's offices in Rockefeller Center to bid their latest departing chief a reluctant farewell. In a rare show of unanimity, all the assorted elements of command, including the trustee, Irving Trust, conceded that Leo Spitz was largely responsible for steering the bankrupt corporation from its dubious financial position, after the scuttling of the Sarnoff era, to the profitable present. It was common knowledge that Spitz, whose Chicago law firm, Spitz and Adcock, was one of the biggest in the Midwest, had been anxious to return to his law practice. Nevertheless, the feared yet highly regarded Odlum–Lehman leader had assumed temporary charge of the studio in the days immediately following Sam Briskin's resignation, with Pan Berman pinch-hitting as production head in the emergency situation. Following a round of conferences at the first of the year between the Odlum–Lehman top brass and a Rockefeller representative named W. G. Van Schmus, it had been announced in February 1938 that Leo Spitz would continue as president, and Pan Berman would remain in charge of the studio.

Yielding to the wishes of the trustee, some bitter medicine had been added to the Spitz–Berman blend: a financial aide in the person of the unpleasant J. R. McDonough. In fact, so swiftly was the former production executive elected a vice president and member of the board of Radio–Keith–Orpheum that canny observers of the coalition surmised it had to be a "Sarnoff-inspired" maneuver. Although Deak Aylesworth was no longer at the beck and call of David Sarnoff—the radio-film executive had severed his show business connections the previous year and joined the Scripps-Howard newspapers—he still served as a director of Irving Trust and, as such, could accommodate his old RCA friends. Spitz had reached the inescapable conclusion early in February that the reorganization might be "a long, drawn-out affair," since it was still under attack by attorneys of minority stockholders. Accordingly, the Atlas–Lehman option to purchase RCA's remaining holdings in RKO had been extended for another year. It was believed that McDonough's appointment was only for the period of reorganization. Adding to the touchiness of the situation, it was intimated that Spitz had sought to avoid any development that might lead to divided authority and executive conflict within the company. Since the trustee was anxious to retain Spitz, McDonough's new authority, Sarnoffian or not, had been well defined beforehand.

Now, in the fall of the year, with the invaluable Spitz on his way out, another long and tedious series of meetings resulted in the selection of a new president, the veteran Paramount sales chieftain George J. Schaefer. A true pioneer who had entered the film business in 1914 as secretary to Lewis J. Selznick, Schaefer was a big, robust bulldog of a man with a reputation for driving his sales force like a Prussian riding master, earning him the nickname "the tiger." Schaefer had resigned his post as vice president and general manager of American sales for United Artists a week earlier at a propitious stage in the negotiations and gone fishing off the Carolina coast while awaiting final developments.

On October 18, *The Hollywood Reporter* flashed the word that the forty-nine-year-old dynamo was expected to "step in with both feet immediately [as soon as] Judge Bondy gives the word on the reorganization." Another report, seemingly with plenty of foundation, was that after RKO was "snatched from its 77B," the lot would go on a total unit basis "with each independent production unit financed by one of the banking groups intimately connected with Atlas–Lehman." Schaefer was said to be more or less the author of the unit concept, which the banks had decided, after a serious investigation of Hollywood and its production costs, would "eliminate much of the great waste" entailed in production, "permitting product to come out at the right cost." It was this concept that had made Schaefer especially attractive to RKO's banking and Rockefeller interests. On October 20, Schaefer took over Leo Spitz's desk, even though Judge Bondy had yet to make his decision.

In mid-January 1939, Schaefer, accompanied by the long-lasting sales head Ned Depinet, arrived in Hollywood for conferences with Pan Berman on production plans for the remainder of the 1938–39 season and the next season's possibilities. A revised plan of reorganization had finally won the court's approval, with certain modifications, and reports of $10 million in new finances had reached the industry's ears.

Schaefer was received at the studio with some apprehension. The no-nonsense Berman had established a strong rapport with Leo Spitz, and it was because of his close friendship with the older man that he had agreed to take up the production reins again. It had been said of the former president that he appreciated his lack of production knowledge; since he had the good sense to appreciate that Berman did, they had worked well together.

In August 1938, the energetic young production chief could flatter himself on having more big features in various stages of production than at any time in the little major's history. Ready soon for release was the film version of the Broadway hit *Room Service,* bought for the announced all-time high sum of $255,000, for the Marx Brothers, who were on loan from MGM. Their young leading lady, Lucille Ball, who had mugged her way through four RKO pictures since 1937's *Stage Door,* was not deemed worthy of mention. *Gunga Din,* starring swashbuckling Cary Grant, Victor McLaglen, and Douglas Fairbanks Jr., currently clashing swords on the mountainous terrain of Lone Pine, California, with hundreds of artillery, infantry, and cavalry extras engaged in sweeping camera range, would be the studio's most expensive undertaking since *Cimarron.* This epic blockbuster, inspired by Rudyard Kipling's famous poem and given substance by a team of big-name writers that included Ben Hecht, Charles MacArthur, Anthony Veiller, Dudley Nichols, and William Faulkner,* had originally been assigned to producer-director Howard Hawks, who had come onto the lot the previous year to steer Hepburn in *Bringing Up Baby,* her comedic debut opposite Cary Grant. Quiet but forceful in style, the great director had gone far over the budget. RKO had settled his contract and Berman transferred *Gunga Din* to George Stevens, who, along with Leo McCarey and Gregory La Cava, constituted the studio's brand-new trinity of producer-directors with profit participation deals.

Stevens's first production wearing both hats, *Vivacious Lady,* in which timid botany professor James Stewart becomes romantically entangled with showgirl Ginger Rogers, appeared to be the comedy hit of the year. Reports from the field stressed that "Stewart seems so plain, realistic and decent, that he shouldn't miss real stardom," and that "little Ginger shows she needs no dance opus to really 'give out.'" Stevens, on *Gunga Din,* was proving to be as slow-moving and as unmindful of the budget as Hawks. But he was said to be delivering the most spectacular battle sequences since Errol Flynn stormed the heights of Balaklava in 1936 in *The Charge of the Light Brigade.* Said the *Herald:* "Over at RKO, everyone seems to be in the mood to bet that *Gunga Din* will outgross any rival attraction."

Leo McCarey's first picture under the RKO banner, *Love Match,* announced without cast and fanfare, was scheduled to roll in the fall.

Carefree, reuniting Fred and Ginger, was set to close the 1937–38 season, and the series as well, with the key elements of their production unit gradually breaking up. Director Mark Sandrich, who had never received a percentage deal, was leaving RKO. Astaire's departure, following completion of the period

*Joel Sayre and Fred Guiol received the final screenplay credit.

story of the glamorous Vernon Castles (*The Story of Vernon and Irene Castle*) had been announced as far back as January, the month after the team's sudden fall to number seven on the exhibitor's Top Ten box-office poll was made public. Fred's solo effort, *A Damsel in Distress,* had not fared well. Even in an "Astaire town," such as Parker, Indiana, "they did not come out, and those that did were not enthusiastic." "The same old romantic setting" was another complaint being aired with more frequency. "Astaire wants to meet Rogers, and Rogers don't like Astaire. Finally Rogers admits she's in love with Astaire. The story is the same as all the rest of them," said a malcontent theaterman in Elgin, Oregon, about *Shall We Dance.* Berman knew that the series had reached its dead end. He didn't have to hear from some wiseacre that "Maybe they shouldn't fall in love next time."

Nevertheless, that August the RKO star roster was still headed by the Astaire–Rogers combination, while Katharine Hepburn's name was missing. On May 3, the Independent Theater Owners Association had "awakened" Hollywood with a list of stars they considered "box-office deterrents"; Hepburn's name followed those of Mae West, Edward Arnold, Greta Garbo, and Joan Crawford—players whose "dramatic ability is unquestioned, but whose box-office draw is nil," the hard-hitting report stated. In spite of Hepburn's "excellent performances" in *Stage Door* and *Bringing Up Baby,* both pictures had "died." Although she could be headstrong, opinionated, unduly aggressive, and often arrogant, Berman still found Kate an altogether fascinating star. She had plagued him to buy *Gone With the Wind* for her, a property he well realized would be far too expensive an undertaking for the little studio. Instead of Scarlett O'Hara, the top role of the year, Hepburn had been "requested" to star in a folksy, B-plus programmer, *Mother Carey's Chickens.* Under the circumstances, it was the best that Berman could offer. Rather than be reduced to making B pictures like Warner's Kay Francis, another tarnished star, Hepburn had bought off her contract.

With the loyal Leo Spitz gone, Berman had no great desire to continue as production chief. The new president, however, assured Berman that he would not set foot in his domain and that his authority would never be intrusive, and Berman succumbed to promises. In mid-January 1939, following his initial meetings with Berman, Schaefer announced a 1939 program of approximately forty pictures. Sounding like Early Sam Briskin, he proclaimed that the big budgeters would take precedence over the B's. In step with his pronouncement, the mammoth *Gunga Din,* which the studio's ad chief bragged it took all of 1938 to make, was opening at the Music Hall in a few days. Even without benefit of McCormick's $200,000 publicity campaign, the $1.9 million epic was earmarked for the big time. The *Herald* had advised exhibitors that the film was "fast, furious and fascinating," its 135 minutes "taut as a regimental drumhead." This was a picture an audience could "sink its teeth into"; and regardless of all the carnage, "utterly clean in every particular." The following week, Berman announced the largest feature on his new schedule, a remake of Victor Hugo's immortal horror story *The Hunchback of Notre Dame,* in which the late and great Lon Chaney had displayed his terrifying art.

In March, Berman launched a solo starring vehicle for Ginger Rogers, tentatively entitled *Little Mother,* with David Niven, then in *Wuthering Heights,* as the other half of the love interest team. Its young director, Garson Kanin, called by the studio "a sensational find," had turned out one of the previous year's surprise pictures, *A Man to Remember,* an intelligent B scripted by another newcomer, Dalton Trumbo, formerly a baker. Even Anne Shirley had profited, receiving recognition from the *New York Daily Mirror* as "one of the most ringingly true little actresses in films." The studio was celebrating two box-office champions, *Gunga Din* and *Love Affair.* The latter was formerly titled *Love Match* and starred Irene Dunne and Charles Boyer. It had run into serious censorship problems when the French embassy vetoed the script, which depicted a tragic affair between the French ambassador and a married American woman, set in the 1850s. The resourceful Leo McCarey called his writer pal Delmer Daves, who hastily devised a variation on the forbidden love theme, a bittersweet shipboard romance based on an affair of a woman he had just met on a boat coming back from Europe. Shooting in continuity, without a finished script,* McCarey improvised some of the early sequences, permitting Irene Dunne as the "soiled" nightclub singer to develop a thoroughly convincing, well-rounded character, thus earning for herself a fourth Academy Award nomination.

In New York, the home office was celebrating the approaching end of Radio–Keith–Orpheum's six arduous years spent in the courts. Judge Bondy finally confirmed the reorganization plan, signing the final papers in April. Approved also were the officers and directors for the "new company," while the opposing minority stockholders were brushed aside by the judge. Ignoring their declarations to take their grievances to the Supreme Court, Atlas attorney Rickaby later emphasized that finalization of the plan would proceed regardless. The new directorate, headed by Floyd Odlum as chairman, was a precarious balance of Atlas, Lehman, RCA, and Rockefeller power, plus the necessary nuisances of reorganization: representatives of the stockholders' protective committee and unsecured creditors. Last-minute additions to the hefty board added weight to the Atlas camp with socialite magazine publisher Condé Nast and gave Time, Inc., the holder of about $1.250 million in unsecured RKO notes, a spokesman in Thomas P. Durrell.

The trustee's report for the previous year revealed an alarming downward

*Daves and Donald Ogden Stewart received screenplay credit; Mildred Cram shared story credit with McCarey.

trend in the company's fortunes: a profit of only $173,578 in 1938, compared with 1937's $1.821 million and 1936's whopping $2,514,734 million. But the new president was too busy deal-making in the millions—"writing new history in swift, bold strokes," as Depinet spouted off in one of his pep rallies to the field force—to consider the onslaught of another downward turn. "RKO Radio is geared for a place close to the very top," said Schaefer in a statement on the new season's objectives. Under *his* guidance, the little major would "proceed with greater courage and daring showmanship."

In June, Schaefer announced a new season's program of fifty-eight features and an increase in production budgets of about 40 percent, to give the company a greater number of big pictures. "RKO will spend a minimum of twenty-one million dollars on the 1939–40 product, six million more than this year," Schaefer informed the delegates at the annual sales convention at New York's swank Westchester Country Club. While Berman winced, Schaefer told about a big deal closed with two distinguished Broadway producers, Max Gordon and Harry Goetz, bringing them into the RKO fold, and with them, Robert E. Sherwood's Pulitzer Prize–winning play *Abe Lincoln in Illinois,* in which Raymond Massey would recreate his stage role, and another play, the patriotic *The American Way.* "RKO has spent five-hundred thousand dollars for the rights to these great properties," Schaefer added, "and is prepared to spend up to three million to produce them."

Distinguished though Gordon and Goetz were on Broadway, Berman realized that they had never made a picture in Hollywood. The Lincoln project was decidedly noncommercial, but Schaefer had made the deal without so much as a backward glance in Berman's direction. Schaefer had signed plenty of other "top-bracket specialists," with more misses than hits among their credits, without consulting his production chief. The delegates heard about the new author-producer team of Gene Towne and Graham Baker and their program of children's classics, as well as the new Boris Morros unit, which would produce remakes of French pictures, some with Laurel and Hardy. RKO would participate with Herbert Wilcox's British company, whose *Nurse Edith Cavell,* starring British import Anna Neagle, was already in the works.

Meanwhile, the one and only Charles Laughton had been signed for the remake of *The Hunchback of Notre Dame* and had arrived in Hollywood to begin work under the direction of the gifted and important William Dieterle. The British star had yearned to play the bestial Quasimodo since the role had first been suggested to him by Thalberg in 1934. At his insistence, Perc Westmore was engaged to create the hideous makeup intended to make audiences shriek with horrified delight. At Laughton's urging, Berman had cast Irish-born Maureen O'Hara in the role of the gypsy girl, Esmeralda. The strikingly beautiful nineteen-year-old was under contract to Laughton's Mayflower Productions in London and had just played the Irish ingenue in his

Jamaica Inn. A gigantic $250,000 outdoor replica of the medieval Notre Dame square, as conceived by RKO's Van Nest Polglase, was under construction at the studio's eighty-eight-acre ranch at Encino, in the San Fernando Valley.

This would be Berman's final production for RKO. His relationship with Schaefer had deteriorated early in the year, and in February Berman had asked to be released from his contract but had later agreed to remain at the studio until the first of December. He disagreed with Schaefer's policy of overdosing the studio with independent production units, which he felt created a divided organization. It was obvious that the president was motivated to take over production and would be delighted to have him out of the way. A new berth awaited Pan at MGM, for the far-sighted Louie Mayer had been courting him faithfully through the years. Berman's cool head and production wisdom were needed more than ever since the premature death of Irving Thalberg. The realization by Schaefer that he was losing one of the studio's major assets—a fact he would be forced to confront at the next meeting of the board of directors—came too late. Berman firmly rejected his pleas to remain as an independent producer, as well as his offer of a lucrative new deal. He wanted nothing further to do with "the tiger." It would be a sentimental leave-taking; the lot had been his second home, a part of his family tree. He would be leaving seventeen years of memories and old friends, but by December there would be two new, big releases to add to his string of successes, *Bachelor Mother* and *The Hunchback of Notre Dame*. At the very least, Berman would be leaving in a blaze of glory.

22

Early in September 1939, George Schaefer joined the conclave of pessimistic movie chieftains assembled in New York to take emergency steps to meet the onslaught of a second world war in Europe. A cable received by the RKO president from Ralph Hanbury, the United Kingdom's managing director for RKO Radio Pictures Ltd. in London, contained news of the utmost gravity: "All cinemas closed by Government decree...the chief constable in each city empowered to reopen some...according to the vulnerability of air raids...." With England and France at war with Germany, the distribution offices in London and Paris—key points through which most of the European market had flowed in recent months—virtually suspended operations. Before the month was over, Schaefer released a statement in which he dwelled on a "drastic falling off in foreign revenues, the drop in foreign exchange, and possible restrictions on transfer of funds...." The RKO chief ended his litany of ill fortune by announcing upper-level salary cuts, some of more than 35 percent, but promising that no employee receiving $4500 a year or less would be affected.

Taking pains to ignore Schaefer's noble gesture, the *Herald,* on September 23, reviewed with customary perception industry actions in a world so swiftly reshaped by war:

> From Hollywood come tidings of payroll amputations. The first to fall were some of the court jesters [and] golf, polo and card instructors. The West Coast and New York home offices did a bigger long distance telephone business than usual. It appeared probable that Lady Hollywood might get her allowance cut, regardless of pouts and protests. The conversations grew hot in spots. One New York executive hung up the phone with the observation, "The whole damn outfit out there is nigger-rich, and now's the time they'll have to learn to get over it." One acute film-buyer, dealing for large interests, observed: "We must remember that this is a lucky business. As an industry it has had one break after another. Maybe it will be getting another one now. The first world war made it, for America."

As the war news grew progressively worse, any optimistic outlook lost its supporters. A 27 million–foot drop in exports of "positive" film (theater prints) from Hollywood was reported in November. By spring 1940, the Nazi march into Norway and Denmark, the blockading of Sweden, and the Russian grab of part of Finland, it was predicted, would cost the American film industry $4 million a year. Arriving in New York in May, on the heels of total war that had now engulfed Western Europe, Reginald Armour, RKO's foreign sales head, hesitated to predict the future. The major portion of a once-blooming film market had been dealt a deathblow. The picture could hardly be any blacker than it was at present. Only in England, where the industry had a strong ally in the British ambassador, could anyone expect to make any profit.

Hollywood had regarded the December 1937 appointment of Joe Kennedy to the post of Ambassador to the Court of St. James with comforting anticipation. True; the *Herald* viewed the big event with mixed emotions: "It is pleasantly entertaining that from Boston goes the American to sit in the world's greatest 'tea party'—in London." Still, there was no denying that the industry's continued problems with the all-important British market would now receive the skilled attentions of one of Hollywood's own. Consequently, the movie community publicly sympathized with Joe's "absolute refusal" to wear those traditional knee breeches when he presented his credentials to the king, in spite of his "mighty shapely calf." His hole in one, on his first round of golf at Stoke Poges, was treated as an everyday Kennedy occurrence. "He has been shooting like that in considerably more complex games ever since he sold Pathe to Mr. David Sarnoff," remarked the *Herald*'s editor on March 12, 1938.

Kennedy came through on Hollywood's behalf with a tough monetary agreement that covered the withdrawal of $17.5 million in film revenue in 1939, almost as large a sum as if there had been no restrictions. Furthermore, in the fall of 1940, it appeared likely his "splendid efforts"—Will Hays's expression—would reap $12 million for another year. Shortly afterwards, his popularity eroded both at home and abroad by his intense pursuit of his own business—movies and liquor—and his pessimistic isolationist views, Kennedy arrived in Washington, submitted his resignation on November 6, and later in the month was in Hollywood meeting privately with the moguls. Although the trade press respected the "strictly confidential" nature of their talks, Drew Pearson and Robert S. Allen were not so obliging. On November 26, their syndicated newspaper column reported that the moguls were "almost pop-eyed with Kennedy's confidential views on the outcome of the war and appeasement." Kennedy told them that England was going down in defeat; therefore, the U.S. should curtail aid to Britain and build its own arsenal in order to be in a "better position to do business with the Axis victors." He warned them to stop making pro-British and anti-Nazi movies, and keep their "Jewish rage" to themselves. He described anti-Semitic riots he had witnessed in London.

Before Kennedy left Hollywood to continue his barnstorming across the country "peddling appeasement" —in Joseph Alsop's and other journalists' words—the trades revealed that he had been offered "the Will Hays job" but had refused it, putting in a big plea for his longtime friend.

In this embittered, uncertain world, in which the movie chieftains trod an increasingly narrowed path between fighting and fearing, it may well have seemed expedient to cast out their old front man. In truth, the Hays organization's legal force had set out for Washington the preceding spring, carrying evidence that the industry had been singled out for forty-four different legislative attacks in the past six years. The Justice Department's two-year-old anti-trust suit that sought to force the moguls to separate theater ownership from production had reached an uneasy compromise, formalized by a Consent Decree. Five majors, including RKO, were faced with tough new regulations that would greatly hinder distribution. As Schaefer pointed out at the 1941 RKO convention, "We will have to do business with a block of no more than five pictures now. The old practice of pulling a picture and grabbing another, when one doesn't break records, will not be so easy." Suggested Ned Depinet: "The Consent Decree may be a blessing in disguise requiring better pictures."

The moguls had been harassed and tormented by almost one hundred censorship boards that had sprung up across the country, worn down by a conglomeration of taxes, and victimized by William Bioff. The strong-arm labor organizer and his president, William B. Browne of the International Alliance of Theatrical Stage Employees and Motion Picture Machine Operators (IATSE), had extorted hundreds of thousands of their dollars by threatening studio strikes and had raked in more than $4 million from their studio workers. Only the "protective wings" of the federal court had saved RKO from "paying tribute" to Willie. "Them producers would like to see me dead in every room," Willie boasted to reporter Florabel Muir, whose *Saturday Evening Post* exposé, ALL RIGHT GENTLEMEN, DO WE GET THE MONEY?, hit the newsstands on January 27, 1940. At the government trial of the IATSE union leaders the following year, which ended in "long-term jail contracts"—Alcatraz for Willie because of his Capone connections in old Chicago—several moguls suffered the embarrassment of having to admit that they had covered the "transactions" in the company's books through well-padded expense vouchers. Joe Schenck, the popular head of Twentieth Century–Fox, was forced to leave his palatial home for a short time and take up residence in a jail cell.

Meanwhile, the changing political climate in Europe had bred new enemies that the moguls realized could no longer be handled by the Hays appeasement policies of old. They had dealt personally with Congressman Martin Dies of Texas, convincing him, by means of private talks, to retract his ludicrous statements that their community was dominated by Communists. In the summer of 1941 they disregarded Kennedy's warnings and entered the arena against the witch-hunting group in Washington that was led by two isolationist senators. Gerald P. Nye of North Dakota, for one, dared to call Chaplin's *The Great Dictator,* Lasky's *Sergeant York,* MGM's *Flight Command,* and other films that "sold the American way of life," in 1940 and 1941, propaganda films. If this was "the first Nazi *putsch* against freedom of expression in the U.S.," as Sol Rosenblatt, now a film industry attorney, claimed, they were ready to fight back.

23

Early in 1940, following Pan Berman's departure, George Schaefer hastily constructed a fresh network of executive command—one that left him firmly in charge. By elevating the company's longtime assistant secretary, J. J. Nolan, the man who had served as his assistant for the past year, to vice president in charge of the studio, and placing a former independent producer and agent, Harry E. Edington, in charge of high-budget films, the authoritative president would not have to share his room at the top.

The new Radio–Keith–Orpheum Company had just begun to operate, freed at last from the court supervision of seven years of reorganization and actions by minorities and whatnot having been finally dismissed. In a simple ceremony in the Irving Trust offices in the RKO Building on January 26 that took less than a half hour, a vice president of Irving Trust turned over the assets of the $95 million company to the RKO vice president, W. G. Merrill. With no outstanding indebtedness, its capital structure consisting only of preferred and common stock, and extensive working capital—more than $8 million cash in bank alone, which amounted to approximately twice the current liabilities—the emerging parent glowed with health; and Schaefer's initial statement expressing confidence in the future of the new corporation and its subsidiaries launched high expectations.

Meantime, in Hollywood, Schaefer's world was rapidly turning sour. The previous summer he had signed that "spectacular genius of the show world," Orson Welles, to act, direct, and write, as well as produce four movies. The decision had been made without consulting Berman, but with the enthusiastic endorsement of Nelson Rockefeller, a major RKO stockholder. Only twenty-four, Welles had attained national prominence in the past two years through his Mercury Theater, an innovative repertory company founded with the more experienced John Houseman, and as a producer of radio dramatizations in which he invariably and colorfully starred. His sensationally realistic broadcast on October 30, 1938, of H. G. Wells's *The War of the Worlds* so terrified the country with its simulated Martian landing in New Jersey that CBS had actually been threatened with punitive action by the FCC. It made the young Mercury Theater impresario an instant celebrity. Welles's RKO contract, which yielded concessions unprecedented in movie history, gave him almost total autonomy. Only Schaefer would maintain a degree of control over his "genius." Under the glare of national publicity culminating in a *Time* magazine cover, captioned "Marvelous Boy," Welles burst onto the Hollywood scene as the incarnation of D. W. Griffith, intent on distancing himself from the old Hollywood and its orthodox ways. Welles's extreme youth, coupled with his ruddy, robust, more-than-six-foot-tall attractiveness and unique credentials, brought out the worst in the movie colony. All its jealousy and possessiveness erupted as the press continued to revel in the Orson Welles phenomenon. Alva Johnston and Fred Smith tickled *The Saturday Evening Post*'s readers and alienated Hollywood in January with an account of Welles's precociousness: "He talked like a college professor at two. At three he looked like Dr. Fu Manchu and spouted Shakespeare like a veteran. At eight he started making his own highballs. He was leading man for Katharine Cornell at eighteen. Today, at twenty-four, he has the most amazing contract ever signed in Hollywood."

"One-fifty grand a picture, plus a piece of the action, and he doesn't have to kowtow to New York," grumbled the Brown Derby squatters. Welles's remark, quoted in the *Post* about his first tour of RKO— "It's the greatest railroad train a boy ever had!"—left Hollywood unamused. The town was rooting for "Little Orson Annie" to fail, and by the following spring—after Welles's first project, an adventure drama based on Joseph Conrad's *Heart of*

Darkness, was hit by budget trouble and an English thriller by Nicholas Blake, *The Smiler with the Knife,* reached a casting impasse—Hollywood cheered. But on April 30, *The Hollywood Reporter*'s Rambling Reporter column* advised, "This Saturday, no kidding, Welles is starting to make tests of different players at RKO. His office says 'It's not a picture, just an idea.' In the advance announcement of RKO product just before sales convention time in May, the "idea" was listed as *John Citizen, U.S.A.* When it was announced at the convention, it had become *Citizen Kane.*

On the brink of failure, Welles, hustling plot ideas with a kindred spirit, the enormously creative but self-destructive screenwriter Herman Mankiewicz, had hit upon a daring concept, a film "biography" about a fictitious publisher modeled on the great yellow journalist William R. Hearst. Mankiewicz, with John Houseman providing editorial assistance and co-author Welles dropping in on weekends, spent thirteen weeks in the high desert country turning out a screenplay.

Rudy, the RKO bootblack who, it was reported, won $40 in small bets around the lot when he wagered that Welles *would* do a picture, rejoiced along with Schaefer as cameras finally started turning at Pathé late in June. In mid-October, the Kane company, mostly drawn from Welles's distinguished Mercury players, headed by Agnes Moorehead and Joseph Cotten, moved to the RKO lot for a few days, then returned to Pathé where filming wound up, only four days behind schedule with what was described as an inadvertent Mars stunt. An incinerator had been built on a stage for a scene where old furnishings in a home were being burned. "Fire went off swell," *The Hollywood Reporter* informed the town, "but Orson forgot about the sprinkler system, which took off with the heat and had the entire Culver City fire department out in full blast!"

The fireworks had only just begun. Fortified by a *Newsweek* revelation in September that Hearst had approved the Kane script, the word had spread during production that it was, in fact, based on the life of the opulent press lord and included a loose but harsh portrait of his adored Marion Davies. Welles, who looked upon Hedda Hopper as his family's "only syndicated friend," had promised the powerful *Los Angeles Times* columnist that she would be among the first to view a rough cut of the picture, along with *Look* and *Life,* very early in January. By the time Hedda gave her readers the titillating facts in mid-January 1941, on the "biggest story to break in this little old town in many a day," Hearst's loyal movie editor, Louella Parsons—who, it was felt, might have been called into action by a surreptitious phone call to Hearst from her archrival—had seen the picture in the company of two Hearst lawyers. In a post-preview phone call to George Schaefer, Louella spoke frankly: "RKO is going

*A witty general-news column written by various columnists.

to have one of the most beautiful lawsuits in history if you release *Citizen Kane*."

Said Hedda in her syndicated column on January 15: "All kinds of rumors are flying about town. First, that the RKO studio will be ignored editorially by all of Mr. Hearst's papers. That is being done. Next, that the refugee situation will be looked into.* Nor are the private lives to be overlooked.† These rumors have become so frightening... that it's now become an industry affair and will be dealt with accordingly"—which implied that an alarmed L. B. Mayer had offered to buy the film for its negative cost, $842,000, rather than see it released and take the consequences. To his credit, "the tiger" stood his ground, while Will Hays retreated, reminding *The New Republic*'s Michael Sage of "the sterling fortitude displayed by Neville Chamberlain when Hitler trampled Czechoslovakia."‡

The Rambling Reporter followed the *Kane* squabble almost on a daily basis for the next few months, offering all the latest tidbits culled from Hearst, RKO, and Welles sources. On January 16, old RCA–RKO friend and former leader Deak Aylesworth slipped into town accompanied by an RKO attorney to take full charge of the legal end of the fracas. "It is expected they will fly to the Hearst ranch to have a talk with 'W.R.'" Four days later Aylesworth was spied boarding the Chief bound for New York to make his report. On January 27, Hollywood learned that Welles had skipped to the East over the weekend with a print of *Kane*. His purpose: to "advance-bally the picture without RKO aid." On February 3, it was reported that "the ban placed on RKO publicity by Hearst papers had been lifted, so long as no mention is made of *Kane*," although it would be a good three months before Louella grudgingly mentioned the name "RKO" in her column. "All the furor has resolved itself in the decision by RKO to release the picture on February 14, Valentine's Day, in its present uncut form," the Rambling Reporter advised. However, four days later, a print of *Citizen Kane* was said to be on its way to San Simeon and it was believed that Hearst might suggest changes or deletions, and that RKO would make them, disregarding Welles's contract.

The statement by the Hearst forces that they would sue every theater that showed the film for the stipulated $250 fine and damages caused RKO to cancel the premiere. *The Hollywood Reporter* treated the matter lightly on February 19: "Still no New York house for the flicker's opening, you know." It could not, of course, reveal the ugly rumors that Mayer and others were pulling strings to stop theaters from booking *Kane*. Because the Music Hall had

*At a time when many American-born Hollywood writers were unemployed, the studio heads had given employment to many aliens, including some German-Jewish writers who couldn't speak English.

†The Hearst papers had always protected the moguls.

‡*The New Republic*, February 24, 1941.

rejected the picture, it was said that Louella had threatened Nelson Rockefeller with an unsavory story on his father. It was said that she had telephoned a threat of the same nature to RKO stockholder David Sarnoff.

The showdown *The Reporter* had predicted later in January arrived in March when Welles threatened to sue RKO if it did not release the film. "Under my contract I have the right to force its release," Welles thundered at a press conference in New York on March 11, adding that he might also sue Hearst if it could be shown that the picture was being withheld at his request. He said that a major company—unnamed, but reported to be Universal—and a banking group, had made offers to buy the film from RKO for approximately $1 million and release it themselves. Henry Luce of *Life, Time,* and *Fortune,* and labeled a confirmed "Hearst-baiter," was also rumored to be in on a *Kane* deal. Attacking the alleged resemblance between incidents in the picture and Hearst's life, Welles insisted: "*Kane* was not intended to have, nor has it, any reference whatsoever to Mr. Hearst or to any other living person."

Led by *The Reporter*'s headlined rave on March 12, MR. GENIUS COMES THROUGH, "KANE" ASTONISHING PICTURE, *Time, Life,* and other magazines finally ran their reviews. "Like some grotesque fable, Hollywood last week appeared to be destroying its greatest masterpiece," *Time* grieved. "*Citizen Kane* is the most sensational product of the movie industry...a work of art created by grown people for grown people." *Life* managed to avoid a single mention of Hearst but ran a straight review: "In his first film Orson Welles breaks all Hollywood taboos. Director Welles and Cameraman Greg Toland do brilliantly with a camera everything Hollywood has always said you couldn't do. They shoot into bright lights, into the dark, and against low ceilings until every scene comes with the impact of something never seen before." *Newsweek*'s John O'Hara thought it the best picture he had ever seen, Welles "the best actor in the history of acting."

By late March, *The Reporter* was ready to apologize to "a real genius" while editorializing on the "brazen" picture's fate, which would either brand the RKO powers as "the most stupid in this business, or the most courageous"—they would be damned if they did or didn't release it. After polling public opinion in Ciros, the popular nitery along the Sunset Strip—"the best opinion around this village"—the Rambling Reporter confided that "public pressure has now been whipped up to a pitch where RKO will *have* to release *Kane,* or turn Welles into a national martyr."

At last came the news the show business world waited for: RKO WILL RELEASE *CITIZEN KANE*. However, it was doubtful that the major, producer-owned circuits would immediately play it. One company head, identified by insiders as Harry Warner, let it be known that RKO would have to put up a $1 million bond to protect his houses against possible suits. RKO finally opened *Citizen Kane* at its Palace Theater in New York on May 1. The event was heralded by a color supplement in *The Reporter* dramatizing Welles's persecution and vindication and ending with a tribute from Schaefer: "...You were condemned before being tried! Your triumph is one of the great accomplishments in motion picture history, and proof that America is still the land of opportunity." But in spite of the tremendous advance sale at the Palace, RKO was finding it difficult to convince small-town and neighborhood theaters to book the picture for its secondary run. Although reported on the verge of a nervous breakdown in April, Welles reacted with vehemence: "I'll show it in a ball park with four screens, in auditoriums, at fairs, in circus tents, if necessary. I'm not *Mr. Deeds Goes to Hollywood,* but I'll play Mr. Deeds if I can be sure Edward Arnold will go down to destruction in the last reel."

The overwhelming critical praise heaped on *Citizen Kane* engendered little joy in the New York office, where Floyd Odlum and fellow owners Rockefeller and Sarnoff were grappling with the problem of rapidly mounting losses. The red ink amounted to almost a million and a quarter for 1939 and 1940; and the root of failure appeared to be in Hollywood, on the door mat of Schaefer's executive suite. Neither of his two flunkies, new studio boss Joe Nolan or Harry Edington, in charge of A pictures, had proved effective. Furthermore, Schaefer's highly recommended independent production units, those "top-bracket specialists" he had pinned his hopes on, had let him down badly. Exhibitors had been burned by critical successes, such as *All That Money Can Buy,* William Dieterle's arty film version of Stephen Vincent Benet's short story "The Devil and Daniel Webster," and the RKO sales force was encountering growing resistance in the field to these problem films. Not even the popular success of *Kitty Foyle,* Ginger Rogers' Oscar-winner, the continued distribution of the marvelous Disney product, and an important (if not lucrative) deal for Samuel Goldwyn's prestigious pictures, which Schaefer closed in April 1941, could counter the image of a down-in-the-mouth studio.

It was the opnion of insiders watching the RKO situation early in 1941 that the stock control would shortly be "tossed into a single basket," as *The Reporter* put it, belonging to Odlum and his Atlas Corporation putting an end to this detrimental period of divided rule. Joe Kennedy's name had recently been brought up again in regard to his making one of his famous investigations of the floundering company. Broadway believed that Joe, who was on the friendliest of terms with Odlum, Sarnoff, and the Rockefellers, had an option to acquire a major slice of the stock if he would agree to stay on after he had probed Radio–Keith–Orpheum's vitals.

In Hollywood, Schaefer strenuously denied any knowledge that Kennedy was "headed for RKO," as the press insisted, and in February, the beleaguered president took complete charge of the studio. What followed was a round of wholesale firings and/or walkouts. Schaefer demoted old-timer Lee Marcus, head of the studio's B-unit, who had been with the company since its Robertson–Cole days. Marcus settled his contract and walked off the lot, leaving Gloria Swanson's "major" comeback picture, *Father Takes a Wife,* to be finished by his successor, none other than the Sarnoffian executive, J. R. McDonough. Producer Bob Sisk followed Marcus, leaving a Ginger Rogers starrer, *Tom, Dick and Harry,* still shooting.

According to the Rambling Reporter, the picture's audacious director, Garson Kanin, stuck his head into the executive dining room at lunchtime to see who else was missing and couldn't resist shouting: "I just had a hot tip that 'R' is pulling out, leaving the company only the 'KO'." Schaefer graciously treated Joe Nolan, the erstwhile production chief, to a testimonial dinner in the commissary before his departure in July, with entertainment by RKO radio stars Kay Kyser and Edgar Bergen and Charlie McCarthy. Nolan's replacement took Hollywood by surprise—it was none other than gruff, hearty Joe Breen, the Hays Office's lord high censor, until his sudden resignation in the spring.

At an informal press conference the big Irishman indicated that it would be *his* policy to stress entertainment. He would not personally produce but intended to secure the services of the finest production talent available, dropping the names of Gregory La Cava, Leo McCarey, and John Ford. Orson Welles was definitely staying on at the studio, Breen said; in fact, "the wizard of RKO" would make three or four pictures a year. Welles had completed a script for a Mexican picture he wanted to make and was already at work on another, which Breen emphasized would not follow the pattern of "shocking Hollywood." Then there was the possibility of an adaptation of Eric Ambler's tense thriller *Journey Into Fear.*

The number-two position, formerly occupied by Harry Edington, now sitting out his contract, was handed to another independent producer, Sol Lesser, a veteran whose credits ranged from the likes of *Tarzan* to Thornton Wilder's sensitive *Our Town.* J. R. McDonough, the Sarnoffian executive–turned–producer, was put in charge of outside producers. Other than the important Goldwyn, whose first RKO release was *The Little Foxes,* starring Bette Davis, they would all be subject to the crack of his whip.

By summer, one thing seemed clear in the muddled RKO situation: Schaefer would probably be felled by contractual difficulties. Informed Wall Street circles reported that the present directors were unwilling to hand their president a new long-term deal and tie up the new board, which would come in next year; therefore, they had insisted on adding a seven-month's cancellation clause to Schaefer's contract offer, which he rejected. The annual stockholders' meeting, usually held on June 5, had been postponed, possibly to give Atlas, reported now in full voting control, the chance to buy up controlling interest.

In August, Chairman N. Peter Rathvon, Odlum's alter ego, who had every appearance of the number-one man to succeed Schaefer—should the situation arise—arrived in Hollywood for a short studio visit with production chief Joe Breen. Anticipating an executive shakeup, *The Reporter,* playing with the title of a programmer that director Tay Garnett had just finished shooting, quipped: "RKO executives are frantically trying to decide whether to call it *Week End for Three, Weekend for Three,* or *Week-end for Three.*" However, "the tiger" continued to defend his lair as vigorously as ever, denying that he was on his way out or that a new studio shakeup was imminent that would deliver Joe Breen back to the Hays Office and increase Rathvon's responsibilities.

Nevertheless, a short time after Pearl Harbor, a second shakeup hit the studio, this time claiming J. R. McDonough among its victims. A problem of dual authority between Joe Breen and Sol Lesser knocked out Lesser. Breen, meanwhile, went on vacation, which left Orson Welles in a vulnerable position, since another executive, Charles W. Koerner, RKO's theater head, reputed to be favored by Odlum, came West to take charge of the studio in Breen's absence. Under these circumstances, a sign near the set of *The Magnificent Ambersons* that read "Do Not Bomb, Orson Welles Shooting" was interpreted as having more than one level of meaning.

Early in February 1942, Welles left for Brazil at the invitation of Nelson Rockefeller, President Roosevelt's coordinator of Inter-American Affairs, to make a documentary, *It's All True,* that would promote Latin American goodwill. He had been maintaining an exhausting schedule, working days finishing and cutting *Ambersons,* and nights supervising his third film, *Journey Into Fear,* in which he also played a small role. He had handed over the direction of this feature, which starred Joseph Cotten and Dolores Del Rio, to Norman Foster, an experienced hand with *Charlie Chan* and *Mr. Moto* B's.

After Joe Breen returned to the studio, Koerner failed to relinquish the production reins, so another problem of dual authority arose; and in May, Koerner became Joe Breen's successor.

Throughout the winter and early spring, a management and control battle had raged in New York, with neither Rockefeller nor Odlum interests giving an inch. But now, in June, it appeared more likely that Atlas would come out on top. The latest reports indicated that the Atlas–Odlum empire—having tried, unsuccessfully, to bail out its by now $8 million RKO investment via a sale—might decide to step in and purchase some additional shares, arrange for $3 or $4 million new financing needed for production, and run the company. Much as Floyd Odlum did not want to go in deeper, it looked as if he might be forced to do so in order to protect Atlas's huge investment.

As the result of a special meeting of the board, Ned Depinet, the able sales chief who had stood like Gibraltar through the tumult of the past ten years, emerged as acting president of RKO Radio Pictures, with Rathvon set to perform Schaefer's executive functions. At the stockholders' meeting held in Dover, Delaware, on June 17, all RKO directors were reelected, with the exception of George Schaefer, who had already given notice. A week later, when the new board convened in New York, both Rathvon and Depinet praised Charles Koerner, recommending that the Odlum choice remain in charge of the studio.

In Hollywood, meanwhile, the word was that when Charlie Koerner paid a visit to Charlie McCarthy on the set of Allan Dwan's *Here We Go Again*, the flippant dummy had piped up: "Hello, Mr. Koerner! I'm here for six weeks. How long are you here for?"

PART SEVEN

THE SHOWMANSHIP COMPANY: THE ODLUM-KOERNER ADMINISTRATION, 1942–1946

The Spirit of World War II. RKO morale builders: 1943 starlets. Carole Gallagher (Britain), Elaine Riley (Russia), Shirley O'Hara (USA), and Barbara Hale (China).
Courtesy Shirley O'Hara Krims.

RKO's Irish Starlets (left to righ Patti Brill, Shirley O'Hara, Daun Kenned Elaine Riley, and Dorothy Maloney (wh soon became Dorothy Malon
Courtesy Shirley O'Hara Krir

The N. Peter Rathvons and Floyd Odlum, right, attend the New York world premiere of Samuel Goldwyn's *The North Star,* an RKO release starring Anne Baxter and Farley Granger, on November 4, 1943. Odlum's companion is Annette Downes. Odlum's wife, aviatrix Jacqueline Cochran, whom he married in 1936, is away helping to win the war.
Courtesy Marc Wanamaker, Bison Archives.

Frank Ross, who several seasons earlier turned out *The Devil and Miss Jones* for RKO, starring Jean Arthur, again tied up with the studio on a producing deal in 1943, with *A Lady Takes a Chance* as his first effort. Here seen on location are the stars, Jean Arthur and John Wayne. Director William Seiter, wearing a Western hat, is standing on a camera dolly.

Courtesy Marc Wanamaker, Bison Archives.

A view of RKO Studio, 1945, looking north from Melrose. The standing sets to the right of the water tower are part of the Paramount back lot. A small piece of the Hollywood Cemetery is visible north of the studio. KHJ radio faces Melrose just east of the Melrose entrance leading to the truck gate.
Courtesy Marc Wanamaker, Bison Archives.

Director Fritz Lang (far left) with Edward G. Robinson and Bobbie Blake on the set of Nunnally Johnson's *The Woman in the Window*, 1945.
Courtesy Marc Wanamaker, Bison Archives.

Director John Cromwell with leads Herbert Marshall, Robert Young, and Dorothy McGuire between takes of *The Enchanted Cottage,* producer Harriet Parsons' first picture for RKO, 1945.

Courtesy of the Academy of Motion Picture Arts and Sciences.

Left to right: director Mervyn LeRoy, Louella Parsons, Claudette Colbert, RKO production head Charles Koerner, and Jesse Lasky during the filming of *Without Reservations,* 1945.

Courtesy of the Academy of Motion Picture Arts and Sciences.

24

Before the end of June 1942, Floyd Odlum took over the steering wheel of the battered show business machine that neither he nor his co-owners wanted but could not seem to get rid of. Peace was restored with the election of Peter Rathvon, Ned Depinet, and Charles Koerner; and although none of the posts carried contracts—all could be removed in the event of a sale—there was rejoicing in Hollywood.

"This new setup looks like the best RKO has ever had," *The Hollywood Reporter* raved. President Rathvon was regarded as a sound businessman, as capable of commanding Radio–Keith–Orpheum as the many large corporations he had served as counsel and officer through the years. Everyone agreed that the affable Ned Depinet, now heading RKO Radio Pictures, was not only one of the best-equipped film men in the industry but also had the appeal of a popularity-contest winner. As for Charlie Koerner, RKO's newest production chief, who, in the opinion of *Variety,* had stepped into "this hottest spot, probably, in the industry," he possessed the winning attribute: common-sense showmanship, gained during his twenty-five years of contact with the moviegoing public. New Orleans born, Koerner had been in the exhibition and theater-management end of the business almost exclusively since 1914, when he had begun operating a small movie house in Havre, Montana. From all evidence during his short stay at the studio, it was felt that the tall, gray-haired forty-five-year-old executive with the physique of a boxer and a friendly manner would put the company back where it belonged: in show business. As Koerner told the press: "When we decide to make a picture, I try to think of what the exhibitor can put up in his lobby to sell tickets."

"There's no 'genius' stuff about Mr. Koerner," the inevitable studio spokesman explained. The boss was like a businessman in the movie business. "Our production forces will be leveling off at only one major target, the exhibitor, and, through the exhibitor, the public!"

From the looks of things, it was felt that this new chief shared a few of the qualities of one of the studio's most successful leaders—Pan Berman. He appeared to have Berman's solid sense of the little major's limitations, and what was possible to achieve within its boundaries. Berman had always been concerned about doing the financially responsible thing. The unstable Schaefer regime had undercut Pan's smooth-running operation. Film production had been sporadic; toward the end there had been months when the stages were dark. The dearth of leading men, which forced postponement of a number of productions, had been so acute that in desperation Schaefer had tried to sell *Rio Rita,* the studio's big moneymaker of 1929, to MGM, hoping to obtain the stellar services of Robert Young, Robert Montgomery, and Jimmy Stewart in the deal. A year later, with its losing streak worsening, the studio sold both *Rio Rita* and *Cimarron,* its Academy Award winner, to MGM, but no male leads changed hands in the deal.

RKO had signed a number of promising young male players with the idea of giving them extensive buildups. Among them were Paul Henreid, who had attracted attention as the Gestapo agent in Fox's *Night Train* in 1940; Dennis O'Keefe, who appeared opposite Lucille Ball in RKO's *That's Right, You're Wrong*—bandleader Kay Kyser's screen debut in 1939—the Mercury Theater's Joseph Cotten, and Edmond O'Brien, a Berman discovery brought from the New York stage to play Maureen O'Hara's poet lover in *The Hunchback of Notre Dame.*

During his short stay at the studio, Koerner had set about stabilizing operations, aided by an influx of $3 million that Rathvon negotiated from Boston banking interests, and further working capital amounting to $2 million from unfrozen coin in Great Britain. Unlike his predecessor, there would be no disasters creeping up on him. Those "interesting film events," such as Gloria Swanson's ill-advised return to the screen, would find no place on RKO's $12 million program of forty-five features for 1942–43. Nor would the expensive Broadway hits that hadn't always panned out as screen material. Original stories tailored to what the canny theaterman knew the box office was crying for—war and service features to kindle the patriotic spirit of the home front, with direct appeal to servicemen on leave and war workers with fat pay envelopes—these types of films would dominate the new season's product.

Koerner fully expected to start erasing the red ink with three promising features currently on the production agenda: *The Navy Comes Through,* in which Pat O'Brien, George Murphy, Jackie Cooper, Max Baer, and Desi Arnaz would be hustling U-boats to the bottom of the Atlantic; *Seven Days' Leave,* to star Twentieth Century–Fox's Victor Mature (as the enlistee), Lucille Ball, and a raft of radio names; and another Pat O'Brien war feature, *Bombardier,* with fellow officer Randolph Scott and RKO's compliant contract-lead, Anne Shirley. Officially, grown-up Anne was now listed as one of RKO's "woman contractees," which placed her in the company of Ginger Rogers, the studio's most glowing asset, Maureen O'Hara, and Lucille Ball; but in reality she seldom stepped out of the programmer division. Ginger Rogers, now on a nonexclusive pact with RKO, had returned in triumph following the success of Billy Wilder's daffy comedy *The Major and the Minor,* made at Paramount. The studio announced that its top box-office star would costar with Cary Grant in a big-budget Leo McCarey comedy-drama, *Once Upon a Honeymoon.* Maureen O'Hara, whose contract was shared with Twentieth Century–Fox, had, of course, been catapulted into stardom by that studio's *How Green Was My Valley.* Lucille Ball, soon to be seen in an "emotional" role opposite Henry Fonda in Damon Runyon's *The Big Street,* after a spate of unchallenging B's, would shortly be leaving RKO. Lucy's seven-year pact, signed in 1941, had risen to $3,500 weekly. The "good commercial product" in the studio's bright future, Koerner realized, could be headlined by less expensive featured players. The dynamic redhead had already been announced for the Ethel Merman role in MGM's version of the Broadway hit *Du Barry Was a Lady.* It would be "the first on a definite MGM ticket," the trades had revealed in May.

Koerner's belief in the box-office pull of radio personalities led to increased emphasis on B pictures adapted to favorite "airer" stars. Harold "Great Gildersleeve" Peary, of the manic baritone giggle, smooth songstress Ginny Simms, Freddy Martin's and Les Brown's radio-famed bands, and two of radio's most popular programs, Ralph Edwards' "Truth or Consequences" and "The Court of Missing Heirs," would add to the general appeal of *Seven Days' Leave.* The smash business turned in by the Fibber–Molly–Bergen film *Look Who's Laughing,** one of 1941's most profitable productions, had proved that the multimillion radio audience would rather "escape" to Wistful Vista, radio habitat of Fibber McGee and Molly (Jim and Marian Jordan), and J. Throckmorton Gildersleeve than share Abe Lincoln's long-suffering prairie years in Illinois.

Lest anyone take his slogan "Showmanship in Place of Genius" lightly, Koerner took swift action against the enemy—in this case, the cinema's "eccentric" but "universal genius." Using the pretext that the space was urgently needed for Sol Lesser, who had been signed to make two Tarzan pictures, on July 1 Koerner ordered the Orson Welles Mercury Productions unit to vacate its offices on the Pathé lot. The news conveyed by *The Reporter* the next day in a story informally headlined RKO BOOTS WELLES UNIT OFF THE LOT hardly surprised Hollywood; therefore, the Wellesian response from Mercury officers Jack Moss and Herbert Drake, "We are Leonardo da Vinci, evicted from his draughty garret," brought a minimum of chuckles. As did Welles's telephone call of reassurance to his forlorn staff from Brazil where he was

*Starring Fibber McGee and Molly, Edgar Bergen and Charlie McCarthy, J. Throckmorton Gildersleeve, and Lucille Ball.

filming *It's All True:* "Don't get excited. We're just passing through a rough Koerner on our way to immortality." Even though Mercury attorney Lloyd Wright stressed that the order came "at a time when *Citizen Kane* has been judged one of the outstanding pictures in 1941... *The Magnificent Ambersons* is receiving unusually high praise from the critics" and emphasized the importance of the film work Welles was currently completing in Brazil, spelling out that he had gone at the request of the Washington Coordinating Office to make a picture in the interest of hemispheric solidarity, Hollywood was unmoved.

It had been known for some time that the heavily talented youngster was living on the edge of a volcano of his own making. Sure, he had created a memorial to little RKO—to the whole damned industry, for that matter! *Kane* was a hot textbook—its sensational use of new techniques were variously imitated on Hollywood sound stages. No one could argue, either, that at $686,000, Welles's movie masterpiece had not set a record for cost efficiency, despite the tales drifting off the lot that Welles had no possible conception, naturally, of economy, money, resources, talent, energy, space, or time. "None of them means anything to him, whether they are *his* for the disposal, or belong to somebody else," Mercury actor George Coulouris blabbed to the *New York Times*. The catch to *Kane* was that it had not earned its cost because it had yet to be booked by a major-chain distributor. As *Time,* a staunch Welles defender, pointed out: "Most moviegoers have never been given a chance to see *Kane*."

Ultimately, Welles had failed to heed the line that guarded the Studio System from a perilous border, beyond which lay freedom of self-expression. Thus, George Schaefer's boy wonder had fast deteriorated into the new regime's "bad boy" who would have to be dumped.

The tip-off had come in a poetic *Reporter* headline the previous March 6. WELLES SO TIRELESS, CUTS AMBERSONS BY WIRELESS brought an exchange of knowing glances from those who knew the score. "Orson Annie" was overreaching himself, behaving like a super-genius. He had toted a print of *Ambersons* down to Rio and had actually thought that he could edit it over the telephone with cutter Robert Wise in Hollywood.

On April 16, the trade paper reported that the studio was "putting several un-Orson touches into retakes on *Ambersons,* while Welles works in Rio." The "un-Orson touches" triggered a dispute, while the references to "work" brought laughter, since everyone knew that upon arriving in Rio, the flamboyant Welles had abandoned himself to the bacchanalian spirit of carnival-time, while directing his second units to film the excitement of the samba-ing crowds converging on the city and gyrating through its cobbled streets. An expensive fleet consisting of two chartered planes carrying cinematographer Harry J. Wild, cameramen Eddie Pyle and Harry Wellman, Technicolor specialist W. Howard Greene, and four Technicolor cameras, plus twelve other planes loaded with equipment had flown down ahead. A ship carrying additional materials arrived later.

Schaefer had warned Welles to hold the cost of *It's All True* to $600,000, but Welles, carried away by the carnival experience, decided to enlarge the scope of his theme. Wellesian second units trekked into the steaming jungle to trace the source of the samba rhythms. Then Welles staged additional carnival scenes in a Rio theater, and a carnival extravaganza in the biggest studio in the city. And in mid-May Schaefer was jolted by the news that Welles had already spent $526,867 and that another $595,000 would be required to finish the documentary.

Ironically, Welles was working for nothing, receiving neither salary nor percentage. That famous contract, which guaranteed him $150,000 against 25 percent of the profits, had been "adjusted" the previous summer, and Welles had made his last two pictures as a hired hand. But shortly after his arrival in Hollywood, to the dismay and anger of industry agents, he had agreed, as a gesture, to do a free picture for RKO, and the company had held him to it.

True to form, Welles refused to permit any changes on his faithful adaptation of Booth Tarkington's 1918 prize-winning novel, insisting that *The Magnificent Ambersons* be released the way he wanted. But the Welles version, more than two hours long, had played badly at sneak previews. George Schaefer, in the last days of his reign, had faced in Pomona an onslaught of irreverent moviegoers who had hooted and talked back at the screen. With $1.125 million tied up in *Ambersons,* Schaefer, disregarding Welles, who no longer had the right of final cut, had prescribed retakes and cuts that would give the picture a commercial ending and bring it down to the double-bill length of eighty-eight minutes.

"RKO breaks out in a cold sweat whenever Joe Cotten goes near a studio phone," *The Reporter* informed Hollywood on April 21. "He calls Welles in Rio to tell him what goes with *Ambersons* and *Journey Into Fear.*" The latter picture had also been confiscated by the studio and was being edited without Welles's supervision.

Meanwhile, the town buzzed with tales of Welles's wild behavior in Brazil. It wasn't until mid-July, however, that *The Reporter* alluded to some of his antics, which it suggested would probably cause considerable embarrassment to his sponsors, the Rockefeller group, in its attempt to establish better relations between the Americas. "It seems that Orson did a Lee Tracy down there, not once but on several occasions, resulting in his being tossed into jail for a matter of hours. Too, he delighted in the prank of throwing every highball glass out the window, once he finished his drink," the item concluded with plenty of etceteras.*

*Lee Tracy, who played fast-talking, crack reporter, and other aggressive types in both lead and supporting roles, was also well known for his drunken behavior off screen. In one well-publicized

To insiders, this read like an anticlimax. The worst mishap had befallen Welles several months earlier, receiving wide news coverage but strangely enough overlooked by the vigilant trade press. An accident during the filming of a battle between a shark and an octopus, by one of Welles's second units off the coast of Rio, had resulted in the death of a native taking part in the sequence. The man had been spilled from his unwieldy sailing craft (called a *jangada)*, caught in a treacherous current, and swallowed by the sea. But days later, when a 440-pound shark caught off Barra da Tijuca was opened, "there rolled out," said *Time* graphically, "a decomposed head and two half-devoured arms," the dubious remains—unfortunately for Welles—of a national hero.*

Manoel Olimpio Meira, called "Jacaré" (alligator), had become the modern savior of Brazil's poverty-stricken *jangadeiros,* "share-cropping" fishermen, after sailing 1,650 miles with three comrades on the flimsy *jangada* they used for seining fish, without benefit of a compass, from Fortaleza south around the hump of Brazil, all the way to Rio, to tell President Getulio Vargas about their sad plight. By the time they reached the presidential palace, the press had made them famous, and the astute dictator granted the *jangadeiros* full union rights and pensions. Intrigued by their exploit, Welles signed Jacaré and his three companions. He had decided to adapt his carnival episode, which he had already augmented with a colorful history of the samba, to include their story.

After hearing the news of Jacaré's death, Welles, deeply distressed, dedicated his unfinished film to "An American hero." But the repercussions were felt in Washington and Hollywood. In its aftermath, his film company lost its hold on Brazilian sympathies. Early in June, the trade press reported that the Welles crew had shrunk from twenty-eight to three, and the final scenes of *It's All True* were being shot by only one cameraman. Members of the crew who had been recalled to Hollywood by order of Charles Koerner told how they had been afraid to venture into the streets of Rio after the death of Jacaré, while Welles with his crew of three (his faithful assistant Richard Wilson, Wilson's wife, Elizabeth, and his secretary) impetuously journeyed to Fortaleza, Jacaré's home town, to complete the episode left unfinished by his death. Instead of being met by a lynch mob, they were actually well treated by the primitive community of fishermen, who assisted Welles in his effort to record the daily life of the *jangadeiros*. For its part, RKO's Brazilian office inserted a formal ad in prominent newspapers serving notice that it was not responsible for "any acts committed by Orson Welles in Brazil."

Tragically, the footage of *It's All True,* which had been flown back from South America by every available express, turned out to be an editing

escapade, he was said to have urinated onto a parade from his hotel balcony in Mexico.

† *Time,* June 8, 1942.

nightmare that had no end. Welles had attempted several scripts, rashly tossed them aside, and decided to film his picture first and worry about continuity and dialogue later. "My film will be comprehensible to the eye and not necessarily the ear of the audience," Welles had explained in a May 5 press release. "It will be a polyglot movie, completely understandable, no matter what the language of the audience... It will not be necessary to be able to read to understand."

In mid-August, Welles slipped into Hollywood and tried to salvage his incompleted film. The Office of Inter-American Affairs had pledged $300,000 to RKO against loss on completion. After investigating the facts in a closed budget session of the House Committee on Appropriations the following summer, Nelson Rockefeller and Francis Alstock, the new director of the Coordinating Office's motion picture division, reneged. The movie that Welles had intended for "all the people of all the Americas" was committed, in its unfinished state, to the studio vault, together with footage from another Welles project—the incompleted Mexican story, entitled *My Friend Bonito,* which director Norman Foster had started before taking over *Journey Into Fear.*

It was too late for Welles to salvage *The Magnificent Ambersons* when he returned to the States. It had already opened in tandem with a lowbrow Lupe Velez comedy, *Mexican Spitfire Sees a Ghost.* Welles rushed to a theater to see what "the Savage of Gower Gulch" had done to him. He later emerged shaking his fist at the studio's bourgeois mentality, commenting, "It looks as though somebody had run a lawn mower through the celluloid."

A handful of critics disagreed with his harsh appraisal. Obviously motivated by the need to separate Welles's work from Hollywood's run-of-the-studio product, *Time*'s young intellectual James Agee stopped short of pronouncing *Ambersons* another *Citizen Kane* but nevertheless thought it "a magnificent movie" that continued Welles's "important exploration" of new cinema technique—the "novel use of side-lighting and exaggerated perspective" that had lifted *Kane* from the ranks. "It has all of *Kane*'s rich technique," he said of Stanley Cortez's camera work. But, like the *New York Time's* young Tom Pryor, who also dwelled on *Ambersons'* magnificence, Agee pointed out the consequences of Welles's refusal to meet his audience halfway. The film was almost humorless, almost without physical action, its subject matter a character study of a declining American Midwestern dynasty during the formal 1880s and the coming of the motor age, and it did seem that Welles was asking too much of wartime moviegoers. Final damaging praise came from the *Los Angeles Times's* Edwin Schallert, who felt that *Ambersons'* "philosophical comments on the effects of the advent of the automobile" almost entitled it to the description "epical."

In a quandary, RKO advertising tried various approaches to deliver itself from this arty evil. Early poster displays emphasized the prestige of the Orson Welles name. But the ads concentrated on minor sensationalism: "Scandal played no favorites when that high-and-mighty Amberson girl fell in love once too often!"

Welles suffered the final humiliation at the hands of Hollywood with the release of his third film. "Suspense is there, so is confusion. That's *Journey Into Fear,*" *The Reporter* decreed. Welles had played a small role in the Eric Ambler thriller before rushing off to South America, and he had also collaborated with Joseph Cotten on the screenplay. Nearly all the trade critics agreed with *The Reporter.*

Koerner reacted promptly by pulling *Journey Into Fear* out of the first 1942–43 block of pictures, which included a Herbert Wilcox British production, *Wings and the Woman,* starring Anna Neagle and Robert Newton; Damon Runyon's *The Big Street,* with Henry Fonda and Lucille Ball; and two uncertain programmers, *Highways by Night,* with Richard Carlson and Jane Randolph, and Lupe Velez's *Mexican Spitfire's Elephant.* While waiting for a strong block in which to sell the weak product, he permitted Welles to shoot a new ending to his film. Meanwhile, Koerner demonstrated his commonsense showmanship by replacing *Journey Into Fear* with *Here We Go Again.* The Fibber–Molly–Bergen combination, he knew, was a box-office natural.

25

"The next time some political windbag shoots off his big mouth in Washington about the movie industry, ask him what the hell he's doing for the boys out here in New Guinea, at Guadalcanal, at Munda, and the other fighting fronts, who are fighting and dying to win this war against the Japs. We know what Hollywood is doing. And those sanctimonious patriots so swift to smear any man who happens to be an actor, let them take our word for it that an actor like Rooney or Bogart can do a million times as much good mugging in front of a camera as he can behind a gun.... There is something tragically beautiful about that real soldier boy shedding real tears over the make-believe soldier who is bleeding real tomato catsup." So wrote correspondent Art Cohn in the summer of 1943, in a report direct from the South Pacific and picked up by the Hollywood trade papers. It was sweet music to the studio chieftains again on the receiving end of the taunts and jibes from Washington bigwigs, and the prejudice and misinformation generated by Colonel Robert McCormick's *Chicago Tribune.*

The government had allowed the movie industry, because of its essential nature, to stay in business, and Hollywood had shown its gratitude a thousandfold. In proportion to the number of studio workers "sacrificed" to the armed services and defense plants, purchase of war bonds and stamps, contribution to service and civilian morale, could any other industry outshine Hollywood's war record?

The little major's sacrifices had been made public at RKO's 1942 sales convention. Board member Richard C. Patterson unveiled a plaque listing the names of 385 of its employees then in the armed forces. Sadly, the studio's Service flag carried three gold stars. They were for Harry Oldham, out of construction, killed serving as a ferry pilot, Weldon McNichols of the labor crew, cut down from the Army Air Force, and ex-reader Billy Lynn, who had been valiantly flying a bomber over Germany.

At its sales convention the following year, Radio–Keith–Orpheum's new chairman of the board, Floyd Odlum, conveyed his pride in the stability and strength of the industry in this period of heavy war activity. "The picture companies are getting film to carry on,"* he told the delegates, "because pictures are filling a real need, helping morale, helping build up production, helping the man at the front...."

The industry would shortly be assisting President Roosevelt launch the $15 billion third war loan drive. Plans were underway for hundreds of their exhibitors in theaters in every city to interrupt their screen shows to broadcast the president's message. Hollywood had assumed responsibility for the first forty-five minutes of this projected four-network patriotic extravaganza. Stars thankfully not yet in uniform, such as Bing Crosby, Gary Cooper, Humphrey Bogart, Robert Young, Don Ameche, Charles Boyer, George Murphy, Edgar Bergen, Burns and Allen, and Dinah Shore, would be heard in a series of dramatic sketches highlighting the war to date. James Cagney, president of the Screen Actors Guild, speaking in Washington, would then place the Hollywood Bond Cavalcade and the entire resources of the movie industry at the disposal of the secretary of the treasury, Henry Morganthau Jr. At this stirring moment—the show's climax—the president would speak for ten minutes, calling for "a rededication to the war aims of the United Nations, and for maximum sacrifices"—the war was presently costing the U.S. $200,700 per second—"to hasten an early and decisive victory." Members of the Hollywood Cavalcade at the president's side during the broadcast would include the cream of Hollywood: Greer Garson, Judy Garland, Fred Astaire, Lucille Ball, Olivia de Havilland, Kathryn Grayson, Harpo Marx, Dick Powell, Betty Hutton, and Mickey Rooney.

Yet the Senate Special Committee investigating the war effort in 1943 was responding to Hollywood's patriotic efforts with accusations of various improprieties. Led by Senator Harry S. Truman, the committee brazenly asked

*When Odlum said "film," he meant raw stock.

how some of the brave studio bosses had wangled their officers' commissions, and it delved into the extent of their profits from the military training films they were so expertly turning out for the government on a profit-free basis. Colonel Darryl F. Zanuck, in particular, was singled out. The committee was unhappy that the young Twentieth Century–Fox mogul had not removed himself from the studio payroll while "proving his mettle"—*The Reporter*'s expression—on commando raids. Moreover, he had had the effrontery, in the committee's opinion, to appear in a documentary about the North African campaign, *At the Front in North Africa,* and with the war still raging, had requested inactive status and returned to making Hollywood movies, a smart move in the opinion of his fellow moguls. For wasn't this the job he did best?

The committee grumbled about their monopolizing government work and freezing out the small producers. It was true that the moguls had set up a special Hollywood committee to handle the allotment of government contracts and divided the work among themselves. RKO received a little more than $100,000 from the Army Pictorial Division in 1941 and 1942, as much as MGM, but far less than Paramount or Twentieth Century–Fox, before the Truman Committee enforced competitive bidding. But could they be blamed for wanting to keep their costly movie factories intact, wartime economy or not?

Most distressing was the insinuation of the Truman Committee's Senator Ralph O. Brewster that "recent citizens," such as Russian-born director Anatole Litvak, should be excluded from the cinema battlefront. In his opinion, only "seasoned citizens" were suitable candidates for Signal Corps film jobs. Brewster's views reminded the moguls of the Senate smear campaign of a couple of years back, when they had gone against Will Hays's appeasement policy and their friend Kennedy's advice and talked back to the subcommittee investigating warmongering in the movies. At that time, Senator Nye's attack on their films had embraced the moguls he considered responsible for what Americans viewed when they went to the movies. Those he mentioned were Jews; one fell into the unpopular category of foreign-born.

Their industry now ranked after farming, automobiles, and steel, in importance. Yet the Washington hunting pack had lost none of its appetite for the jugular. The Will Hays jaunts between Hollywood, New York, and the nation's capital no longer seemed to produce results. Their own W. R. "Billy" Wilkerson, *The Reporter*'s intrepid editor, had made it official: "Will Hays is now as dead politically as the Harding administration which spawned him."* Wilkerson had overheard a rumor in Washington that the movie business was going to be "the patsy of this war." And to some industry insiders, this bore the ring of truth. For although the moguls had been given the green light to

***The Hollywood Reporter,* August 23, 1943.

conduct their business of making, distributing, and exhibiting pictures, this could, indeed, serve a sinister purpose. Wilkerson warned that it was to shield the "real plans and motives" that many leftist administration leaders had for the postwar period. The moguls knew that some form of theater divorcement was coming which would prevent them from owning and operating any theaters, an action certain to hamper industry progress and place them in a vulnerable position. According to the Washington source, taking the control of the industry away from the companies that built it, to serve as political fodder for those who now wanted to change the whole world, would be "like taking candy from a baby."

Nonetheless, the second year of the war found the industry essentially preoccupied with the problems at hand: raw stock restrictions and shortages of male personnel, material, and equipment. The little major's loss of manpower to the armed services had risen to 867, including thirteen women. Key technicians were being replaced by assistants, or men hurriedly trained, resulting in delays and extra costs in production. However, the moguls adopted a tight-lipped attitude toward their troubles, and whenever the press bore down on them, the stock phrase was, "The studio has adjusted to the problem."

The first crack in the European market had followed the Allied advances in Sicily and Italy in the summer and fall, when Hollywood films were again shown in Italian theaters. And in the past year, the Soviet market, which received not more than twelve Hollywood movies in the last decade, had been officially opened to American motion pictures.

On the home front, exhibitors reveling in the tremendous box office awaiting anything on celluloid experienced a glut in, of all things, war films. RKO's crop, although rapped by the majority of critics, had figured high among Charlie Koerner's initial money-makers. Glowing endorsements of *The Navy Comes Through* evoked a nostalgic recollection among veteran distributors of the manner in which the Astaire–Rogers product had been greeted across the country. One delirious theater man in Milford, Iowa, wrote in January 1943: "This is the kind that helps pay off my second mortgage. A whiz of a title. The patrons won't kick, and it brings them in, gas or no gas."

Concerning war propaganda features, the RKO studio chief asserted that "war films will continue to be made in the future, if the material warrants it." Two, inherited from the Schaefer regime, were expected to spell big money. *Hitler's Children,* released early in the year, starred Tim Holt, the studio's versatile Western star, former child player Bonita Granville, and Kent Smith and was loosely based on Gregor Ziemer's factual book *Education for Death.* In fact, 50 million copies of the Reader's Digest condensation had been dropped over the conquered countries of Europe by the United Nations, while Edward Dmytryk, a former cutter turned director, was shooting the movie in the fall of 1942. A co-production deal with producer Edward A. Golden, the project had been rescued by Koerner when the banks refused to finance the producer. Indulging in a Koerner praise-fest on August 18, 1943, *The Reporter* avowed that "Charlie Koerner's showmanship brain demanded that the RKO treasury be scraped for the making of this idea show" and predicted that the sensational feature, which had cost $205,000 to make, would do better than $3 million in the U.S. alone.

The gruesome *Behind the Rising Sun,* starring Margo, Tom Neal, and J. Carroll Naish, also directed by Edward Dmytryk, followed in the fall. Hyped as the "first drama to unmask the Japs," it was judged "serious rather than sensational" by the *New York Times,* which had labeled *Hitler's Children* conventional melodrama. For though the picture featured terrifying scenes of tortures and horrors, Emmet Lavery's script dared to present some of the Japanese characters in a sympathetic light, risking criticism, *The Reporter* suggested, from some Americans "who hold that all Japs, without exception, are evil."

Koerner was receiving as much recognition and praise for an imaginative series of low-budget horror movies that were the contribution of a small, close-knit unit headed by a gifted new producer, Val Lewton. Handed lurid, exploitable titles that had been pre-tested on audiences—*Cat People, I Walked with a Zombie, The Leopard Man,* and others—Lewton challenged himself and his talented crew to come up with stylish little movies that would substitute subtle psychological undertones for violence.

It was 1943, and now Frank Sinatra, the King of Swoon, had arrived in Hollywood and reported to RKO producer Tim Whelan for his role in *Higher and Higher,* announced in August as his first on a three-picture deal. The scrawny young crooner had propelled his fans into shrieks of ecstasy at the Pasadena station, and the jaded press into making comparisons with Valentino. Frankie would soon be making his debut as a film personality.

Another promising debut was in sight for Louella's daughter, Harriet Parsons, whose first assignment as a producer on her new RKO contract had just been announced. At thirty-six, the petite producer had paid her dues, grinding out more than a hundred short subjects in the past ten years at Columbia and Republic, and one feature for Republic, *Joan of Ozark* in 1942, starring Judy Canova and Joe E. Brown. Now she would start to prepare a remake of the British dramatist Sir Arthur Wing Pinero's sensitive love story *The Enchanted Cottage,* a property she had discovered while rummaging in RKO's files.

By the mid-forties, Charlie Koerner's formula for bringing the studio out of the red had paid off: President Rathvon was able to report profits of Radio–Keith–Orpheum totaling close to $7 million for 1943, compared with

$736,241 the previous year, when the popular executive had taken over. Furthermore, RKO Radio Pictures was credited for the extraordinary increase in earnings. The company had held much of the financial ground it gained: $5.2 million in 1944, and $6 million in 1945, the year when shattering war gave way to the complicated readjustments of peacetime.

With the studio well out of reach of the sheriff and bolstered by a new seven-year contract as executive vice president, Koerner veered from his established course. Declaring in July 1944 that "It's part of our responsibility to take some chances," he endorsed some artistic projects. Rosalind Russell was set to portray Elizabeth Kenny in a bio of the strong-willed Australian nurse, commonly known as Sister Kenny, who defied the medical establishment in the treatment of polio. Tamara Toumanova, "dancing star" of the Ballet Russe de Monte Carlo, and Gregory Peck, fresh from the New York stage, made initial screen appearances in *Days of Glory,* a war epic in which both died heroically and uncommercially at the end. The film marked the first producing assignment of major screenwriter, Casey Robinson. Playwright Clifford Odets took over the megaphone for the poetic, downbeat *None but the Lonely Heart,* which daringly cast Cary Grant as the Cockney drifter Ernie Mott and marked the triumphant return to the screen of Ethel Barrymore after an absence of twelve years.

Another important releasing deal, announced in January 1944 with "International Pictures," a powerful new independent company piloted by L. B. Mayer's son-in-law, William Goetz, and former RKO president Leo Spitz, brought additional prestige. *Casanova Brown,* a comedy written and produced by Nunnally Johnson and starring Gary Cooper and Teresa Wright, would be their first production.

In the spring of 1945, with Hollywood ruptured by labor strife that bore the taint of Communism, Harriet Parsons' otherworldly *Enchanted Cottage* finally reached the screen. There had been endless delays. Koerner had tried to control the project by handing over Parsons' treatment to a distinguished French director, Jean Renoir, and writer Dudley Nichols, recently turned producer. The two had been responsible for 1943's thoughtful and inspiring anti-Nazi drama *This Land Is Mine,* which had starred Charles Laughton, Maureen O'Hara, George Sanders, and Walter Slezak. Only the quick action of her mother's rival, Hedda Hopper, who dashed off a column in Harriet's defense that lambasted the studio bosses, saved her budding career. By evening of the day Hedda's crusading column appeared, Harriet had *Enchanted Cottage* back. But Koerner, who must have had reservations about what he regarded as the limitations of her sex, assigned an executive producer, Jack Gross, to supervise her projects, placing her in his unit. Finally, Harriet had to bite her tongue while "A John Cromwell Production" was placed before her name on the screen. A few realists, like the *New York Times*'s Bosley Crowther,

Frank Nugent's distinguished successor, who had also failed to see the poetry in Val Lewton's initial chiller-drama, *Cat People,* remained unmoved by the story of the disfigured war pilot, played by Robert Young, and the homely girl, Dorothy McGuire, whose love transfigures them in each other's eyes. Most reviewers found it meaningful and exhalted in motive, scripted skillfully by DeWitt Bodeen and Herman Mankiewicz, and directed feelingly by John Cromwell. Mindful of Harriet's warning, "Mother, please if you go overboard on me, you're going to hear from me," Louella tried to restrain her pride. "... I know if anyone other than my daughter produced this tender, beautiful love story, I would have wanted to urge you to see a film in which the emotions are so fine, the drama so poignant, that it reaches right into your heart."

Following the end of the war in August 1945, Charlie Koerner traveled to Europe to survey the foreign market and meet with the British film magnate J. Arthur Rank on a joint production deal. The bewildering executive shifts that had clouded the little major's past had finally ceased. In fact, so solid was the present administration that on one occasion when a visitor on the RKO lot asked, "What does RKO stand for?" she was informed, "It means Rathvon, Koerner and Odlum."

The rehabilitation of the affairs of the corporation and its subsidiaries had been most gratifying to Floyd Odlum. His Atlas was now the only substantial stockholder in Radio–Keith–Orpheum, both RCA and the Rockefeller interests having disposed of their stock in the company. In April 1943, the *Herald* reported that RCA had sold its entire remaining holdings for close to $7 million.

RKO's Christmas offering to a world at peace was Leo McCarey's *The Bells of St. Mary's,* starring Bing Crosby as Father O'Malley and Ingrid Bergman as Sister Superior. A co-production with McCarey's Rainbow Productions, the result of Koerner's deal-making prowess, it opened with the strength of *King Kong*. But Koerner was unable to savor its success, for he had been suddenly stricken with acute leukemia.

On February 2, 1946, the executive who had shepherded the studio through three-and-a-half years of profitable and popular filmmaking was gone. He would be mourned.

PART EIGHT

THE POLITICAL STUDIO: THE ODLUM-SCHARY ADMINISTRATION, 1946-1948

Dore Schary (right
on location at Petaluma
north of San Francisco
for his production of *The Farmer's
Daughter*, which won an Oscar for
Loretta Young, left
Courtesy Marc Wanamaker, Bison Archives

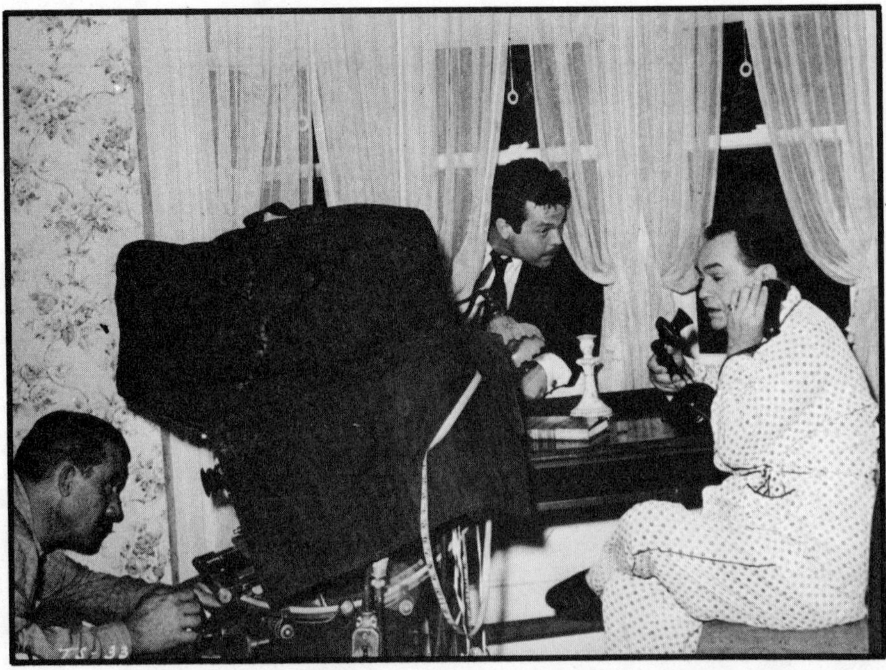

Orson Welles directs Edward G. Robinson in *The Stranger*, an International Production for RKO release, 1946. Welles starred as an escaped Nazi war criminal.
Courtesy Marc Wanamaker, Bison Archives.

RKO president Peter Rathvon, former RKO production head David Selznick, and new production chief Dore Schary (left to right) at a party hosted by Rathvon for Schary, 1947.
Courtesy Marc Wanamaker, Bison Archives.

Floyd Odlum negotiating the sale of RKO to Howard Hughes from the swimming pool of his ranch in the desert near Indio, California, 1948.
Courtesy Marc Wanamaker, Bison Archives.

Cathy O'Donnell and Farley Granger on the set of *They Live by Night,* Nicholas Ray's directorial debut, 1948.
Courtesy of the Academy of Motion Picture Arts and Sciences.

26

Hollywood had lost its heart to "lovable Charlie Koerner," as Louella called him in a eulogistic column, and shock waves passed through the community when the word came. At forty-nine, the executive seemingly born to success was dead. On Tuesday, February 5, 1946, the home office closed at 2:30 P.M. so that Radio–Keith–Orpheum's employees could pay their respects at the same time the funeral service was taking place in Hollywood. The studio had been closed all day, and, as Louella noted, the grief of everyone, from the most humble employee to Koerner's closest aides, demonstrated the affection the entire work force felt for their fallen chief. The list of honorary pallbearers read like a who's who of the movie industry. L. B. Mayer, Harry Cohn, Jack and Harry Warner, Walt Disney, Darryl Zanuck, Sam Goldwyn, Jesse Lasky, David Selznick, RKO's "Big Three"—Floyd Odlum, Peter Rathvon, Ned Depinet—and at least thirty others buried their hatchets and joined in honoring one of their own.

Then, indulging in that time-honored ritual of postmortem praise, the movie colony paid tribute to Koerner's memory. "Charlie had such a capacity for friendship. If he had any enemies, no one ever heard about them," wrote Louella. "Few men in our industry would be missed more than Charlie Koerner will," remarked Hedda with her usual candor. His aides recalled that he never let the importance of his job overwhelm him. He had been accessible to the lower echelons, and he made it his business to understand their problems. His sense of humor never deserted him. Stars who worked on the lot remembered his charm and generosity. None had started a picture without a bouquet of flowers and a personal note of good wishes from the studio boss. Said Pat O'Brien, the Irish seer: "RKO will die without him," or words to that effect.

But Odlum, above all, anxious to avoid an air of crisis at the studio, acted promptly, engineering what *The Reporter* called "the greatest elective officer shakeup in the history of RKO." President Rathvon moved to the West Coast to take active charge of production and assumed Ned Depinet's post of president of RKO Radio Pictures, while the responsible Depinet became chief executive in New York. A further reshuffling of the theater subsidiary and the home office appeared to justify *The Reporter*'s extravagant claim. The significance of Rathvon's transfer from New York to Hollywood hinged on Odlum's desire to retain the imposing list, which Koerner had built, of independent outfits turning out pictures for RKO release; for these days the studio's better product was being supplied by its "sharecropping" producers.

Walt Disney's latest Technicolor cartoon feature, *Make Mine Music,* would be arriving for Easter. Goldwyn offered his comic prize, Danny Kaye, in *The Kid from Brooklyn,* also for Easter release. Goldwyn's *The Best Years of Our Lives,* with an all-star cast, would be heading into New York for Thanksgiving. Said to be a labor of understanding and love from director William Wyler and writer Robert E. Sherwood, it dealt with the problems of veterans returning home from the war. Frank Capra of Liberty Films, back from the war, was preparing *It's a Wonderful Life* for James Stewart, another war veteran. Top entertainment was promised for spring from Jesse Lasky and his associate Walter MacEwen, who, with director Mervyn LeRoy, were delivering *Without Reservations,* a romantic comedy co-starring Claudette Colbert and John Wayne.

Hedda correctly prophesied in her column that RKO would not go outside the studio to replace the irreplacable Koerner. Said she: "His position will probably be filled by Bill Dozier, who's mighty smart, but very young for Charlie's job." True, the thirty-eight-year-old former talent agent who had served as Koerner's executive assistant for several years stepped into his shoes only briefly, because in May, the personable young executive eloped to Mexico City with actress Joan Fontaine, terminating his contract "by mutual consent and in a friendly fashion," then moved over to Universal–International.

In the ensuing months, Rathvon observed that a bright young producer, on loan from David Selznick, had made several exceptional pictures. Dore Schary, a former Academy Award–winning screenwriter, had come to the studio as part of an unusual package deal in which Selznick provided the properties, the stars, and Schary's services while RKO supplied the rest of the picture-making ingredients and split the profits. RKO had already reaped a financial harvest from an earlier agreement with Selznick that secured director Alfred Hitchcock for two films in 1941, the frothy *Mr. and Mrs. Smith* starring Carole Lombard and Robert Montgomery, and *Suspicion,* that year's most profitable picture, which earned Joan Fontaine an Oscar for her performance as the threatened wife of a dashingly dangerous Cary Grant. Hitchcock's current release, *Notorious,* a mystery melodrama co-starring Cary Grant and Ingrid Bergman, was well on its way to outstripping the latter film. Producer Dore Schary's *The Spiral Staircase,* a first-rate period thriller, elegantly directed by Robert Siodmak and starring Dorothy McGuire, George Brent, and Ethel Barrymore, was doing smash business as well. Schary's second production, *Till the End of Time,* made a big impression in its treatment of the plight of returning World War II vets—it featured Selznick's Guy Madison and RKO's Robert Mitchum and Bill Williams and caused *Daily Variety* to remark: "[The picture] is an achievement for Dore Schary from a production standpoint." Schary's third film on the lot, not yet released, was a romantic comedy entitled *Katie for Congress,* but nevertheless, with a strong point of view. In casting Swedish Katie, the Minnesota farmer's daughter who gets a notion to run for Congress, Selznick had had to veer from the obvious choice, Ingrid Bergman, who refused the role, to the petite skating star Sonja Henie, a lightweight actress whom Schary had refused to hire. He had held out for Loretta Young, who was not a Swede, had no Swedish accent, and was neither blonde nor robust. Schary was just as adamant about changing the title to *The Farmer's Daughter,* which Selznick considered vulgar.

Schary's reputation as a hard-nosed picture-maker, earned during his three years on Selznick's staff, was not lost on Rathvon. The studio jurisdictional strike, still a nagging thorn in Hollywood's side, was driving production costs through the ceiling. B pictures only looked cheap, while some A's now cost more than $2 million. To compound this problem, Rathvon noticed that the bulk of the features that RKO itself produced to round out its program were of inferior quality. As head of the B-picture unit at MGM, prior to working for Selznick, Schary had contributed a unique crop of low-budget successes. His creed, expressed to the press, that "there can be a happy blending of entertainment and a message," had been put to the test in *Joe Smith, American,* a realistic study of a war worker, *Pilot No. 5,* the first picture to talk about American Fascism, *Bataan,* one of the best early World War II movies, in which Schary daringly cast a Negro as one of the soldiers, and other pictures. Then Schary clashed with Mayer over a script he developed with novelist Sinclair Lewis; it was to be his first A picture on a new production deal.

Storm in the West proposed to tell the story of the rise of Fascism in terms of a Western, and with a cast of characters who bore uncanny resemblances to Hitler, Churchill, Mussolini, and Stalin. This was 1943. Such bits of business as the mention of a hammer and sickle in "Slavin's" wagon (a takeoff on Stalin) brought an anguished outcry from the New York office. Rather than surrender, Schary left the studio.

At thirty-eight he had a reputation of a maverick who did not like to take orders. He could be tough to deal with, L.B. said. But Rathvon, a cultured man with style and taste, found Schary warm and charming. The attractive six-footer, who looked something like a lovable bloodhound with glasses, had nothing of the cheap Brooklynese quality that Rathvon associated with so many producers, but rather a kind of university personality. It was hard to believe that this New Jersey–born son of Russian immigrants had struggled upward from the Borscht Belt to reach the Bel-Air circuit. He was bright to the point of brilliance, and he was eloquent. He spoke quickly and with an educated accent, and his conversation revealed an enormous compassion for humanity, a deep sense of social responsibility—concern with the world. Rathvon was well aware that Schary was extremely liberal, a dedicated Democrat, a worshiper of the late FDR. He knew that the old guard, the Republican right wing, regarded Schary with suspicion. But Rathvon eventually asked himself if this enlightened executive might not be the perfect heir to Koerner. Rathvon consulted Floyd Odlum; then he invited Schary to lunch.

Isadore "Dore" Schary walked through the RKO gate as vice president in charge of production on January 1, 1947. He had Selznick's unqualified blessing—"You'll do a hell of a job"—and the admiration and support of his peers. In countless writers' homes across Hollywood, telephones rang overtime; for Schary had fought their battles in the Screen Writers Guild and had been instrumental in obtaining their first contract with the producers. Along the Bel-Air circuit, where Schary's intellectual circle held its regular Sunday tennis games, wine glasses were lifted. One of their own, a writer, had made it to the top.

"Dore Schary rhymes in Hollywood with hoary sherry," said *Time*, cunningly distinguishing him from the haberdashers and bankers. In the Holy Tongue (Hebrew), Dore Schary meant "Gate to my Generation." In character, Schary told the press, shortly after taking office, that his mind was open to "new approaches and new styles.... I want to get off the beaten path. Most big successes have been made by producers who took a chance, starting from *Birth of a Nation,* and later *The Informer. The Razor's Edge,*" he said, referring to Twentieth Century–Fox's current hit, "is a spiritual picture and different. You're dealing more with an educated public today, and it's an insult to give them tripe and trash." With his air of quiet authority, this writer–turned–studio boss added: "We have come through troubled times recently, and the writer's point of view has remained as troubled and confused as our world. But my hunch is we are due for a flood of new and important stories about important things."

It was a prophetic statement, for one of the first scripts Schary read dealt with the ticklish subject of prejudice against Jews. The idea—a coldblooded murder motivated by the killer's anti-Semitic prejudices—had been adapted by writer John Paxton and writer-producer Adrian Scott from Richard Brooks's inflammatory 1945 first novel, *The Brick Foxhole,* in which the victim, being a homosexual, was thus an untouchable screen character. It had been Scott's dream to make a film about anti-Semitism on the home front, which he felt was an overwhelming global problem that had to be exposed, particularly in light of the recent Nazi horrors; it was his idea that the victim in Brooks's novel could be made a Jew.

As a creative team, Scott and Paxton, along with Edward Dmytryk, who wanted to direct the film, had established an enviable track record at the studio of two hits and no misses in the past few years. *Murder, My Sweet* had given that faded song-and-dance man Dick Powell a second acting career as Raymond Chandler's hardboiled hero Philip Marlow; it also marked the end of Anne Shirley's movie career. Anne had tried unsuccessfully to trade roles with tough, malevolent leading lady Claire Trevor but had had to settle for the softer role of Trevor's innocent daughter. A month before the picture opened at the Palace Theatre on March 8, 1945, Anne married her producer, young Adrian Scott, and bowed out of films. Scott, Dmytryk, and Paxton followed with *Cornered,* another taut, violent thriller that gave Powell further opportunity to display his "watch-me Bogart" attitude. They had recently completed an RKO–J. Arthur Rank co-production in England entitled *So Well Remembered,* based on the James Hilton novel.

Meanwhile, the option that Scott had taken on *The Brick Foxhole* ran out, and Scott and Dmytryk had to convince Rathvon to gamble $1000, the cost of renewal, on their enthusiasm. When Schary read the screenplay, he virtually made an overnight decision to put it into immediate production. He had lectured on anti-Semitism in Army camps during the war, where he witnessed and heard about incidents of violent bigotry. The vicious, Jew-hating G.I. murderer, Monty, in this script, tentatively titled *Cradle of Fear,* rang true. Schary's interest was stimulated by the knowledge that Darryl Zanuck had bought Laura Z. Hobson's current bestseller, *Gentleman's Agreement,* a genteel, parlor-version exposé of racial and religious prejudice; he wanted to beat it to the screen.

Although Rathvon agreed that Schary's project was "a suspenseful melodrama," he wrote to him that he doubted that it had any value "as a document against racial intolerance" and thought it "might backfire." Prejudiced Gentiles were not going to identify with the "despicable" Monty and so "feel ashamed of their prejudices. Rather they may be resentful, feeling we have distorted the problem by using such an extreme example of race hatred." Rathvon also felt that the script did not actually deal with the racial problem; it was injected "solely for the purpose of furnishing the killer with a motive." Rathvon's conclusion was: "I think it will do more harm than good." Ned Depinet cast his vote with Rathvon, citing depressing statistics from an audience-research-company poll he ordered that showed how small a percentage of moviegoers wanted to see this trailblazer.

But Schary regarded the film as an experiment—it was budgeted under $500,000—and in a matter of weeks, Adrian Scott's brainchild went into production with a hastily assembled cast headed by Robert Young as the police captain, Robert Mitchum as the G.I. informer, Robert Ryan as the rabid Jew-hater, Sam Levene as his victim, and Gloria Grahame as a dance-hall floozy. The terse, explicit title, *Crossfire,* was supplied by Schary. Dmytryk finished shooting in twenty-three days; only 200 feet of film was left on the cutting-room floor. Then came a series of previews for Jewish and Catholic groups, and others, utilizing the latest mechanical devices for testing audience reactions. The results seemed to indicate the need for drastic changes. Schary wavered briefly while Scott, Dmytryk, and Paxton sweated blood. But because of the urgency of getting *Crossfire* into release, it was saved from butchery.

Crossfire opened on July 22, 1947, at the Rivoli and grossed $8007, leading *The Hollywood Reporter*'s New York correspondent, Irving Hoffman, to remark: "There's your answer to whether the public wants to see stale stuff or a timely topic." Shaken from its impact, Cecilia Agar of *PM* wrote: "It feels fine, hearing at last 'Jewboy' and 'Jew' from the screen. It's like hard rain after a long-brooking thunderstorm. It clears the air, it spreads elation. With one clear blow, a long-festering, a sniveling, a contemptible movie taboo is smashed." With few exceptions, the critics crowded their reviews with tributes to the "heavily shaded" pictorial style of director Dmytryk, with its "moods of ominous peril," the "hot ferocity" of Paxton's script, and the superlative cast. Both *Life* and James Agee, writing in *The Nation,* tempered their praise, echoing Rathvon's thinking: By making the murdering sergeant "a villain of deepest dye," the filmmakers assured that audiences would be discouraged from disliking him "solely for being a Jew hater," pronounced *Life*. "He also becomes unbelievable...." Opening a can of worms, Agee pointed out: "This film is not entirely fearless, even with its relatively safe terms. They have the sardonic courage to preach the main [subject] to a Southern boy, taking painfully embarrassing care never to mention Negroes; but they lack the courage to make that omission inescapably clear to the audience."

Crossfire chalked up an all-time record during its twelve-week run at the Rivoli and was well on the way to grossing four times its cost. Its success strengthened Schary's determination to make other movies that took chances, "modestly budgeted but thoughtfully prepared vehicles containing *real* exploitation values": Robert Wise, former *Citizen Kane* editor, was set to direct *The Set-Up* as a starring vehicle for Robert Ryan; he promised a brutal and unromantic look at the dark world of hick-town boxing. Producer John Houseman, a former Orson Welles associate, was proceeding with a sordid crime story, tentatively titled *Your Red Wagon,* that he described as "a love story, also a morality story—in the tempo of our time," which meant that its point of view would be pessimistic and at the same time idealistic.* Houseman

*It would eventually carry the title *They Live by Night.*

had brought Nicholas Ray, with whom he had worked on Broadway, to the studio to direct it.

In August, Schary announced that *Crossfire*'s producer, Adrian Scott, would next tackle "a different type of movie" that would deliver "a message for bettering the world, and still entertain." The "different" title, which confounded everyone off the Bel-Air circuit, was *The Boy with Green Hair.* To direct, Schary selected Joseph Losey, who had just guided Charles Laughton in his stage production of *Galileo*. In the fall, *The Window,* a harrowing thriller, would commence shooting. Its director, Ted Tetzlaff, a well-known cameraman, had chosen the principal location, a condemned tenement block on East 105th Street in New York, for its shadowy, claustrophobic atmosphere. Twelve-year-old Bobby Driscoll, borrowed from Disney, would play the boy who "cries wolf," Arthur Kennedy his tenement father, and RKO's Barbara Hale, a member of the studio's actress stable since 1942, his housedress-clad mother.

Indeed, Schary felt that RKO's newer players suited these "adult" features to a T. Gritty and cynical Robert Ryan, weary and taciturn Robert Mitchum, and grimacing cobra Kirk Douglas looked at home on their ominous back streets, in their murky alleys and harshly lit interiors. The style and mood of this brave new screen world demanded luscious *femme fatale* Jane Greer, husky-voiced and honest Barbara Hale, sensitive and sincere Barbara Bel Geddes, and tough broad Gloria Grahame.

But Schary's satisfaction in getting the daring subject matter he believed in into production was short-lived. One morning he answered his buzzer to be greeted by two grim-faced strangers—investigators of the House Un-American Activities Committee. They informed him that Adrian Scott and Edward Dmytryk, *Crossfire*'s much-praised producer and director, were under investigation.

27

Red hysteria, masterminded by New Jersey Congressman J. Parnell Thomas of the House Un-American Activities Committee, had returned to Hollywood in the spring of 1947, this time with support from within the industry and in an atmosphere that gave credence to the committee's charges. The groundwork had been laid by the U.S. Chamber of Commerce in a 1945 report on "Communist Infiltration in the U.S." that warned of the inroads made by Communists in the entertainment media, in particular the Screen Writers Guild.

Ironically, the moguls had chosen the Chamber's president, Eric A. Johnston, to replace the aging Will Hays, who was "voluntarily" retiring. The new president of the MPPDA,* a lean, thin-faced, sharp-nosed man with a fixed smile, had taken office at a dignified and quiet meeting at the Association's Forty-fourth Street offices in New York on September 19 of that year. "We pass the throttle—and the brake," Hays had said, although he would still keep his advice available for a fee of $100,000 a year for five years. Johnston, who was receiving a salary of $150,000 a year and an expense arrangement for $50,000 annually, responded with "enlightened self-discipline a guarantee"—after which he went over to the Waldorf to lunch. Thus in March 1947, Johnston tried to sway the congressmen from the idea that Hollywood should get rid of any Communists it employed. Exposing them should be sufficient.

Hollywood had formed its own conservative group in 1944 to wage war on "the rising tide of isms" that sought "by subversive means to undermine and change this American way of life." Led by hard-nosed Red-baiters Sam Wood, the formidable producer-director of *For Whom the Bell Tolls,* and MGM executive James McGuinness, 200 "loyal" members of the industry had turned out for the first meeting of the Motion Picture Alliance at the Beverly Wilshire Hotel.

The anti-Communist front gained a convert from the top ranks when that hotheaded mogul Jack Warner stood on the roof of his studio in October 1945 and, with mounting anger, watched police battling, with tear gas and fire hoses, the pickets that threatened to bring Warner Brothers to a standstill. An even more violent strike the following fall stiffened his resolution to oppose the disruptive Commies who, he had been told, were causing the ferment. So, on October 20, 1947, Warner, joined by the conservative L. B. Mayer and Walt Disney, another strike victim, spoke for the moguls as "friendly" witnesses at the full-dress inquiry in Washington.

Before Dore Schary took the witness stand the second week of the hearings, and gave what *The Hollywood Reporter* pronounced "a ringing defense of Hollywood's Americanism," the committee had recommended eight out of ten "unfriendly" witnesses for contempt of Congress. To Schary's dismay, they included Scott and Dmytryk.† The furious thumping of Chairman Thomas's gavel prevailed; the witnesses' outbursts of defiance over the Bill of Rights were silenced. It did not matter that they refused to answer the question "Are you now or have you ever been a member of the Communist Party?" The committee was prepared to exhibit photostats of their membership cards. Cross-examination had been ruled out by the committee. Chairman Thomas, a

*After December, the Motion Picture Producers and Distributors Association became the Motion Picture Association of America (MPAA).

†The others were writers John Howard Lawson, Alvah Bessie, Albert Maltz, Dalton Trumbo, and Samuel Ornitz and writer-director Herbert Biberman.

pudgy, short-tempered man whom *The Nation* called "Undoubting Thomas," smashed his gavel to bits silencing attorney Charles J. Katz, who represented some of the accused writers, ordering him thrown out of the room when he demanded the right to question a "friendly" witness.

L. B. Mayer had testified earlier that he thought that rich screenwriters who followed the Communist Party line must be "cracked." Unhesitatingly, he named as suspect MGM family members Donald Ogden Stewart, Dalton Trumbo, and Lester Cole. Director Sam Wood willingly applied the word *Communist* to Stewart, Trumbo, and Lawson, but he did not stop there. Said this defender of American ideals: "These Communists thump their chests and call themselves liberals, but if you drop their rompers you'll find a hammer and sickle on their rear ends." Wood also aired his particular views on the subject of fund-raising for the Party. Mentioning a Hollywood gathering for Henry Wallace, President Roosevelt's former vice president, who was identified with the Communist Party, he confided that "Katharine Hepburn appeared and they collected $87,000. You don't think that money is going to the Boy Scouts, do you?"

Most of the "friendly" witnesses had been handpicked by Chairman Thomas the previous summer, and on the whole, they did not disappoint him. Director Leo McCarey, volunteering the reason why his hit movie *Going My Way* never played in Russia, explained: "I have a character in there they don't like." Was it Bing Crosby? he was asked. "No," replied McCarey, "God." Veteran actor Adolphe Menjou, by his own admission "a student of Marxism and Stalinism," proved he was an expert Red-baiter by his technique for uncovering them. Fingering his moustache and adjusting his profile to best advantage for the newsreel cameras, the dapper Menjou explained that "Anyone attending any meeting at which Paul Robeson appears, and applauds, can be considered a Communist." Ronald Reagan, president of the Screen Actors Guild, veered from the established stance to sound a note of warning: "I abhor the Communist philosophy, but...I hope we are never prompted by fear of Communism into compromising any of our democratic principles."

As the second week began, the Committee for the First Amendment, a delegation of liberal film stars, including Humphrey Bogart and Lauren Bacall, descended on the capital for a round of press conferences and radio broadcasts attacking Chairman Thomas and his committee. Pennsylvania Representative John McDowell assured Eric Johnston that the industry was coming out of the hearing with "a very fine reputation." Certainly, the nation's press was almost unanimous in its condemnation of the committee's contempt of First Amendment rights. But Chairman Thomas rejected his colleague's opinion. Earlier he had remarked that the industry had used a lot of "underhanded pressure" to get the investigation postponed or toned down. Now, he brusquely told

Johnston to "sit around next week. You'll see more exposing than you've ever seen before. Glamor girls and money will make no difference."*

RKO's liberal chief took the stand the following Wednesday, right after Scott and Dmytryk were benched for contempt. *The Hollywood Reporter,* calling it "the toughest position of the day," delivered Schary's positive statements to an apprehensive movie colony. "There never was a subversive American film made," Schary maintained. "Never saw Scott or Dmytryk ever try to put anything un-American into pictures." The great body of Hollywood's workers were "good, middle-of-the-road Americans," Schary insisted. To pointed questions by chief investigator Robert E. Stripling about RKO's policy regarding employment of Communists, Schary said he personally would refuse to ban writers branded Red by the committee until it was proved that they "are dedicated to the overthrow of the government by force or violence." Until such time, he maintained, he would continue to decide employment wholly on the basis of ability.

The next day, Chairman Thomas snared two more "unfriendlies," writers Ring Lardner Jr. and Lester Cole, and banged his gavel a final time. He had exhausted his evidence for the time being. The committee had failed to establish that the Hollywood Commies had ever planted any propaganda into movies, but it had promoted a climate of fear. And among the first to panic was the industry's own front man, Eric Johnston.

On Monday, November 24, fifty top-level industry chieftains, attended by a fleet of lawyers, met in a closely guarded fourth-floor suite in the Waldorf to ponder how best to rid themselves of the Red menace that threatened economic disaster. But the man scheduled to call the meeting to order had not arrived. On the eve of the hearings, Johnston had indignantly stated that he would "never be party to anything as un-American as a blacklist"†—words that would have to be swallowed in the council chamber of the Waldorf. When Nicholas Schenck, the president of Loew's, caught up with Johnston, he was on his way home to Spokane, Washington, for the Thanksgiving holiday; his flight put down in the Windy City and he was summoned to the telephone. Said Schenck: "Get right back to New York or hand in your resignation."

By Tuesday the capitulation was complete. An impatient crowd of newsmen, jammed into a hallway of the hotel, received from Tom Waller, MPAA publicity aide, a mimeographed announcement. "We deplore the actions of the ten Hollywood men who have been cited for contempt by the House of Representatives," the statement led off, referring to the overwhelming vote of Congress the previous day. "We will forthwith discharge or suspend without compensa-

**Time,* in covering the hearings, did its own detective work and found that Thomas had changed his name from J. Parnell Feeney after World War I and before entering Wall Street.

†Johnston quoted in Gordon Kahn, *Hollywood on Trial,* 1948.

tion those in our employ.... We will not knowingly employ a Communist...." At this point, some of the reporters wanted to know how the producers defined "Communist." Waller shrugged off the question. The reporters read on: "In pursuing this policy... frank to recognize... dangers and risks... danger of hurting innocent people... risk of creating an atmosphere of fear."

Faced with their greatest crisis, the scared studio chieftains had coerced the dissenters among them into uniting in an effort to salvage the picture business. There was no need to exercise their penchant for polls to forecast what would happen if the moviegoers' indignation over Communism in Hollywood reached epidemic proportions. And if the public vacillated, the American Legion, that bulwark of patriotism, would help make up its mind by throwing picket lines around the box office. Nineteen-forty-six had been the industry's biggest year, but it had been followed by an alarming decline in theater attendance. The lucrative foreign market was again slamming its doors against them, this time employing quota laws and special taxes. In August the British government had slapped a confiscatory 75 percent tax upon their film imports. With so much grim news, it was no wonder *The Reporter* lapsed into melodramatics—pleading with the industry to "put aside its family quarrels, forget its politics and unite in an effort to save this business that buys its bread and feeds its children."

Dore Schary had been forced to put aside his own personal convictions at the Waldorf meeting and follow the will of the majority. RKO had already announced that it would not employ known Communists; therefore, his hands were tied. He could do nothing but sit back and allow Scott and Dmytryk to be fired. He could, of course, make a grandstand play, quit his job in protest. But what would that accomplish? The damage had already been done. Besides, Schary liked the picture business. It was worth compromising his principles to carry on at RKO. So he convinced himself that by remaining at the studio he could fight against the blacklisting. As he told his tennis pals, some of whom were stunned by his apparent about-face, a living titan could be a more effectual combatant than an unemployed hero.

To Schary's embarrassment, *Crossfire* was being cited for awards by various institutions all over the country, and he had to collect them alone. Johnston obligingly accepted the Humanitarian Award from Philadelphia's Golden Slipper Club when Schary was forced to cancel his appearance. By the spring of 1948, *Crossfire* had garnered every possible award, it seemed, but the coveted Oscar. Although nominated for five Academy Awards, including the work of Scott, Dmytryk, and Paxton, it won none. Aided by the press, which aimed its big guns at *Crossfire*'s "Commie" connections, the Zanuck juggernaut *Gentleman's Agreement* smashed the low-budget competition, winning three Oscars. Schary's disappointment was overshadowed by the success of his own production of *The Farmer's Daughter;* for despite strong competition from Rosalind Russell for RKO's ponderous box-office flop *Mourning Becomes Electra,* Loretta Young won an Oscar, vindicating his belief in her.*

Harriet Parsons, meanwhile, was collecting tributes from the Hollywood press for the "George Stevens production" of *I Remember Mama.* In a replay of the *Enchanted Cottage* sabotage, RKO, without consulting her, had sold the stage right to Kathryn Forbes's 1943 novelistic reminiscences of her Norwegian immigrant family, *Mama's Bank Account,* which Harriet wanted to produce. Retitled *I Remember Mama,* the Rodgers and Hammerstein production, dramatized by John Van Druten, ran on Broadway for two years, starring Mady Christians as Mrs. Hansen. When Harriet was finally able to get the project moving again, Irene Dunne agreed to play "Mama" only if the autocratic genius George Stevens directed, and Stevens refused to make the film unless he received executive producer credit. By then, Harriet had invested too much time, love, and effort on the project to let anything stand in the way, so she agreed.

Stevens's unfaltering control of the directorial reins stretched the picture's normal shooting schedule to eight months. Harriet was powerless to halt the runaway budget, because Schary had too much "respect" for the formidable Stevens to clip his wings. After several attempts to enlighten the front office, Harriet rolled with the punches, knowing that the movie's excessive negative cost† would wreck its chances of profit.

By the time the overlong but "warm, flowing motion picture" that the critics found "glowing with affection" reached the Music Hall for Easter 1948, a major change was brewing behind the scenes at RKO. Floyd Odlum, the business seer who had engineered the little major's recovery, was ready to sell out—at a profit.

Atlas's big investment in Radio–Keith–Orpheum fell under the category of "special situations" in the company's portfolio. For, as Odlum explained in one of his infrequent interviews: "If we think we can find the reason why a company has slipped, we'll go in for any amount—and for the long pull." It had been a good thirteen years since Odlum and Lehman first dipped into RCA's holdings in the ailing movie company. In 1940, when the new Radio–Keith–Orpheum began to operate, freed from the court supervision, the future had looked promising. Despite the financial crisis in 1942, when Odlum had had second thoughts about staying on the movie roller coaster, the company prospered. Actually, the war had been its salvation. By 1946, Odlum had increased RKO's return on its invested capital from .8 percent to 16.9 percent. That was the year that RKO's profits soared above $12 million. That banner year, Odlum sold 650,000 shares of RKO common stock to a group of underwriters headed by Lehman Brothers and Goldman Sachs. But he pointed

*See references on page 232.

†The cost of the picture alone, before distribution and other charges are added.

out that Atlas would still retain an $18 million "active interest" in company affairs. "This distribution means only that Atlas considers the task which it set out for itself in 1935, in connection with the rehabilitation of RKO, has been completed, and that as a consequence, Atlas must in the natural course of its own business, reduce its holdings," Odlum said. He added that Atlas's remaining holdings in RKO would constitute "the largest single holding" in its portfolio.

The following year, 1947, RKO's profits plummeted to just over $5 million. The company was heading down a perilous road again—at its end loomed a corporate graveyard. Odlum had been dismayed by the Thomas Committee's investigation of Hollywood. He feared the consequences of theater divorcement. And then there was the potential threat of television. RCA's Brigadier General David Sarnoff had retracted his habitual phrase "television is around the corner." Now he was diligently proclaiming: "It is beyond the doorstep! It has pushed its way through the door into the home."

On July 4, the *New York Times* confirmed reports that Radio–Keith–Orpheum's president Peter Rathvon, and an unnamed Wall Street syndicate were negotiating for purchase of a controlling block of stock in RKO. However, the British 75 percent tax in August killed the Rathvon deal. Then, on January 15, 1948, the trade papers reported that RKO's entire board of directors, headed by Odlum, was in San Diego for conferences with Howard Hughes, "who desires to acquire the RKO company."

In New York, meanwhile, a contest was predicted between the forty-two-year-old American multimillionaire plane manufacturer and independent movie producer and British movie tycoon J. Arthur Rank for Odlum's 929,000 shares in RKO. Rank was slated to arrive in the U.S. in March and would accompany an American associate, Robert R. Young, a rail magnate, to Hollywood to make an offer. By spring, the front runner appeared to be "the big oil tool, airplane and Jane Russell man," as Los Angeles columnist Darr Smith described the enigmatic Hughes. Hollywood wits jested: "Hughes will never buy RKO because he can't get it off the ground."

However, on May 10, in a move *Daily Variety* called "the biggest motion picture transaction since 20th Century took over Fox Films," the Hughes deal was consummated: Odlum sold out Atlas's interest in RKO for $8.8 million—$9.50 a share, giving Atlas $17 million total profit on its original investment. The trade paper revealed that the price was the result of bargaining that had started the previous December 1. At that time, Odlum was asking between $12 and $13 a share for his holdings. Since then, RKO common stock had dropped to $8, the lowest in more than a year, and comparable to a high of $15.75 during 1947. Odlum was not "infallible," as *Newsweek* pointed out on March 21, 1949. He would be getting out of RKO far below its 1946 peak of $28 a share.

Odlum still retained 300,000 warrants for purchase of RKO stock at $15 per share, a financial detail the wily business leader stressed in his statement issued May 11, immediately after the opening of the market. "…I accepted the Hughes deal in preference to alternate bids," Odlum said, referring to a recent higher cash offer, "having in mind Mr. Hughes' indicated plans with respect to the future of the company. These plans are important to Atlas, not only because it has been the sponsor for RKO during more than twelve years, but also because Atlas is maintaining a direct and heavy financial interest in the company's progress and future," he remarked, mentioning Atlas's "large block of RKO option warrants." Despite Odlum's plug, RKO warrants, listed on the N.Y. Curb, failed to stray above $2.12½ during the day.

Odlum's words about the preferential treatment given Hughes caused no surprise among insiders. His Trans World Airlines was a highly important customer of Consolidated Vultee Aircraft Corporation, of which Atlas was Number One stockholder. It was clear, therefore, that Odlum would take no undue chances of jeopardizing the important orders TWA could throw to Consolidated.

Daily Variety advised Hollywood that because of the purchase, Hughes was now the largest single investor in their industry, with more than $16 million of his own money tied up in films. Besides his RKO purchase, two movies (made in association with writer-director Preston Sturges), *Vendetta* and *Mad Wednesday,* both unreleased, accounted for approximately $5.5 million. Since its completion in 1941, *The Outlaw,* Hughes's much-publicized Western featuring his protégé, billowing-bosomed Jane Russell, had encountered enough censorship troubles to keep it from playing more than minimum dates. During Hughes's court battles over the film, a Maryland judge upheld a state ban on the movie with the comment that the actress's breasts "hung over the picture like a summer thunderstorm spread out over a landscape…." Later, *Fortune,* in May 1953, linked Hughes's purchase of RKO to "his two abiding interests, prestige and money." RKO owned 124 theaters, plus a share in about 75 others; Hughes needed theater outlets for his unreleased films. As one Hughes observer reasoned, Hughes wanted RKO for one purpose alone, to "shove his *Outlaw* down the throats of the general public. He doesn't give a damn about the studio itself!"

Rathvon followed Odlum's statement with one of reassurance to panicky company employees: "I have had numerous conversations with Mr. Hughes, and we seem to be in agreement in all matters of policy…. Mr. Hughes has no hungry army of relatives looking for your jobs…. I believe he will be a valuable and constructive influence in our company…."

Before Hollywood could recover from Rathvon's poker-faced declaration, Dore Schary managed to top it. For, as one old friend observed, "Dore's bright and he's literate, and he knows what's going on in the world. But he's also the most falsely optimistic rainbow chaser I ever knew." Said the rainbow-chasing executive, in a statement that was a model of brevity, "I have had a number of talks with Mr. Hughes, and we are in complete accord on present policy and on the projected program for RKO."

Actually, Schary's first reaction to the Hughes purchase had been an offer to resign. Recent history suggested that Hughes was a self-indulgent filmmaker, an unmitigated meddler—signifying death to creative people. Schary had no desire to have his interesting record of enlightened production desecrated by an eccentric part-time movie magnate who had spent the past few years trying to stuff the Russell bust into the box office. But after a meeting with the lean, lanky, seemingly shy Texan who he felt resembled a gunhand in a Gary Cooper Western, Schary was won over. With quiet sincerity, Hughes assured him that he had "no intention of taking over."

For the next few weeks the studio program moved forward, punctuated by an unusual pattern of nocturnal visits from the new owner, who, Schary was informed, was viewing the daily rushes. Hughes was also reading scripts and scrutinizing payrolls in the office he maintained at the Goldwyn Studios in West Hollywood. Then, late in June, Schary received instructions from Hughes to postpone production of three films: *Battleground,* a World War II epic, which Schary had asked Lasky and Walter MacEwan to produce, *The Set-Up,* the prizefight story that producer Richard Goldstone was to make with Robert Ryan, and William Pereira's *Bed of Roses,* in which Barbara Bel Geddes was featured. "Fire her," Hughes ordered. The sets had been built for the Bel Geddes picture; it was scheduled to start on July 12.

On June 30, Schary tendered his resignation. He told his staff he was quitting because he would not function under what his statement called "a two-man operation." As long as he was head of production, he wanted no "arbitrary cancellation of pictures" he had scheduled. Schary made it known that *Battleground,* a story of the Battle of the Bulge, which he had developed with writer Robert Pirosh, was his personal project. Hughes had hit his Achilles' heel.

The new management remained silent on the subject of Schary's departure. But as Hollywood started to speculate on what the future might hold for the little major now that the inscrutable Howard Robart Hughes Jr. controlled its destiny, a hint came through his publicist, Dick Davis. "... I'm really cooking at RKO, and things are going to pop. I'll make news for you. The only thing that could stop me would be my death—and even that would be a story."

Only three pictures were in production on the lot. Several were set to start early in July. One, a football yarn entitled *Interference,** starred Victor Mature and would mark Lucille Ball's return to RKO. "Just wait," one Hughes watcher remarked, "until Junior gets his teeth into that one."

*Final title: *Easy Living.*

PART NINE

THE OUTLAW REIGN: THE HUGHES ADMINISTRATION, 1948–1955

Howard Hughes, producer, on the set of *Sky Devils,* 1932.
Courtesy Marc Wanamaker, Bison Archives.

Howard Hughes with Bette Davis.
Courtesy Marc Wanamaker, Bison Archives.

Promotion for *The Outlaw*,
Howard Hughes style.
San Francisco, 1942.
Courtesy Marc Wanamaker, Bison Archives.

Howard Hughes in the editing room.
Courtesy Marc Wanamaker, Bison Archives.

The northwest corner of Melrose and Gower, 1949. The billboards feature *I Married a Communist,* Hughes's response to "the enemies of America."

Courtesy Marc Wanamaker, Bison Archives.

RKO–Pathé studio in Culver City, 194

Courtesy Marc Wanamaker, Bison Archiv

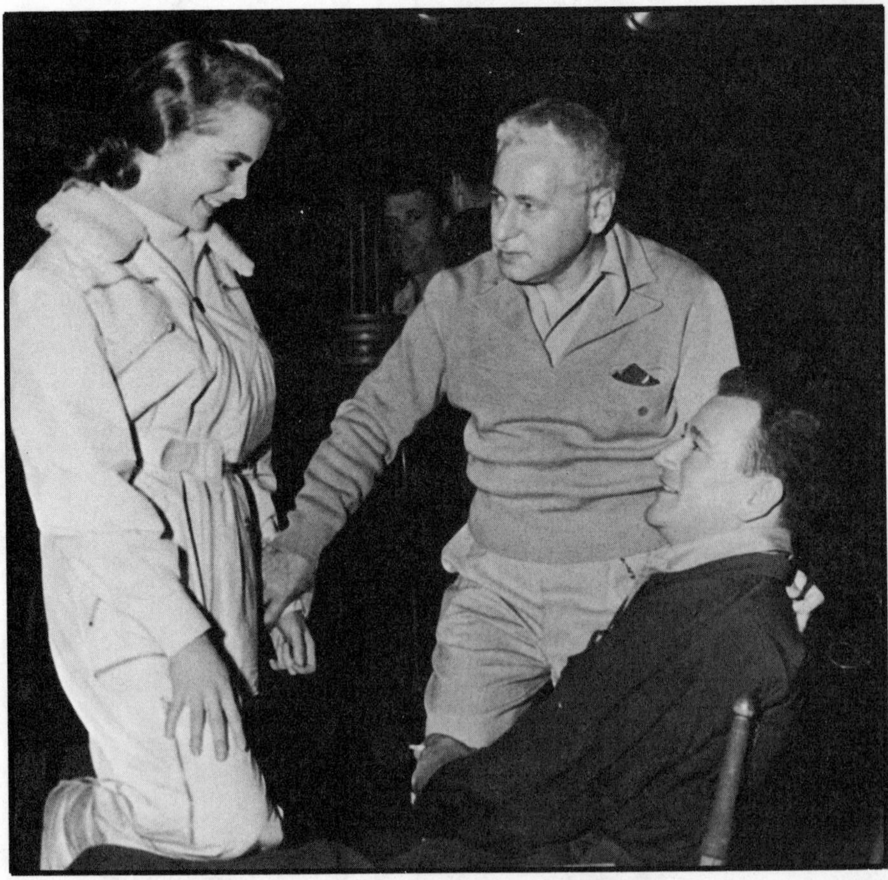

Janet Leigh, John Wayne, and director Joseph von Sternberg relax on the set of *Jet Pilot,* filmed under the production guidance of Howard Hughes from 1949–1951 but not released until 1957.

Courtesy of the Academy of Motion Picture Arts and Sciences.

The author congratulates her father after he received the first Milestone Award from the Screen Producers Guild for his historic contribution to the American motion picture, September 12, 1951.
Jesse L. Lasky Collection, courtesy of the Academy of Motion Picture Arts and Sciences.

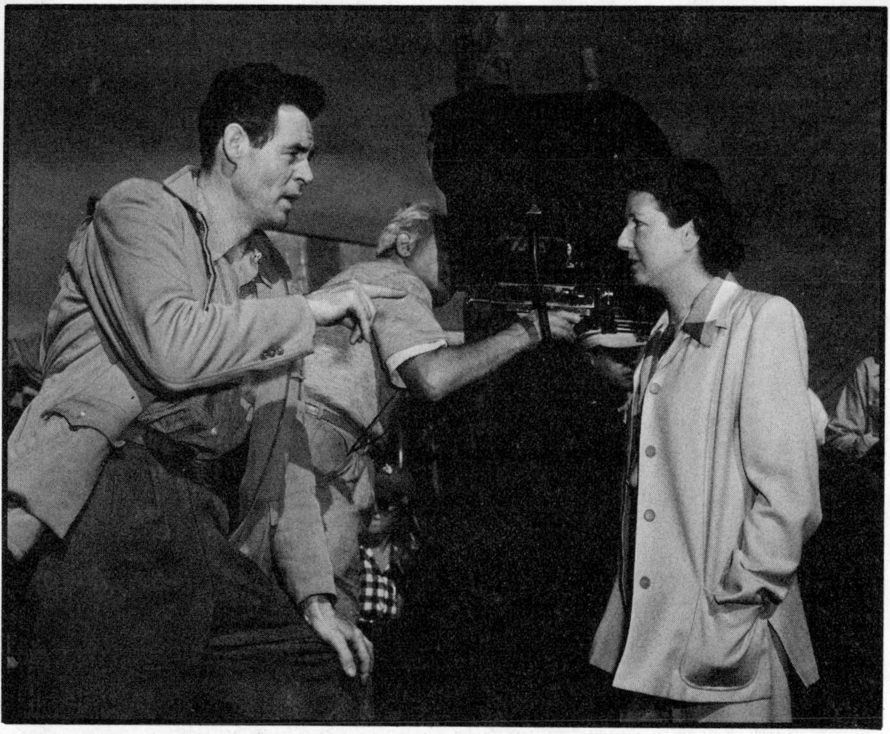

Producer Harriet Parsons with Robert Ryan on the set of *Clash by Night*, 1952.
Courtesy Evelyn Farney.

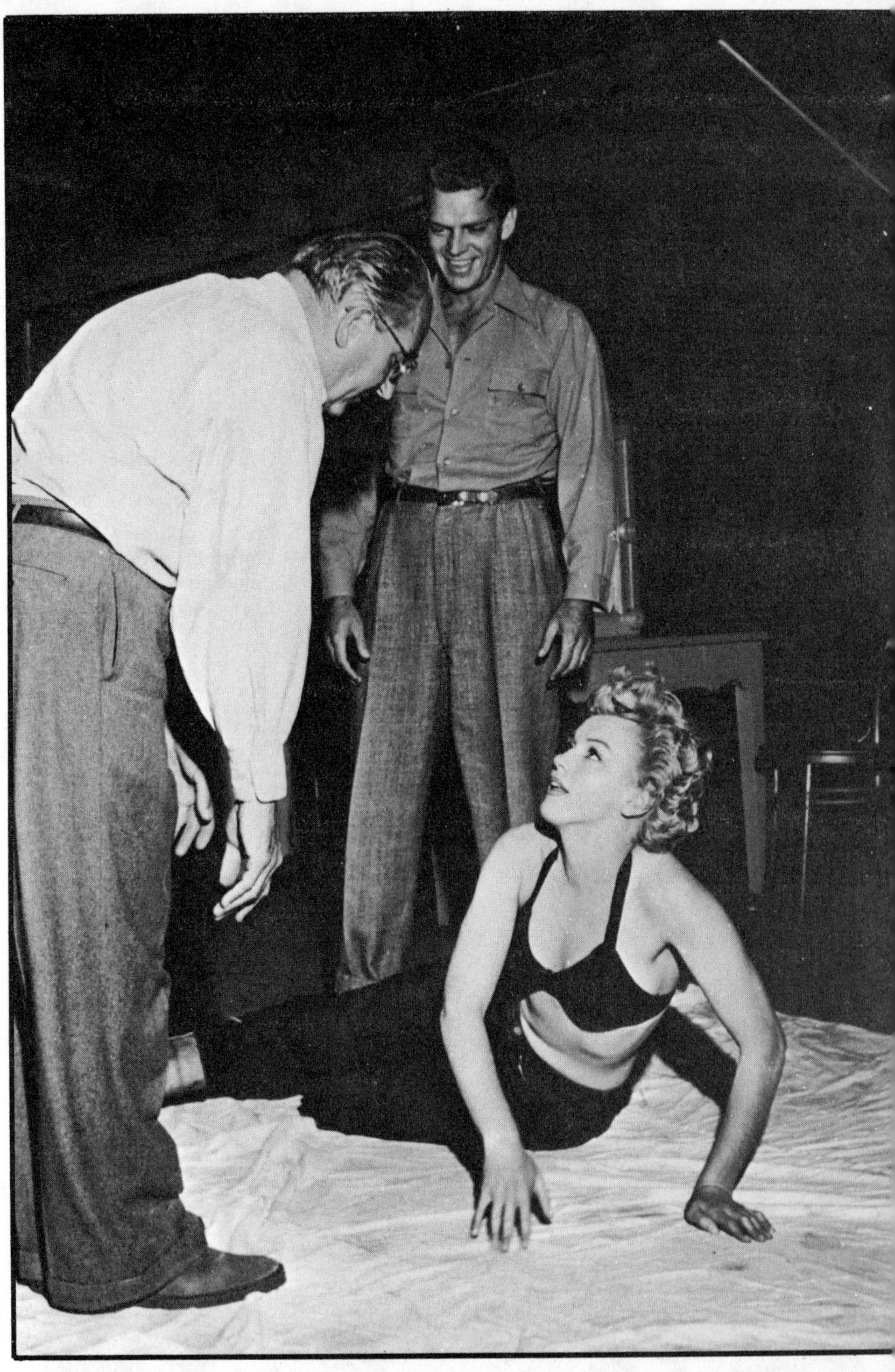

The legendary Fritz Lang coaches newcomer Marilyn Monroe in an intimate scene wit
Keith Andes in *Clash by Night*, 1952. Based on a play by Clifford Odets, it starre
Barbara Stanwyck, Paul Douglas, and Robert Ryan and was produced by Harriet Parson
Courtesy of the Academy of Motion Picture Arts and Science

The camera catches a close-up of Robert Mitchum as he gallops in *The Lusty Man*, a story of life on the rodeo circuit that also starred Susan Hayward and Arthur Kennedy. Produced by Jerry Wald and Norman Krasna and directed by Nicholas Ray, 1952.

Courtesy of the Academy of Motion Picture Arts and Sciences.

A view of the RKO ranch in Encino, 1953, looking north from Burbank Boulevard. Louise Street is at left. Right corner: the *Hunchback of Notre Dame* sets. Left and center: Western town sets.

Courtesy Marc Wanamaker, Bison Archives.

28

The RKO banner, which proudly traced its origin back to the epical day in 1883 when Benjamin Franklin Keith opened his first vaudeville theater in Boston, still topped the Gower Street lot in July 1948, but all who worked under it felt the passing of the Odlum administration. It was the fifth time a new owner had taken over the once spit-and-plaster studio that the English outfit Robertson–Cole had built in a citrus grove in 1920. The trade papers had duly recorded the changing of the guard as well as some of the highlights of the little major's intricate twenty-eight-year history— "the most complex in the industry." To insiders, it read almost like an obituary. In fact, a reminiscence of the mottled dynasties of Robertson–Cole, FBO, RCA, and Odlum and their self-serving management and vast array of transient executive talent only served to heighten the feeling that Floyd Odlum could not have passed his scepter to a more unprepossessing candidate than Howard Hughes.

The studio employees had been piecing together what they thought they knew or had heard about the new owner, and it hardly put their minds at rest. Hughes was a man of stark contrasts and inconsistencies, and it had always been difficult to gauge where the legendary hero began and the real Howard Hughes ended. Nonetheless, there was enough evidence to conclude that the real Hughes was a charlatan—a man who would go to any lengths to protect his image as a "genius of the aviation industry." Hollywood had caught a frightening glimpse of this Hughes in action the previous summer when he had crushed Senator Owen Brewster in an infamous congressional squabble over his wartime plane-building record. The Senate committee never did find out why the government had received nothing in return for the $40 million of taxpayers' money handed Hughes for two military-aircraft projects. Masterfully alternating his articulate venom with the naïveté of a small boy, Hughes had managed, at the end, to make his accusers feel ungrateful; and he departed Washington with his reputation unsullied, smiling and waving to his admirers at the airport.

What had happened to the national hero who had established all those speed records in "the perfect machine," the small, silver racer he had created? The man who won a special Congressional Medal of Honor for his record-breaking, world-girdling flight in his "World's Fair of 1939" flying laboratory? Only a vestige of that romantic figure had been pulled from the wreckage of the controversial XF-II, the first photo-reconnaisance plane, which Hughes was building for the Air Force and finally tested in 1946. His own negligence had caused the near-fatal crash, according to the findings of the Air Force investigating board. But it had not discouraged Hughes from taking the giant Hercules flying-boat—his other government order, and the object of the senators' scorn—aloft for a one-mile spin over Long Beach Harbor in November 1947. He had shown them that the big boat could fly—if only at an altitude of about seventy feet—before storing it at enormous cost in a special hangar, like an aged dinosaur in a museum.

Hollywood had been questioning the meaning and extent of Hughes's accomplishments ever since the 1930 premiere of *Hell's Angels,* which featured, among other excesses, a seventy-two-hour-running cocktail party for the press at the Hotel Astor in New York, and stunt pilots buzzing Grauman's Chinese Theater on Hollywood Boulevard. This, his most pretentious production, steeped in World War I fighter planes—$3.8 million worth—and provocative glimpses of Jean Harlow's swooping neckline, was claimed by Hughes's public relations force to have made a profit of more than $2 million. It had been nearly three years in the making, and Hughes's obsessive need to control every aspect of the production had caused two directors to quit, and his wife of two years (Houston socialite Ella Rice, whom he had completely shut out of his life) to leave him. After Hughes took over directing the picture, his demand for realism cost three pilots and one mechanic their lives. Hughes himself crashed in a vintage scout plane that he foolishly insisted on taking up in one of the aerial scenes, and he had had to undergo facial surgery. Although Hollywood would have shrugged off the news that Hughes had manufactured figures to give his burgeoning legend a box-office smash, as his personal "financial advisor," Noah Dietrich later revealed, citing a loss of $1.5 million, the town was taken aback by the young mogul's published confession: "Making *Hell's Angels* by myself was my biggest mistake. Trying to do the work of twelve men was just dumbness on my part. I learned by bitter experience that no one man can know everything."*

Hollywood fastened the "man of mystery" label on this odd young man, who combined the flair of P. T. Barnum with a modesty unheard of in the movie business, and put out the welcome mat. At parties he "inclines his head

**American,* April 1932.

out and down and looks at the ground. Seated, he clasps his hands between his wide-spread knees and stares at his knuckles," wrote Henry F. Pringle for *Collier's* on March 9, 1932. Marion Davies regarded him as a "big, awkward, overgrown country boy." Marian Marsh, one of the string of beautiful actresses he courted, thought him polite and charming, if hopelessly unconventional. As she put it, "How can I marry him? He has never sent me flowers." The only person who could see the real Hughes behind the party mask was his famous uncle, screen writer, and biographer, Rupert Hughes, and he guarded the pertinent facts. Rupert Hughes had known his brother's only child to be indulged and overprotected; he had seen young Howard at sixteen, when his mother, a confirmed hypochondriac, died prematurely, bequeathing him the phobias about his health and emotional condition that were beginning to sprout in the Thirties. He had seen eighteen-year-old Howard traumatized by the sudden death of his father—now obsessed by the fear that he, too, would die prematurely. In the next year and a half, all before his twentieth birthday, Howard had willfully rejected college, alienated his relatives, seized control of his father's Hughes Tool Company (the mainstay of his fortune), pursued Ella Rice, and written a will.*

By the mid-Forties, when the Howard Hughes of *The Outlaw* held center stage, his behavior pattern had hardened. Hollywood had come to realize that he was a multimillion-dollar accumulation of eccentricities with powerful influence. Crazy as it sounded, Hughes had gained control of a major studio for only a million dollars more than he had spent completing his huge flying boat. Hollywood was not holding its breath waiting to see what this aging, neurotic-looking man who wore rubber sneakers to nightclubs and held business appointments in jalopies and seedy hotel rooms would do with his latest toy. It was already the subject of nightmares.

The handwriting was on the Gower Street gate and it could not have been plainer, but Rathvon, for reasons doubtless known to himself and Floyd Odlum, preferred not to see it. "The entry of Howard Hughes into the organization ensures the continued growth of RKO. One thing the industry can be assured of. We propose to maintain RKO as a leader in the business." This was the message on July 8, 1948. The following day *The Hollywood Reporter*'s big headline screamed that RKO was cutting personnel by 75 percent, despite Rathvon's assurance to employees only a month earlier that their jobs were secure. The manpower cut, already in progress, moved into high gear over the weekend when approximately 800 more studio employees were dropped from the payroll. The lot was in turmoil. In a matter of weeks, a skeleton crew of an estimated 600, instead of a normal roster of 2500, was left to keep the studio

*It directed that most of his fortune be used to set up the Hughes Medical Research Laboratories for the prevention and cure of dangerous diseases.

on its axis. Said *The Hollywood Reporter*'s Rambling Reporter, indulging in black comedy, "Our ears are bent all day with more intrigue rumors concerning RKO, as Howard Hughes cuts pictures and budgets. Wonder if H.H. thinks you can operate a studio on instruments like you do a plane?"

Rathvon's tenure under the new regime lasted exactly two weeks. On July 23 the harassed president tendered his resignation following what was described by the trade papers as a "sharp disagreement with Hughes over studio policy." Hughes had gone over his head and approved a loanout of Robert Ryan for a picture deal Rathvon had already rejected. Although Odlum—still chairman of the board because of the 300,000 stock warrants Atlas retained—tried to make peace overtures, the new boss refused to consider any concessions. Rathvon would later spin a yarn to the effect that both Odlum and he had actually believed Hughes to be a "responsible buyer, although we knew he was not an experienced executive.... I agreed to remain as president on the understanding that I would function without interference from Mr. Hughes...."* Hughes had told him that he intended to devote himself "almost exclusively to his aviation interests"; he did not even *contemplate* becoming a board member.

Late in July, Hughes placed an executive committee of two henchmen, C. J. Tevlin and Bicknell Lockhart, and RKO executive producer Sid Rogell in charge of the studio. Rogell, who had first come onto the lot in 1936 as studio manager, was to actively direct production. Weighting the combination even more in his own favor, Hughes sent in his official "talent" executive, the affable Walter Kane, a former well-known talent agency head, to assist in an unofficial capacity. Kane not only made deals for motion picture productions but earned a reputation in Hollywood circles for providing ladies of the evening for Hughes.

The new ruling trio faced an immediate problem of how to meet the studio's star commitments in the face of the retrenchment winds that were knocking out production. The studio held deals with twenty-five stars for forty-three films. Other than Ginger Rogers, whose two-picture deal gave her story approval with no expiration date, most were "pay or play" agreements more likely to give the stars vacations at RKO's expense.

The word had already gone out from Tevlin and Lockhart that RKO would not schedule any more "so-called message pictures." Entertainment values and box-office potential would be the watchwords of the new regime. On orders from Hughes, Hollywood agents were notified to stop submitting stories. RKO's ten contract producers were instructed to utilize the stockpile of 400 unproduced properties and 1250 produced pictures that were available for remakes. A few weeks later, RKO offered for sale on the open market fifty story properties valued at $1.5 million. They included scripts and remake rights to

**Fortune*, May 1953.

some of the little major's finest efforts: *Alice Adams, Morning Glory, Stage Door, The Informer,* and *Gunga Din.* A particular group of new scripts developed in the Schary era, including Schary's favorite *Battleground,* which Hughes had shelved, were expected to land at MGM; Dore Schary, now L. B. Mayer's production head, had put in a strong bid for them.

By fall, eight producers had been assigned twelve pictures; three were shooting. *The Clay Pigeon,* a thriller starring studio contractees Bill Williams and Barbara Hale, and *Stagecoach Kid,* a Tim Holt Western programmer, were from producer Herman Schlom. Richard Goldstone had finally put *The Set-Up,* the Robert Ryan prizefight story, into production.

Early in September Hughes selected RKO's crack distribution head, Ned Depinet, to replace Rathvon. Looking for a silver lining, the trade papers viewed the choice of the "universally popular film veteran" for president as "a major step" by Hughes to retain the little major's position as an industry leader.

Floyd Odlum's resignation, which surprised no one, was announced on November 1 as a momentous board meeting got underway at the Beverly Hills Hotel. The Atlas group of two directors obediently followed their leader out of the company just before Hughes topped off his broken promises by the election to the board of himself and his financial alter ego, the shrewd Noah Dietrich, ruler of the $81 million Hughes Tool Company. A formal announcement had already been made of Hughes's scheme to terminate the government's anti-trust suit, which had been pending for more than ten years, by dividing the company into two units—splitting the theaters off from the production–distribution end. Although Depinet backed this "important step" with positive statements to the press, the feeling in the film community changed from surprise to anger. In fact, Hughes, by entering into a consent decree with the Justice Department, had deserted the moguls, whom he personally disliked, in their united opposition to the government. RKO's defection meant that all the other studios would have to hoist the white flag. Odlum and his Atlas directors were reported to have resigned over the terms of a proposed agreement, vehemently opposed by Hughes, which limited the warrant-holders to exercising their option either for the new production company *or* the new theater company after the separation was completed.

In the ensuing months, a tale of intrigue gradually unfolded, revealing that the groundwork for his divorcement plan had been carefully designed by Hughes when he bought RKO. At that time, Odlum had quietly entered into an agreement with Hughes to purchase the controlling interest in the proposed new theater company for a cash price to be determined by offers from at least two other sources, but not to exceed $4.5 million.* The consent decree gave

*The consent decree that RKO entered required that Hughes dispose of or trustee his stock in either the new theater or the new picture company.

RKO a year in which to complete the divorcement. However, by February 1949, three or four big bidders for the RKO theater properties were already standing in line. Odlum felt threatened. At his ranch in Indio he flatly told *The Hollywood Reporter* that he stood ready to purchase Hughes's 24 percent stock interest. "I will certainly exercise my option, but the price will have to be a fair one," he said.

Meanwhile, the dutiful new president (Depinet) envisioned the "happy future," predicting "Our picture company, operating separately, will continue as one of the industry's most reliable sources of high-grade product." Hughes's response was to sell RKO his two sex-and-violence–packed movies, *The Outlaw* and *Vendetta,* and Harold Lloyd's leaden film finale, *Mad Wednesday,* which Hughes had financed. Hughes also ordered RKO to hand over $100,000 to Hughes Tool for Jane Russell's services. Skirting the issue, the Rambling Reporter remarked, "Jane Russell's contract with Howard Hughes is on Hughes Tool Co. stationery. What is she—an oil well?" In a brilliant stroke of offbeat casting, Hughes put his 5′7″ sex goddess opposite the undernourished Frank Sinatra and a leering Groucho Marx in producer Irving Cummings Jr.'s *It's Only Money.*

Besides meddling in Sid Rogell's production domain, which Hughes accomplished by assiduous use of messenger and telephone from his offices in the Goldwyn Studios a mile westward, he also got back into production himself. Purchasing *Jet Pilot,* an unfinished screenplay, Hughes set out to create nothing less than a modern version of *Hell's Angels.* As set-dressing for the thrilling aerial scenes he visualized, Hughes cast John Wayne in the role of the American test pilot who falls for a Russian Mata Hari in the unlikely but shapely figure of Janet Leigh. By December 1949 the project finally taxied to a takeoff with the veteran self-made "genius" of the screen, Josef von Sternberg, at the controls after a retirement of eight years. But the man who had directed Marlene Dietrich in *The Blue Angel* was no match for Hughes; they eventually clashed, and Hughes gleefully took command. Wrestling with cumulus cloud effects so that the zooming jets could swoop and play hide-and-seek with fleecy white clouds for cover, Hughes still managed to thoroughly frustrate production on the lot.

As his childhood phobias intruded more urgently on his behavior, making themselves felt in his intense need to insulate himself from germs, Hughes would remain incommunicado for weeks at a time. While he spent his days devising means of controlling dust and avoiding human contact, or tinkering with the latest draft of his will, the studio was losing momentum. Yet Hughes continued to insist that he be the final arbiter of decisions. In a highly competitive business where an immediate reply was often necessary in order to secure a star or option a story property, Hughes might ponder over the matter for weeks. However, if a producer was lucky enough to get Hughes's permission to proceed, Hughes bombarded him with incessant phone calls, particularly in the middle of the night. As one battle-scarred producer explained after checking off the lot, "Working for Hughes was like taking the ball in a football game and running four feet, only to find that the coach was tackling you from behind."

RKO had leaned heavily on its backlog of completed pictures in 1948, the year when Hughes bought the studio. In 1949, although forty-nine pictures were announced, only twelve made it past the starting gate. Schary's message-oriented pictures were, because of Hughes's doctoring and indecision, still finding their way into theaters. In July of that year, despite mounting studio deficits of more than $3 million, the RKO directorate elected Hughes to the newly created post of managing director of production. Again, President Depinet backed his employer to the hilt. The board had acted in recognition of "Mr. Hughes' outstanding ability in the field of motion picture production," the obliging president stated, although he failed to come up with any examples.

At Hughes's request, the deadline for divorcement was postponed until December 31, 1950, bringing another onslaught of bids from prospective buyers for the theater company while it was still undervalued. With various purchasing groups outmaneuvering one another to grab the theaters, Odlum hurled a threat of legal action at Hughes if he sold his 929,000 shares of RKO Theatres stock to one of the interlopers. Indeed, the situation had become quite complicated. Industry observers reasoned that Odlum's deadline on his option to buy the theater stock had probably expired. The enigmatic Hughes was reported as "sitting tight" in the eye of the storm, and not the least bit worried. Said *The Reporer* emphatically, "The next step will definitely be his."

29

By the summer of 1950, the little major had moved farther down the deficit lane. No longer a catalytic force in an industry struggling against the inroads made by television, it had dropped from third to fifth place in gross receipts from the previous year. The tempestuous Hughes administration proved too much for Sid Rogell, chief studio executive, who made a sudden exit in May, the day after an explosion in which he told Hughes to stop rousing him in the middle of the night to talk business. His serviceable replacement, Samuel Bischoff, a veteran quickie specialist and former associate producer at Warner Brothers, moved into a modest office, leaving Rogell's quarters vacant. Hollywood deduced that Hughes had something up his sleeve, and he did. In an outstanding feat of negotiation, credited to his studio aide C. J. Tevlin,

Hughes closed a deal on August 13 to bring Warner Brothers top talent—the new Jerry Wald–Norman Krasna production unit—to RKO.

The "Whiz Kids," as Wald and Krasna were called, had been responsible for some of Hollywood's most sparkling hits. RKO's *Bachelor Mother* and *The Devil and Miss Jones* numbered among Krasna's long list of screenplay triumphs. Jerry Wald's first-rate Warner Brothers productions included *Destination Tokyo, Mildred Pierce, Key Largo,* and *Johnny Belinda.* Hughes had paid Warner Brothers the grand sum of $150,000 for the remaining twenty months of Wald's contract. Hollywood was impressed. *The Hollywood Reporter* rated the deal, which would bring the "wonder boys" to RKO for five years to produce sixty features for $50 million, as "the biggest independent production transaction in industry history." Even more astounding was the news that in addition to weekly salaries of $2500 apiece, the two young fellows would share the profits with RKO on a fifty-fifty basis. This was an industry first. So was the primary financing by Pittsburgh's potent Mellon Bank, which expressed confidence in Hughes and the industry in general and agreed to a partnership with New York's Bankers Trust Co.*

At their press conference staged by studio publicity chief Perry Lieber, Wald and Krasna could not contain their enthusiasm. The fast-talking pair vowed to assemble "the smartest people since the Greeks." Teams of reporters would "scout the world for story material." Nine pictures were already set. "In Hollywood," Krasna declaimed, "twenty percent of the people carry the other eighty. Twenty percent are real hot." In answer to the all-important question of the script and star approval Hughes was said to have retained, Wald retorted loftily, "Mr. Hughes is busy with big war contracts—I mean really big [and] important.... This deal could only be done in a time of disaster [in the industry]. Everybody's frantic. Mr. Hughes is taking a big look at the thing and he took the jump." The two shouted in unison: "We'll have even more autonomy than Zanuck."

It was true. Hughes had shifted his interest to Hughes Aircraft that summer, where a major expansion was under discussion because of the Korean War. Yet RKO still demanded a great deal of his time and energy. Enormous quantities of aerial footage for *Jet Pilot* were arriving in Hollywood from fourteen air bases as far apart as Alaska and Eglin Air Force Base in Florida as his photographic unit continued filming. He now faced the difficult but to him engrossing task of trying to decide which scenes to use and which to eliminate. Also requiring his personal attention were the RKO films that were tailored to the unpolished screen charms of his particular protégées and other actresses he favored: *Vendetta*'s sultry Faith Domergue, Janet Leigh (MGM's property, on loan to RKO for several pictures), and his abiding interest, the "robustly

*Security–First National Bank of Los Angleles, former partner of Bankers Trust, had temporarily withdrawn from motion picture financing because of the box-office slump.

curvaceous" Jane Russell. That August the twenty-nine-year-old actress was starting an exotic melodrama, *Macao,* with Robert Mitchum, RKO's hottest attraction, with Josef von Sternberg directing. Of particular concern to Hughes was the twenty-six-pound dress of metallic cloth that Jane, as a cabaret singer, was to wear in her principal scene. Applying himself to the problem of her frontal contours as they related to the gown, he wrote his studio aide C. J. Tevlin:

> The dress is absolutely terrific and should be used, by all means. However, the fit of the dress around her breasts is not good and gives the impression, God forbid, that her breasts are padded or artificial. They just don't appear to be in natural contour. It looks as if she is wearing a brassiere of some very stiff material which does not take the contour of her breasts.
>
> I am not recommending that she go without a brassiere, as I know this is a very necessary piece of equipment for Russell. But I thought, if we could find a half-brassiere which will support her breasts upward and still not be noticeable under the dress, or alternatively, a very thin brassiere made of very thin material so that the natural contour of her breasts will show through the dress, it will be a great deal more effective.
>
> Now, it would be extremely valuable if the brassiere, or the dress, incorporated some kind of a point at the nipple because I know this does not ever occur naturally in the case of Jane Russell. Her breasts always appear to be round, or flat, at that point so something artificial here would be extremely desirable if it could be incorporated without destroying the contour of the rest of her breasts.
>
> You understand that all the comment immediately above is with respect to the dress made of metallic cloth. However, the comment is equally applicable to any other dress she wears, and I would like these instructions followed with respect to all of her wardrobe.
>
> Regarding the dresses themselves, the one made of metallic cloth is OK, although it is a high-necked dress, because it is so startling. However, I want the rest of her wardrobe, wherever possible, to be low-necked (and by that I mean as low as the law allows) so that the customers can get a look at the part of Russell which they pay to see and not covered by cloth, metallic or otherwise.

It was this very diligence that Hughes demonstrated toward his protégées that knocked Wald and Krasna off their shaky pedestal. Hughes insisted that they use the "beautifully stacked" Terry Moore for the lead in their feature *High Heels.* Wald and Krasna declined. Hughes, armed with "picture and star casting approval," rejected their choices. The movie project died. The dejected team spent more than a million dollars in the next year trying to get their initial program of twelve pictures launched. But only two made it into release in 1951: *Behave Yourself,* a light-hearted canine comedy starring Farley Granger and Shelley Winters, and *The Blue Veil,* a classy weeper with spunky Jane Wyman devoting her best years to other people's offspring.

By the fall of 1951 Wald and Krasna had had their fill of the famous Hughes elusiveness. "They can't get to him to present their requests or problems when he turns down their ideas—if they get any answer at all," explained *The Reporter.* The "Whiz Kids" were hopelessly behind schedule and reported seeking an exit from their five-year contract. Their third picture, *Clash by Night,* a powerful triangle story, to star Barbara Stanwyck, Robert Ryan, Paul Douglas, and a newcomer, Marilyn Monroe, was being readied for the cameras, along with a fourth, *The Lusty Men,* a red-blooded rodeo story with a realistic Horace McCoy script. It starred Susan Hayward, Robert Mitchum, and Arthur Kennedy. Producer Harriet Parsons had been loaned to Wald and Krasna for the former hard-hitting vehicle, based on the play by Clifford Odets. The legendary, gentlemanly Fritz Lang was signed to direct. He was a hero to film devotees, and Harriet had been in awe of him; to her relief, they got along famously.

About this time, Hughes pulled *It's Only Money,* his Jane Russell package of cleavage and corn, off the shelf, where it had been languishing for three years awaiting his final instructions. A dubious Christmas offering, it arrived at the Paramount Theatre decked with a fresh Hughes-inspired title, *Double Dynamite,* and lest anyone overlook the Russell attributes, the Hughes-inspired ads informed them: "Double Delicious, Double Delightful, and Double Delirious." As the *New York Herald Tribune* jested: "Jane Russell tries so hard to act that it's touching, but farce is not her *pianissimo.*"

The studio had been operating under its separate production-distribution structure for a year now, following the divorcement. Two new parent companies had been created: RKO Pictures Corporation and RKO Theatres Corporation. Of course, the old Radio-Keith-Orpheum Corporation had been put to death. The new order brought a veritable phalanx of Hughes lieutenants onto the board of the new picture company, which further angered Floyd Odlum. Hughes had thwarted the financier by placing his 929,000 shares of theater stock, which Odlum had hungered after, into trusteeship. Hughes could now bide his time, let the offers pour in, and allow the bidders to outbid one another. It was said that Odlum was so frustrated he was uprooting the date palms on his Indio ranch in Coachella Valley, California. Though Hughes was forced to carry on a running battle with the Justice Department over the length of time he could retain his theater stock, the studio still held his attention. *Jet Pilot* was completed at a reported cost of $4 million, but Hughes was intent on re-editing it and making changes. Then, in the spring of 1952, Hughes came out of hiding to lead a Red-hunting crusade on the lot.

The alleged Commie in the RKO woodpile that inflamed his political passion was screenwriter Paul Jarrico. Hughes had fired Jarrico just before he had taken the Fifth Amendment before the House Committee on Un-American Activities the previous April. Jarrico had been working on *The Las Vegas Story*, a melodrama intended for Jane Russell and Victor Mature. After Hughes removed Jarrico's name from the credits, the writer struck back with the support of the Screen Writers Guild. Enraged, Hughes launched a lawsuit asking for a declaratory judgment, arguing that the screenwriter had violated the standard morals clause in his contract by refusing to answer the questions of the Congressional committee in Washington. Eleven days later, on March 28, 1952, Jarrico answered Hughes and RKO with a $350,000 damage suit. However, before Superior Court Judge Orlando H. Rhodes dismissed Jarrico's complaint—finding nothing improper in Hughes's actions—this "savior of the morals of the American public," as Jarrico angrily labeled Hughes, broadened his offensive. Challenging the Guild to call a strike against RKO, Hughes placed some one hundred "loyal" studio employees on "leave of absence" while he developed and installed a "screening" system. "We are going to screen everyone in a creative or executive capacity.... It is my determination to make RKO one studio where the work of Communist sympathizers will not be used."*

Eyeing the dwindling roster of employees, one cynical film executive commented, "It looks like a move to make a virtue out of a necessity." "Howard Hughes has thrown a mantle of Americanism over his own ragged production record," charged Guild president Mary McCall Jr. *Variety* commented with foresight: HUGHES' COMMIE BLAST VIEWED AS CUE TO EXIT RKO.

Even while Hollywood grumbled about Hughes's publicly stated reasons for curtailing production, a persistent Wall Street report alerted the industry that L. B. Mayer, in partnership with the millionaire San Francisco realtor Louis A. Lurie, was ready to strike a deal to purchase control of RKO from Hughes.† Hughes ignored Mayer's bid to regain some semblence of his former glory. Nevertheless, Hughes spent the summer dickering with a five-man syndicate headed by Ralph E. Stolkin, a thirty-four-year-old Chicago mail-order millionaire whom *Fortune* had recently spotlighted, in an article titled "New Rich," as "one of the outstanding young industrialists in the U.S."‡ Stolkin's syndicate associates were his father-in-law and mail-order partner, A. L. Koolish, Texas oil partners Raymond Ryan and Edward G. Burke, and a Los Angeles exhibitor, Sherrill C. Corwin.

*For Hughes' entire statement, see *The Hollywood Reporter*, April 7, 1952.

†The sixty-seven-year-old Mayer had been cruelly ousted from MGM ten months earlier after a power struggle said to have been engineered by Dore Schary, who replaced him.

‡*Fortune*, January 1952.

On September 23, as RKO's 1952 losses surged above the $4 million mark, Hughes closed a deal with the Stolkin group for $7.35 million. The purchase price was $7 a share for Hughes's 1,013,420 shares;* Ned Depinet joyfully contributed his 37,000. At 1:30 A.M. in his carefully guarded bungalow in back of the Beverly Hills Hotel, Hughes accepted a $1.25 million check as down payment. The syndicate could take two years to pay the balance. Furthermore, Hughes generously offered to lend RKO $8 million to pay off a $5 million bank loan and provide some working capital.

Hollywood was nonplussed. On the strength of a $1.25 million downpayment, Hughes, a notorious penny pincher, had agreed to extend credit of $14 million to a purchasing group that included only one "picture man." Equally disturbing was the fact that the quintet put that down payment on the line without looking at the books.

On October 16, two weeks after the new management took control of RKO—with Stolkin replacing Depinet as president and Arnold Grant, an ambitious young lawyer, succeeding Noah Dietrich as chairman of the board—Hollywood awoke to learn the worst. In the first of what the *Wall Street Journal* promised would be a series of "revealing stories," the industry was horrified to discover that three of RKO's new owners had been involved with "organized crime, fraudulent mail-order schemes, and big-time gambling." Part One of the series of articles linked Koolish to an Illinois insurance fraud. Ray Ryan's reputation as a blue-chip gambler and associate of racketeer Frank Costello rated him extensive coverage in the second of the series. Part Three claimed that Stolkin had made his fortune through masterly use of mail order and the punchboard, "a yokel gambling device."

To an industry striving to present a clean image to the predatory House Un-American Activities Committee, the possibility of one of its major studios' being under the management of organized crime was inconceivable. All the quintet except Ryan had taken seats on the RKO board. But with a wave of unfavorable publicity embarrassing their proposed operations, Stolkin, Koolish, and Ryan's representative, William Gorman, resigned. Wald and Krasna did a double-take and took advantage of the scandal to get out of their RKO contracts and scurry off the lot.†

On November 13, RKO rocked from fresh explosions. Grant, protesting that the two remaining syndicate board members, Burke and Corwin, had "manacled" his hands, abruptly quit as chairman. Within a few minutes, his hand-picked executive vice president, Arnold Picker, followed him out the door. Almost simultaneously, a trio of minority stockholders, alarmed by Hughes's September sale, filed two actions in New York's Supreme Court. One

*Nearly $3 per share more than the stock was selling for on the open market.

†See references on page 232.

suit sought the appointment of a temporary receiver for RKO. The other, aimed directly at Hughes, asked for an accounting "of his stewardship" of the company and for the recovery from him of about $3 million.

The only tranquil voice that day was that of *The Hollywood Reporter*'s Billy Wilkerson. RKO would not be permitted to "sink in this sea of confusion," he assured the town. The sun would break through in a couple of days with "announcements, policies, and sound backing by sound businessmen" that would put the company back on its feet. Wilkerson knew that some responsible bidders for the Stolkin group's stock were lining up in New York.

But by December, no rescue operation was in sight. The Stolkin group, unable to manage the company itself and unwilling to accept any independent directors, returned "temporary" control to Hughes, who returned to the board as chairman and brought back his yes men. Former President Depinet took a look at the Hughes-dominated board and declined an invitation to return with the tactful statement "I am sure Mr. Hughes intends to give RKO good management, and I hope with all my heart he succeeds."

On February 12, 1953, the inevitable happened: The Stolkin syndicate capitulated and handed back the stock to Hughes. According to the terms of the deal, Hughes pocketed the $1.25 million down payment. At this point, insiders were ready to believe that Hughes himself might have tipped off the *Journal*.

Meanwhile, on Gower Street, where only one picture, *Split Second* (on which Dick Powell was making his directorial debut), had gone before the cameras since the preceding fall, a new Hughes-appointed president radiated optimism. RKO was "in fine shape," declared James R. Grainger, former executive vice president of distribution at Republic Pictures, conveniently forgetting the previous year's loss of $10.178 million—which brought the Hughes regime's losses to a grand total of $22.324 million. "In six months, I assure you, things will be humming around here," he said. Grainger's son, executive producer Edmund Grainger, would be going into production in a matter of days with a Technicolor crime film starring Robert Mitchum and Linda Darnell and using the industry's new life preserver, 3-D. Its title, *Second Chance,* elicited only a small amount of laughter around town. RKO Pictures' stock was down to $3.85 a share, and although the receivership suit had been dropped, five new lawsuits had been filed by unhappy shareholders; they contended that Hughes "spent exorbitant sums" of the firm's money for movie actresses and other talent never used and ran RKO as if it were his own personal property. Cracked Dick Powell "RKO's contract list is down to three actors and 127 lawyers."

Rather than fight the lawsuits, Hughes maneuvered to convert RKO into a one-man show by offering to buy out the rest of the stockholders. In a letter to the corporation dated December 7, he made a bid for sympathy, declaring, "I have been sued by certain of the stockholders and accused of responsibility for the losses of the corporation." Hughes emphasized that he wanted all the stockholders to receive more for their shares than they were worth when he bought into the company, offering to purchase all its assets for $23½ million, and all 3,914,913 shares. That would give every stockholder $6 a share for his stock.*

The newspapers broke the big story on February 8, 1954. Under a threat of pending court suits that could halt the sale, Hughes had set a deadline of February 15 for the RKO board's acceptance of his offer. Approval would have to come from a majority of the stockholders by March 30. Wall Street reacted immediately—and amazingly—with the heaviest demand for RKO shares in history. As 723,000 shares were traded in the next four days, RKO stock shot up from $2.87 a share to $5.37. Said the *Los Angeles Daily News* excitedly, "Movie maker Howard Hughes and his stable of bosomy beauties stole the limelight from staid old rails and utilities."

The RKO board gave its assent after twenty-four hours of secret and uncommunicative deliberations. On March 18, despite a dire warning from one minority proxy holder to "beware of Greeks bearing gifts" that might be "oil or real estate developments on the RKO property," 97 percent of the minority stockholders voted to accept Hughes's offer. Hollywood ruefully noted that after writing his personal check for $23½ million, the man who had single-handedly destroyed the studio would become its sole owner.

Yet total victory eluded Hughes. His plan, according to financial circles, was to merge RKO Pictures Corp. with his mammoth Hughes Tool. The huge loss could then be absorbed as a tax deduction. Financial experts estimated that Hughes could make $7–$17 million from the RKO corpse. But only Floyd Odlum stood in the way. Hughes had broken his promise to give the financier first chance to buy the RKO theaters. In fact, the previous November, Hughes had sold the valuable theater stock to Albert A. List, a New England industrialist, for $3.372 million cash, plus a gift of List's 198,500 shares of the picture company stock. Odlum was offended, so much so that he had immediately enhanced his portfolio of RKO stock. Before Hughes finally announced his offer to buy all RKO stock, Odlum already held 78,000 shares. By May he had several hundred thousand. By July Odlum was said to own or control 1,200,000 shares. Furthermore, Odlum suggested to other stockholders that they hold their shares instead of cashing them in at $6 each: "Atlas Corp. does not feel the parent company of RKO should be liquidated," but would prefer to have it "use its cash [the $23½ million asset] to operate for a profit." Odlum's Atlas associates explained that by taking over RKO Pictures

*By this time, Hughes owned 1,262,120 shares, or effective working control.

Corp., Odlum would be all set to move the corporation into any business endeavor he chose.

"The most exciting plot in Hollywood today is behind the cameras—a real-life fight between two financial wizards for control of RKO," wrote United Press correspondent Aline Mosby, comparing their tug-of-war to that depicted in MGM's big business box-office hit *Executive Suite*.

The battle for total control of RKO reached the deal-making stage, then simmered down in the fall; for the two industrial giants appeared unable to come to terms. In December, Odlum, who Hollywood felt desired to get back into the picture business with both feet,* told Atlas stockholders that there was little possibility of his reaching an agreement with Hughes on a buyout of the picture company. The two adversaries had also discussed, but did not negotiate, the takeover of the Hughes Tool Company, Odlum confided. He added that an oral agreement had been reached for Atlas's acquisition of Hughes Aircraft, but "we never could get that meeting of minds into a definitive form."†

His dealings with Odlum stalemated, Hughes took the only avenue left open. He had no alternative but to sell the little major's remains. True, the studio had limped into 1955 with only a skeleton crew running the lot and a few producers making "token" pictures. Sam Goldwyn had severed his long relationship after the distribution of *Hans Christian Andersen* in 1952. Disney had terminated his following *Rob Roy, The Highland Rogue,* a 1954 Technicolor adventure film. The famed location ranch in Encino had been sold to a real estate company. But still the RKO carcass had enough meat left on its bones to attract a buyer. Along with the Hollywood and Culver City lots, RKO Radio Pictures' assets included part ownership of the Churubusco Studios in Mexico City,‡ its worldwide distribution system (consisting of 101 domestic and foreign exchanges), and a library of about 900 theatrical motion pictures, including a number of completed but unreleased productions, such as Hughes's overworked and by now dated epic, *Jet Pilot.*

The latter assets proved an irresistible attraction to a dynamic but unassuming young man with an Irish name, Thomas F. O'Neil, and his father's tire and rubber background in business. As head of General Teleradio, the entertainment subsidiary of Akron's General Tire and Rubber company, forty-year-old Tom O'Neil had, in eight years, built up a $35 million chain of six TV stations and a 569–radio station network that stretched from New England to the West Coast. Young Tom had known how to move in television. He had

*Odlum had been financing a proposed Leo McCarey production of *Marco Polo* and Frederick Brisson's Rosalind Russell starrer, *The Girl Rush.*

†Hughes owned 75 percent of Hughes Aircraft and 100 percent of Hughes Tool.

‡Rathvon had been responsible for its construction, which had cost RKO $1.250 million in American money for half-interest. It had never been profitable.

discovered a cache of thirty bankrupt old movies in the Bank of America's vaults and turned one of his stations into a lucrative movie house called "Million Dollar Movie."

"That Tom, he knows how to make money," said his father, William O'Neil, approving the deal his son closed with Hughes for $25 million on July 18.* To his credit, Tom had first angled for the film library alone; but Hughes had got his way. To get the golden egg, Tom was forced to swallow the whole goose.

The moguls shuddered. This was the breakthrough they had dreaded. Hollywood watched, fascinated. Was it the end of an age?

Said *Motion Picture Herald,* with false cheer: "There's a new look at RKO Radio. Mr. O'Neil is marrying General Teleradio to the picture company; and, in a sense still to be fully realized, television to the picture industry."

*Said *Variety* the next day, summing up Hughes's systematic seven-year rape of RKO: "What it totals up to is a final profit to Hughes of $6.5 million."

BIBLIOGRAPHY

A full bibliography of the works consulted would extend for many pages; therefore, I have chosen to list only the books and other printed sources that were of particular help in my research. My friend Randy Rogers introduced me to Robert Sklar's *Movie-Made America: A Cultural History of American Movies* (Random House, New York, 1975). This remains the most valuable and reliable research tool I have had. The following works—books listed first—have been placed in some order of their importance:

Alexander Walker, *The Shattered Silents: How the Talkies Came to Stay* (William Morrow and Co., 1979); John Brooks, *Once in Golconda: A True Drama of Wall Street, 1920–1938* (Harper & Row, New York, 1969); Abel Green and Joe Laurie Jr., *Show Biz, from Vaude to Video* (Henry Holt and Co., New York, 1951); Rudy Behlmer (ed.), *MEMO from David O. Selznick* (The Viking Press, New York, 1972); Arlene Croce, *The Fred Astaire & Ginger Rogers Book* (Galahad Books, New York City, 1972); Donald L. Barlett and James B. Steele, *Empire: The Life, Legend, and Madness of Howard Hughes* (W. W. Norton and Co., New York, 1979); David E. Koskoff, *Joseph P. Kennedy: A Life and Times* (Prentice-Hall, Inc., Englewood Cliffs, N.J., 1974); Richard J. Whalen, *The Founding Father: The Story of Joseph P. Kennedy* (The New American Library of World Literature, Inc., New York, 1964); Joseph P. Kennedy (ed.), *The Story of the Films* (A. W. Shaw Co., Chicago and New York, 1927); Ron Haver, *David O. Selznick's Hollywood* (Alfred A. Knopf, New York, 1980); Richard Meryman, *Mank: The World and Life of Herman Mankiewicz* (William Morrow and Co., 1978); Charles Higham, *Films of Orson Welles* (University of California Press, Berkeley, 1970); Jesse L. Lasky with Don Weldon, *I Blow My Own Horn* (Doubleday & Co., Inc., Garden City, New York, 1957); James Robert Parish, *The RKO Gals* (Rainbow Books, New Jersey, 1977); John Kobal, *Gotta Sing Gotta Dance: A Pictorial History of Film Musicals* (The Hamlyn Publishing Group Ltd., Feltham, Middlesex, England, 1970); Joseph McBride, *Orson Welles* (The Viking Press, New York, 1972); Thomas Quinn Curtiss, *Von Stroheim* (Farrar, Straus & Giroux, 1971);

Victor S. Navasky, *Naming Names* (The Viking Press, New York, 1980); Larry Ceplair and Steven Englund, *The Inquisition in Hollywood* (Anchor Press–Doubleday, 1980); Gordon Kahn, *Hollywood on Trial* (Boni & Gaer, New York, 1948); Gloria Swanson, *Swanson On Swanson* (Random House, New York, 1980); Desi Arnaz, *A Book* (William Morrow and Co., 1976); Donald Hayne (ed.), *The Autobiography of Cecil B. DeMille* (Prentice-Hall, Inc., Englewood Cliffs, N.J., 1959); Eugene Lyons, *David Sarnoff* (Harper & Row, New York, 1966); Will H. Hays, *The Memoirs of Will H. Hays* (Doubleday & Co., 1955); Dore Schary, *Heyday* (Little, Brown and Co., Boston, 1979); Jesse L. Lasky Jr., *Whatever Happened to Hollywood?* (New York: Funk & Wagnalls, 1973); Budd Schulberg, *Moving Pictures: Memories of a Hollywood Prince* (New York: Stein and Day, 1981); Ephram Katz, *The Film Encyclopedia* (New York: Putnam Publishing Group, 1982); and Ben Hecht, *Child of the Century.*

Publications include *Motion Picture Herald, The Hollywood Reporter, Variety, Daily Variety, The Film Daily, Exhibitors Herald-World, Moving Picture World, Photoplay, Films in Review, American Film, Fortune, Time, Newsweek, The Saturday Evening Post, Collier's,* the *Wall Street Journal,* the *New York Times,* the *Los Angeles Times,* the *Boston Evening Transcript, The Congressional Record, Material from the RKO Archives.*

The text on pages 198–203 refers to information taken from the following sources: "Hollywood Alliance to Wage War on Isms," *Motion Picture Herald,* February 12, 1944; *Time,* October 27, 1947, p. 25, and November 3, 1947, pp. 22–23; Robert Sklar, *Movie-Made America,* pp. 257–58; Victor Navasky, *Naming Names,* pp. 87, 96, 146; Dore Schary, *Heyday.* The text on pages 224–25 refers to information taken from the following sources: *Fortune,* May 1953, p. 123; Richard B. Jewell, *The RKO Story,* p. 244; Donald L. Barlett and James B. Steele, *Empire: The Life, Legend, and Madness of Howard Hughes,* p. 184; the *Wall Street Journal* series, October 16 and 20 and November 14, 1952; *Variety,* October 28, 1952.

INDEX